# AGING SIDEWAYS

## Changing
## Our Perspectives
## on
## Getting Older

### JEANETTE LEARDI

# What Others Are Saying About *Aging Sideways*...

"Jeanette Leardi challenges us to look at aging from a new perspective, revealing some of our misconceptions and biases. The sideways view of aging invites us to redefine our own aging, embrace the beauty etched upon our faces, and live to our full potential at all ages and stages. After years of writing and lecturing about aging, Jeanette has accumulated stories, anecdotes, and meaningful data that encourage us to transform our culture into a pro-aging society. Her approach to a subject so familiar to me still left me feeling more enlightened than when I began."

— from the Foreword by Tracey Gendron, PhD; gerontology chair at Virginia Commonwealth University and executive director of the Virginia Center on Aging and author of *Ageism Unmasked: Exploring Age Bias and How to End It*

"In this entertaining and provocative book, Jeanette Leardi unpacks what most of us think getting older is all about, and why it matters so much. (Spoiler alert: Most of what we know is wrong.) A social gerontologist, Leardi draws on solid research, startling comparisons, and engaging stories to reveal later life as a time of growth and purpose. Exposing the forces that frame long life as decline, she offers clear-eyed strategies for aging with dignity and purpose. I heartily recommend AGING SIDEWAYS to everyone who wakes up a day older and hopes to make the most of the years ahead."

— Ashton Applewhite, pro-age advocate and author of *This Chair Rocks: A Manifesto Against Ageism*

"Jeanette Leardi provides a sharp and provocative take on the scourge of ageism and what we can all do to defeat it. She offers a refreshing, entertaining, and thought-provoking approach for how to explore and perceive growing older, combining her research and analysis as a gerontologist with her personal experience. To follow her advice, you may need to start thinking very differently about aging and ageism and changing your ways, but that's a good thing."

— Richard Eisenberg, "The View From Unretirement" columnist at MarketWatch

"Even though I study aging, when I read AGING SIDEWAYS, I immediately thought, 'This is the book I need to give my family and friends.' It is a book that talks with you, not at you. It's an honest, approachable, and well-researched look at getting older and being judged for it. But make no mistake. This is not a book that calls on us to defy aging, ignore aging, or forget aging. Instead, Leardi challenges us to recognize and confront the negative societal messages about aging that tell us that aging is bad, that we should be ashamed of our age, or that we, as aging people, no longer matter."

— Kate de Medeiros, PhD; gerontologist and professor in the department of sociology and anthropology, Concordia University, Montreal

"In a world in thrall to youth, AGING SIDEWAYS is a welcome blast of fresh air. It torpedoes the myth that growing older is just a downward spiral. Jeanette Leardi reminds us that aging can be an extraordinary journey: rich, complex, contradictory, magical, thrilling, beautiful. And she shows us how to make the most of life at every stage. AGING SIDEWAYS is a timely, bracing read. Whatever your age, grab a copy now!"

— Carl Honoré, author of *Bolder: How To Age Better and Feel Better About Aging*

In memory and honor of…


my grandmother,
Giovina Simone Modè,
who was my first inspiration,


and my parents,
Americo Leardi
and
Rosina Domenica Modè Leardi,
who led me to discover what aging is
and to appreciate all that it can be

# A Word About the Text

**AND THAT WORD** is *pronouns.*

I love the fluid nature of language and the way it adapts new forms to meet our changing needs. Pronouns relating to gender are a recent example. Although I have consciously tried to avoid as much as possible using singular third-person pronouns, nevertheless on inescapable occasions I have opted to use *s/he, him/her* and *his/hers* rather than *they/them/their,* all the while asking the gracious indulgence of any reader who self-identifies using the nonbinary form or otherwise prefers it.

A thornier challenge has been to decide when to include myself as an older adult in a general discussion. I have no qualms about getting personal in many places in this book by using *I, me,* and *my.* However, *Aging Sideways* is primarily about you, not me, and I don't want to assume that all my readers are older persons, or even identify themselves as such. So please note that when I use the terms *older adults, older persons,* and *elders,* I'm not distancing myself from them. Instead, I'm placing the focus on a general segment of the population (which includes me) that deserves attention in its own right.

I appreciate your understanding.

# Contents

# Foreword

**HAVE YOU EVER LOOKED AT A PAINTING** or a piece of art and found yourself tilting your head to one side? If you have, it's likely you noticed things you hadn't before, such as a new color, angle, or hidden meaning. All too often, we walk through life looking at things from one point of view. But there is beauty and wisdom in looking at life from a different angle.

When viewed with an all-too-common eye, aging is seen as the process of decline over time until we leave this world. In reality, aging is far richer and more nuanced; a multi-directional process that is complex and idiosyncratic. It is a personal journey of things gained and lost, things found and unfound, and things learned and unlearned, which unfolds uniquely and often unexpectedly for each one of us.

Although aging is something that we all experience every moment of our lives, awareness of our aging happens in small increments and fleeting moments. Author Thomas Moore refers to this as "the first taste of aging." It may be a moment when we realize that something we used to be able to do with ease is now more difficult. Just as likely are moments when we swell with pride over a hard time endured in which we came out stronger and wiser. Aging is a subjective experience that touches everyone, yet its nuances often remain misunderstood.

Ageism is a force that keeps us from seeing the beauty inherent in our aging. It is powerful and often driven by profit-driven industries that promote myopic thinking and behavior. Ageism thrives by keeping us on the metaphorical hamster wheel chasing the elusive gold standard of looking, acting, and feeling "young." Ageism lurks in the shadows, waiting to rob us of years of happiness, health, and longevity. It permeates our culture and our institutions. Yet, despite the pervasiveness of ageism, it remains overlooked and sometimes trivialized in the broader discourse about discrimination.

In *Aging Sideways*, Jeanette Leardi challenges us to look at aging from a new perspective, revealing some of our misconceptions and biases. The sideways view of aging invites us to redefine our own aging, embrace the beauty etched upon our faces, and live to our full potential at all ages and stages. After years of writing and lecturing about aging, Jeanette has accumulated stories, anecdotes, and meaningful data that encourage us to transform our culture into a pro-aging society. Her approach to a subject so familiar to me still left me feeling more enlightened than when I began. You will find solace in Jeanette's personal experiences and empathize with her challenges.

As you embark on this journey through the labyrinth of aging, I hope you emerge with a deeper understanding of its complexities and beauty; and with a commitment to fostering a world where every individual is allowed to thrive.

So, tilt your head sideways or even fully upside down. See the new angles, sharp corners, and gentle slopes of your personal story of aging and feel empowered to embrace it with renewed purpose and meaning.

Tracey Gendron, PhD
Chair and Professor, Department of Gerontology
Virginia Commonwealth University
Executive Director, Virginia Center on Aging
Author of *Ageism Unmasked: Exploring Age Bias and How to End It*

# Aging Sideways

> When you change the way you look at things, the things you
> look at change.
>
> — Max Planck, quantum physicist

**THIS IS NOT A BOOK** about midlife, mid-torso weight gain. It's a book about perception and direction.

If we think about aging at all — and I believe each of us does at various points in our life — we tend to consider it reluctantly. The process is something we rarely face head-on unless and until those moments when our culture demands otherwise. Like when we notice a wrinkle or strand of gray hair and wonder if others see it, too. Or get turned down for a job for being "too experienced." Or told that our aches and pains are something we should expect at our age.

We live our lives in mostly predictable ways and according to well-established patterns. Where do those ways and patterns come from? None of us grows up in a vacuum. No matter who or where we are, we move through an environment of shared social customs and cultural beliefs that constantly send us messages about what is real.

Unfortunately, our society tells us nonstop that because aging is real — too real, in fact — it instructs us to deal with that reality by mocking, postponing, denying, and most of all, fearing it. Such reactions block us from living authentically, boldly, and productively far into our later years. Furthermore, that pervasive fear manifests itself in ageism: the prejudice, bigotry, and discrimination toward people solely based on age.

It's hard to escape in our culture. According to a research team led by Julie Ober Allen, then–assistant professor of health promotion at the University of Oklahoma, analyzing survey data from 2019, "Among 2035 adults ages 50 to 80 years…, most participants (1915 adults [93.4%]) reported regularly experiencing 1 or more forms of everyday ageism," including being exposed to demeaning jokes or to assumptions about their poor sight/hearing/memory/cognition or their lack of competence, technical savvy, or social importance or value.[1]

Of course, we like to think that we as a society respect and revere our elders, and many of us do. But current data show that many older adults today endure precarious socioeconomic situations and under- or over-treated chronic diseases. And these conditions will intensify if we don't do something about them very soon. In this century, we are at the threshold of dramatic developments regarding longevity and the size of the population aged 65 and older.

Let me give you a few statistics.

Because of significant improvements in the quality of acute health care over the past century, older adults are living longer. In 2021, the average life expectancy for people who make it to 65 years of age was 84.8 years for women, and 82 years for men.[2]

In 2020, 56.1 million people, about 17% of the American population, were aged 65 and older,[3] but sometime between the years 2030 and 2035, that number will increase to 73.1 million, or 21%[4] when, for the first time in American history, there will be more people above the age of 65 than below the age of 18.[5] Currently, the fastest growing population among all Americans is the 85-and-older group, sometimes called the "oldest old."[6]

All these figures are remarkable in themselves, but even more important are the social impacts of getting older in America. In 2020, about 9% of all people aged 65 and older lived below the poverty level.[7] The rate doubled for older African Americans in general[8] and quadrupled for older Hispanic or African American women who live alone.[9]

Furthermore, 1 in 6 oldest old Americans are living in institutional settings such as assisted living centers and nursing homes.[10] In 2011, the first members of my Baby Boomer generation (born between 1946 and 1964)[11] turned 65, and if you've followed the longstanding health care reform debate, you know that this demographic trend is predicted to dramatically affect the future solvency of Social Security and Medicare.

I rattle off these figures to give you an overall idea of the trends that are causing us to rethink what it means to age in this millennium. The short- and long-term repercussions of such socioeconomic conditions, as well as the widespread scourge of ageism that marginalizes and impoverishes older adults, diminish the lives of all generations and weakens the social fabric itself.

Something needs to be done to change all that. And I want to be among the catalysts for that change.

What can I contribute to the subject of aging, about which I'm so passionate? To begin with, I'm in my 70s — an older adult. I'm also a gerontologist. So I can speak with both personal and professional authority about what living in our society as an old person entails.

While much has already been written in a comprehensive way by other pro-aging leaders, I wouldn't presume to create a book that merely repeats what they've already profoundly and eloquently expressed. That being said, the more unique voices we add to that chorus, the louder and more compelling becomes the song. The more facets of understanding we add to the jewel of enlightened aging, the more brilliantly that gem shines.

My contribution is not so much to the "what" of rethinking aging, as to the "how"; in order to overcome the age discrimination, or ageism, that permeates our society, we need to follow Max Planck's advice and "change the way we look at" what it means to grow old. This book approaches the concept of age from many different angles by reconsidering its impact in unpredictable, slightly askew ways.

And here's where I take my lead: In her 1979 groundbreaking book *Drawing on the Right Side of the Brain: A Course in Enhancing Creativity and Artistic Confidence*, art teacher Betty Edwards proposed an exercise called Upside-Down Drawing, in which readers are asked to turn upside down an illustration or photograph of something (e.g., landscape, face, chair) and draw what they see.[12]

The point of the exercise is to disorient the brain by removing the right-side-up cues our brain uses to determine the top, bottom, left, and right of an image, as well as the spaces in between the image's shapes and the relationships between light and shadow that fall on them.

The effect of this topsy-turvy shifting can be great enough to make familiar faces unrecognizable and familiar places unidentifiable. Our perceptions are thrown off and, in fact, thrown away.

Exactly. And that goes for aging, too.

This is precisely the kind of exercise we need to do to understand what becoming an old person is all about. Too often most of us buy into the negative, stereotyped characteristics of older adults; we accept gross generalizations of what old people are like, what they want, and what they are (or aren't) able to contribute to society. We may believe they are slow, frail, incompetent, kindly but ineffective, or cranky and technology averse. So the pictures of them we have "drawn" in our minds are distorted by our judgments.

Here's the remarkable thing about the Upside-Down Drawing

exercise: The pictures that Edwards's students drew when first looking at right-side-up subjects turned out to be *less accurate* and *less real* than those they later drew of the same subjects in their inverse positions. That's because when the images were presented upside down, the analytical, judgmental parts of the students' brains were suspended, thus allowing their minds to see the lines and shapes exactly for what they were.

What if we could "see" age in the same way — exactly for what it is, nothing more and nothing less?

As you read the following pages, I'm not asking you to do a complete Betty Edwards 180-degree turn of your brain, but merely to tilt it sideways — just enough to put your observations and feelings into slightly altered and unfamiliar positions and to get used to this right- or left-angle cocking of your mind. I'm counting on the fact that you'll get the same remarkable results.

And that's why this book is called *Aging Sideways*: to catch your attention. Anything unexpected slightly jars one's mind enough to permit a temporary suspension of one's assumptions. I'm hoping to do the same with you. Because no matter what any of us thinks about aging, we can all benefit from a minor shifting of the ground beneath our feet to remind us that our perceptions are fluid, and that our beliefs, situations, and actions can change, hopefully for the better, if we're open to a repositioning and rebalancing of our own stance.

In daily life, this repositioning and rebalancing can take many forms. For example, if you are an older adult, you might be caught off guard and feel somewhat disoriented when someone calls you "kiddo" or "young lady," a remark that's usually meant to be a compliment. But if instead you turn it "upside down" and see the assumption behind it for what it is — that being younger is better than being older — you'll realize that such a statement reflects the speaker's own discomfort with aging, and thus you might feel freer about your age.

Or if you are denied opportunities or treated as incompetent or worthy of pity, you can realize the ageist nature of this situation more immediately and react to it by applying strategies that advocate for yourself as an individual and not as the representative of a stereotyped, misunderstood population.

What are some effective strategies for aging "sideways"? It helps to think of them as embodying the following skills:

- sidestepping a deeply embedded obstacle you're approaching rather than retreating from it or futilely trying to remove it

- redefining a term or concept in a way that makes its meaning more accurate or more relevant to you

- looking peripherally as you move forward rather than only straight ahead or in the rear-view mirror

- being open to the unexpected rather than controlling what you encounter in the moment

When we make the effort to apply these skills, each of us can form a comfortable relationship with aging in our own way.

In the following chapters, by revealing surprising, often positive truths about aging and offering you examples of the above skills in action as well as some quirky ways to approach the challenges that preoccupy us as we get older, I hope to dispel any overarching belief you may have that living longer results solely in deterioration and decline. Additionally, I'll provide you with memorable images and arguments — useful tools for talking about aging with your family, friends, coworkers, caregivers, health care providers, and anyone else you encounter.

Feel free to move around in this book as you wish, in the same way you would guide your pencil when doing an Upside-Down Drawing. Or think of the brief essays in these chapters as pieces in an eccentric mosaic. Up close, they are shapes in their own right. But step back a bit, and you will find that they form a more surprising, inviting, holistic picture to explore and enjoy.

Or better yet, think of them as offerings in a buffet that may have some of the same ingredients but prepared in different ways. Although it helps to enjoy these servings in order, you can start wherever you like (who says you have to eat dessert last?) and skip around them as your appetite stirs you. By the time you read them all (and I hope you do), you may find that you have a greater appreciation of aging as the complex yet nourishing and empowering process it is and of becoming old as something to aspire to — and savor — rather than dread.

I'm no quantum physicist, but if Max Planck was right (after all, he won the Nobel Prize in 1918), then what happens to perception and reality at the subatomic level most likely applies everywhere else in the universe, including in our individual lives. If that's the case, each of us has the power to change the trajectory of our later years in a significant way by first viewing them with fresh eyes.

In the journey across *your* lifespan, ask yourself: "Am I driving down this road, or am I being driven?" Moreover, think about what directional instructions you encounter and choose to follow. Wouldn't you rather encounter fewer "Stop!" and "S-L-O-W" signs and more "Merge," "Alternate Route," and "Off-Ramp" opportunities leading to new experiences and wider explorations?

If, like most of us, you've always considered getting older with some trepidation, once you begin to perceive the process with a mindset guided by different motives and goals, you can get off the culturally entrenched, misguided, fear-based highway you may have been on for too long, and instead change the landscape of aging so that it offers you more realistic and hopeful directions to take throughout the rest of your life. And by following that approach, you can help lead the way down newer, wider, easier — and freer — roads for future old people to travel in their days to come.

# CHAPTER 1

# It's All About Stories

**WE TEND TO ASSUME** that because aging is a universal process (we all experience it), it's a uniform one (we all do it in basically the same way). But that belief couldn't be further from the truth. Aging involves an intensely individual progression determined by factors that are genetic, historic, economic, biographical, psychological, and cultural in nature. When it comes to the experience of growing old, no two people are alike. Sure, there are established scientific methods for measuring some of the predictable biological changes to any person's body over time, but the only way to get a more complete picture of how that same individual is really maturing is to include that person's ongoing story. And that's where the *real* variation is revealed. Don't take my word for it. Check with any scientific researcher.

Formal work relies on one or both of two kinds of research: quantitative and qualitative.

Quantitative research involves counting, measuring, and arriving at results that are numerical. It seeks to answer such questions as "Yes or no?", "How many?", "How long?", and "When?", and its results can be expressed in numbers.

Qualitative research involves describing and opinion gathering and seeks to answer "Why?" questions, and its results are best expressed in language rather than figures.

Storytelling is a distinctly qualitative endeavor because it reveals emotions, intentions, and perceptions that are hard to capture using math. Stories are a way we get information that isn't codified into charts, graphs, or other types of display. Clear-cut, concise data certainly have vastly important value, since they form the blueprint of a house of ideas. Stories, on the other hand, possess a special value all their own. Who tells them; the occasion, purpose, and audience for that telling; and the way they are told provide the colors, furnishings, and resulting ambience of that home.

We think of fiction as the main realm where storytelling happens. But is that really the case? Real life is full of narratives. Consider how many stories of all kinds you hear or tell in the course of 24 hours.

You wake up and turn on the news as you get ready for work. What comes into your home are narratives — objective or biased — about the latest crimes, natural disasters, political controversies, and celebrity gossip. At the breakfast table, you may share with your family your individual plans for the day. You work out a schedule of errands. At work, virtually or in person at the water cooler, someone tells you a funny story. You recount experiences of watching last night's ball game or favorite TV series' latest episode. All this, while in the greater world, courtroom witnesses are testifying, salespeople are hawking their goods, patients are discussing their symptoms with doctors, clients are revealing their fears to therapists, and professors are lecturing. In the evening at the dinner table, your family recaps the important personal events of the day. You fall asleep watching a movie or talk show. And *still* the storytelling doesn't end, because while you're asleep, you dream.

Many stories, told many ways, and for many purposes.

As we age, our personal stories differ remarkably from those of others, and because of this, sharing them is a powerful way to help us to form — or change — our ideas of what aging is all about.

In my training and work as a gerontologist, I've had access to information that has enabled me to rethink my ideas about aging. Just like the vast majority of us, I've had some distorted ideas of what it means to grow old. But I was also lucky to have had early and ongoing positive role models in my life that defied the stereotypes, namely, those people to whom this book is dedicated: my maternal grandmother and my parents. By sharing these few narrative vignettes about them, I hope to show that any older adult's story, when examined in a slightly different and specific light, can reflect a three-dimensional person who defies categorization.

As you read them, think about the older adults *you* have known. Do the stories of their lives merely reflect those negative tropes about old people that our anti-aging culture is all too often eager to promote? Or, if you look deeper, do the details of how they live or have lived reveal more subtle — and perhaps truer and more powerful and admirable — aspects of their character?

It's your turn to be a researcher, to discover for yourself what is real about living over the course of time. Select an important moment in your own or someone else's long life and focus on its unique impact. Although it's true that assessing an individual's aging process involves some especially important quantitative information (e.g., physical health, years of education, socioeconomic level), having a truly complete understanding requires including qualitative experiences and points of view.

And that means one thing: It's all about stories.

# OLD STORIES, NEW LIVES

I come from a family that loves to hear and tell stories. My mother, who was the first to teach me how to read, also made it a point to share with me her love of old movies. Some of my fondest memories growing up in New York City in the 1950s through '70s are of curling up with her on a sofa, watching Rick Blaine bid goodbye to a tearful Ilsa Lund as she boarded the plane out of Casablanca, Dorian Gray defiantly stab his terrifying portrait, Rhett Butler carry a thrashing Scarlett O'Hara up the grand staircase, and Norma Desmond descend her staircase for the last time.

So nothing seemed unusual that day, when I was in my 30s and she in her 60s, as we watched her favorite actor, John Garfield, being seduced by Lana Turner in *The Postman Always Rings Twice*. Nothing, that is, until my mother absentmindedly blurted out, "You know, John Garfield once told me that I could act."

"WHAT?"

"John Garfield said I had real talent. He told me I'd make a good actress."

Stunned, I immediately turned away from the TV and demanded to hear the whole story.

It was 1938. Garfield, who had been appearing on Broadway in *Golden Boy*, visited his old junior high school, P.S. 45 in the Bronx, N.Y., and dropped in on an acting class taught by his favorite teacher, Margaret O'Ryan. My mother happened to be onstage delivering some lines from that year's hit play, *Our Town*, and he sat in the back of the room and listened to her. Then he came up to her and delivered those words she cherished for the rest of her life.

Four decades after hearing her story, I find that what stuns me more than this revelation is the fact that it took all those years for her to mention what was clearly a significant moment in her life. And to say it in a way that was almost an afterthought. Did she think no one would find that exchange remarkable? Or had she chosen to repress for so long the memory of a thwarted ambition? More than anything else my mother later said or did, that disclosure forever changed my understanding of who my mother was, expanding my perceptions of her beyond the role of wife and mother and into a person independent of my identity, in her own right. And it had a lasting positive effect on our relationship.

My mother has long since gone, yet I continue to be amazed and humbled by the stories I hear my older adult peers tell about their lives. I listen to them whenever I can, including during the journaling and memoir writing classes I teach. I encourage my students to use their compositions to transform feelings of reticence and vulnerability into those of empowerment and wisdom. And I've been privileged to witness more than one intense catharsis.

One such reaction overcame an octogenarian woman who throughout her life in the States harbored a fear of being discovered as the daughter of a Nazi soldier, despite the fact that he deserted and defected to Switzerland by stealing a German officer's motorcycle and making a *Great Escape* of his own. In sharing her story with the class, she found acceptance and even admiration for her emotional endurance. As she read her essay through tears, she found healing.

And as we listened, we learned more about what it means to be human.

Most of us older adults, I suspect, are yearning to share our life stories with others. The tragedy in our society (a disgrace, really) is that we often deny elders the opportunities to do so. Or we minimize the value of what we hear. Or want their stories to meet our expectations. How might their lives be enriched if they knew that others were genuinely interested in what they experienced and the lessons gleaned from them? Moreover, how might *our* lives be enriched by those stories and lessons?

I'm now older than my mother was when she told me the John Garfield story. And while so far nothing in my life can compare with that tale, maybe someday I'll get a chance to tell about the summer day in New York City when a 20-something me ran into — and I mean literally collided with — ballet great Mikhail Baryshnikov in the doorway of a newsstand/candy store as I was entering and he was rushing out to hail a cab. Holding my torso to steady me, he asked me if I was all right and then if I was a dancer and complimented me on my "dancer's muscles." I never saw my body in the same way again.

I'll look forward to sharing that one.

# LESSONS FROM MOM

The Florida sunset reds and oranges filtered through the window blinds, casting horizontal slits of shadows on my mother's hospital bed. In the quiet, late afternoon, while my father was resting at home, I kept her company, sitting on the bed, facing her, watching as she fed herself from her dinner tray. With very shaky hands and an intense expression, she carefully negotiated the challenges of a wrapped straw, a tightly covered soup bowl and the heavy lid that concealed her main course: a colorful though bland meal of steamed vegetables and nondescript beef.

She was silent. I was silent. Only the regular beep of her heart monitor punctuated the stillness.

As I watched her, a tired, emaciated patient, I thought: *This is my mother. And this Mother's Day will probably be her last.*

A hard thought. An awkward one, since Mother's Day for me had always been a one-sided celebration, having had no children and being unlikely to ever become a stepmother. Thus, honoring my mom on that day was always akin to honoring my dad on Father's Day: something not to relate to from the inside out.

But as I studied my mother's face with its pure look of dignity and concentration as she set to the now-monumental task of eating a meal, I thought about how my views of Mother's Day, and of my mother, were usually rather limited. Too often I chose to define her by that role rather than see her first and primarily as the individual that she was.

Now, in that bed, dealing with terminal breast cancer that had spread to her brain, she was less my mother or a mother at all. What I witnessed was an autonomous, determined person, courageous and disciplined, unsentimental yet very much connected emotionally to the intensity of living a life.

This woman taught me many things over the years, mostly about caregiving and nurturing. Hopefully, albeit in contexts unrelated to having children, I've applied those lessons well.

But that particular day, in the growing purple darkness of a solitary hospital room, I learned something powerful from that same woman about inner strength, resolve, and most of all, the quiet dignity and grace of a unique and limitless soul.

One month later, she taught me something else; this time not about identity but about healing.

When I was a child, I loved to sing. Melody or harmony, solo or with others, it was all the same to me — to reach into my heart and bring out my passion through my voice in song.

But somewhere along the way, probably as a teenager, I began to feel self-conscious about my voice. I don't remember a particular instance in which someone criticized or made fun of me, but something made me slowly retreat to a place where, if I sang at all, it was only when I was alone or in a very small group of close family or friends and even then, I'd only sing along with someone, never solo. This self-consciousness lasted for decades, until a turning point in June 1995, when I was 43.

My mother was in a nursing home in Florida and in the last few days of her life. She had gone through five months of painful, traumatic deterioration of her cancerous brain. She had lost lots of weight, her head was shaved and bandaged from the many surgical procedures done to alleviate the buildup of fluid and pressure in her skull. Her arms were black and blue from all the many intravenous tubes put in her. She was in a wheelchair, unable to walk. She moved in and out of consciousness, sometimes not being able to speak or know who or where she was, or who anyone else was.

The last time I saw her, we were alone. It was midmorning, and I wheeled her into the communal dining room. It was in between mealtimes, and no one was there. I wheeled her up to an old piano in the corner of the large room.

I took my place at the piano and began to play some of the old songs, American and Italian, that my parents taught me when I was a little girl and that my family used to sing all throughout my childhood. I played and sang those songs — and my mother sang.

Up to that time, my mother had always had a beautiful soprano voice. So beautiful, in fact, that when she was 15, she had an appointment to audition for a radio program in New York City. But her father died that week, and her dreams of a career ended because of her obligation as the oldest child to help her mother care for her five other siblings.

So now, years later, in this empty nursing home dining room, here was this brave, dignified, albeit confused and disoriented woman, trying to remember the words and melodies that only months before were second nature to her. She stumbled, stuttered, hit many flat notes.

She cried, perhaps because she was frustrated, because she was aware of how she sounded, or perhaps, too, because she knew her end was near and this might be the last time she would ever sing, that *we* would ever sing together.

I was crying, too, as I sang with her.

At that moment, something remarkable happened to me. I was fully aware of the fact that my mother's passion for music had endured the ravages of her body and mind. Her passion came through, despite her conflicted feelings of embarrassment and dread. It didn't matter how she sounded; it only mattered that she sang. And the example of her effort was a glorious gift to me, as well as a legacy.

For at that moment, as I sang through tears, I swore to myself that I would never let the fear of others' judgment intimidate me enough to keep me from singing. I still get anxious, but I sing anyway.

To this day, sometimes people who once heard my mother sing tell me that I sound a lot like her. And while I consider that a great compliment, as I now approach the age of her longevity, my greater wish is to be more like that woman, embracing her passion to the very end.

# VINTAGE RX FOR AN ELDER BODY AND SOUL

"You think they'll say I can have a glass of wine now and then?"

I remembered this poignant, often-repeated question of my father's as I came to pick him up and drive him home from a gathering of his Italian club. It was 1997, and for half a year his query had lingered in my mind like the aftertaste of an unforgettable vintage. At that moment, as Dad finished his meal and introduced me to a few of his newly made friends, I noticed his glass, nearly empty, the last mouthful of pinot grigio calling to be savored. Despite the social distractions, my thoughts reeled back to a time just six months earlier when I doubted that my dad would live to share another meal again.

He was 80, living near me in Charlotte, N.C., and in the hospital for emergency open-heart surgery. His cardiologist and cardiac surgeon debated the necessity vs. the futility of doing such an extensive invasive procedure on someone his age. After all, the surgeon argued, why should they be wasting their time and effort trying to save someone who probably had only a few years left?

Fortunately, his cardiologist argued emphatically for treatment. He knew my father much better than the surgeon did. A retired railroad worker, Dad was a renaissance man — a voracious reader, master woodworker, dedicated gardener, and lover of music. To that doctor, my father was a vibrant individual, and he asserted that no matter how much longer my father might live, he deserved a chance at extending his quality of life. Dad knew the risks and had an advance directive that said if he didn't have a decent shot at maintaining his life the way he wanted to live it, he was willing to let go. His cardiologist supported the decision to opt for quality over quantity.

During that 12-week ordeal, my father was in intensive care more than half that time, on a respirator on three separate occasions, and went into congestive heart failure twice and cardiopulmonary arrest once. And yet here he was, six months later, laughing and joking and sipping the last drop of Italian wine.

Remarkable? Perhaps. Or perhaps not. You see, all the while that my dad's doctors were relying on their vast medical knowledge and skills to save his life, my father was self-prescribing. I understood him completely. His need for occasional wine was not alcoholic but spiritual. Wine took him back to his identity, to the roots of his Abruzzo homeland and to his years in New York City, when every autumn our family would make our own wine. First-press. No additives. Pure. As Dad slowly got stronger, he was telling me by his repeated question exactly what would be healing to his soul. He wanted to feel autonomous and whole again. Would the doctors understand? Each "We'll see" from me was like yet another big pill he had to swallow or injection to endure.

To the credit of my father's surgeon, cardiologist, pulmonologist, and internist, they took a holistic approach, each at the appropriate time giving their consent for moderate consumption of wine, along with recommendations that he sing and walk and putter in the garden and participate in all the other activities in life they knew mattered to him. He took their advice and lived another five active, highly engaged years that brought him joy and the benefits of his wisdom to everyone around him.

The physicians' person-centered prescriptions renewed my father's faith in his own power to heal. They renewed my faith in the enlightened direction it's possible for modern medicine to take. For when science and spirituality are joined in the service of healing an elder's body and honoring an elder's soul, there is no more potent protocol humanity can devise.

Except maybe an occasional glass of good Italian wine.

# A BOUNTIFUL DILEMMA

"It looks like we have to make another delivery to the doctors."

My father said this with a kind of amused annoyance, as he and I checked out the two small garden plots he cultivated at his retirement community. The 5-foot-by-9-foot areas were rampant with tomatoes, peppers, string beans, basil, and zucchini, and only the week before, we had stopped by the hospital to deliver a first harvest to the physicians who saved his life three years earlier and continued to maintain his health.

"I mean, what are we gonna do with all these vegetables?"

Beneath his pseudo-frustration I could hear the pride in his voice, of an octogenarian's accomplishment in maintaining high-yield patches of growth in a city to which he'd suddenly been transplanted four years before.

His life was a series of uprooted experiences. At first, he was used to the rocky struggles of a small town in Italy, then the gritty life of New York City, finally the sandy comfort of retirement in Florida. But two years after my mother died and his own health took a tenuous turn, I brought him to Charlotte, N.C., and the possibility of closer monitoring and higher-tech health care.

In response to his summertime dilemma, I resisted the urge to remind him for the umpteenth time that it was his idea to ask for that extra plot of garden no one else in the retirement community had claimed. That he was the one who insisted we buy more plants after I had brought home what I thought was a reasonable amount to care for. That during the previous year he had similarly complained about the abundance and the quandary of how to share it.

No doubt about it, he'd grafted well to his new environment: starting a new life, making friends who spoke with Southern accents hard for his native Italian ears to understand, digging in and meeting challenges of all kinds as he put new roots in a strange land of hard, red clay.

For all his setbacks, he was determined to remain productive as long as he'd draw breath. Being 49 years old, I marveled at his tenacity, courage, and stamina, even as I did the heavier groundwork while he watered the soil and reaped the blessings of his harvest. So what if what resulted was a bunch of food he couldn't possibly consume all by himself? He reminded me that it was the gardening, preparing, and allowing for growth that mattered.

Whether we know it or not, all of us cultivate gardens. The things we choose to grow and the ways in which we care for them define our lives and who we are. Ironically, for many of us as we age, the urge to cultivate and produce doesn't wane; it intensifies. Yet social pressures, misperceptions, and restrictions trim and prune us of opportunities until the struggle to grow with dignity can be more daunting than a seed's attempt to push its first tender shoot through dry, packed soil.

It takes more than a green thumb to survive. It takes the will and wisdom of a master gardener. My dad was a natural.

What to do with all the fruits of his labors? It was obvious from his wink that he had a plan. We'd just make more trips to the hospital, this time to the nurses in the intensive care units, the chaplains, the volunteers — anyone who had nurtured, watched, and tended him as carefully as he did his plants.

As for me, I, too, was spending some quality time in cultivating: one living thing, 84 years old.

And thriving.

# A GUIDING STAR

For age is opportunity no less
Than youth itself, though in another dress,
And as the evening twilight fades away
The sky is filled with stars, invisible by day.

— Henry Wadsworth Longfellow
excerpt from "Morituri Salutamus:
Poem for the Fiftieth Anniversary
of the Class of 1825 in Bowdoin College"

When I was a toddler, I used to sit for hours on the floor of my maternal grandmother's Bronx, N.Y. apartment living room under her frame of stretched cloth and look up to watch her sew beads and spangles onto fabrics that became wedding gowns, banners, flags, altar cloths, and other decorative pieces.

This is how she worked: The top side of the material, which faced her as she sat at the frame, contained a drawn design, which she followed with her needle and thread. With her other hand, she applied the beads and spangles to the underside, which she didn't see but felt, and caught them with her needle. Her artistry, therefore, consisted of two skills: the knowledge of how to follow a pattern and the intuitive, kinesthetic wisdom to know how to bring that pattern to life. For my part, it was like watching a sky full of constellations forming right above me. And I was mesmerized.

It's been decades since I thought about this vivid memory, although my grandmother, long since gone, remains a real presence in my life as

I continue to benefit from the many intangible gifts she shared with me, the most important one being her life's example of aging as a rich and complex process. A widow who struggled to remain independent, she was my first role model of a person meeting the challenges of growing older with personal dignity and strength in a society that didn't offer her much support.

As I matured, she continued to enrich my life. She empathized with my childhood frustrations and teenage emotional swings while reassuring me that they would soon pass. She knew the patterns of life and how to make those patterns her own. She, along with my parents, formed the constellation of love that gave me my bearings. She was a guiding star.

It was precisely because of my grandmother's positive influence in my life that older adults were *never* invisible to me. Far from it, in fact. Through my formative years and into midlife, my grandmother came to mind almost every time I met someone whom I considered to be old. I naturally accepted that person's dignity and sometimes even wondered what challenges s/he faced and what valuable knowledge s/he might possess.

For these reasons, I'm sad for any youngsters who are oblivious to the presence of older people. I may be wrong, but I can't help but assume that if they have no close, positive relationships with one or more older adults, their sky is devoid of important markers by which to navigate their lives. As a result, they may think that the possibility of reaching a satisfying elderhood is more remote than visiting the stars.

Constellations are forming above the heads of young and middle-aged people all the time — constellations of role models who can instruct them on how to chart their own course as they age and can inspire them along the way. The challenge for our society is to help younger generations become aware, in the daytime of their lives, of what they think is invisible and therefore unimportant. By providing them with meaningful everyday opportunities to work, play, and otherwise mingle with older adults, we can help them focus past a flat horizon of youth-centric concerns and cast their gaze higher.

Much higher.

# CHAPTER 2

# What's Age Got to Do with It?

**SINCE EVERYONE'S PERSONAL STORY** of aging is unique, is there anything that can be said about the condition in general? After all, it's becoming more common for people, usually those in their later years, to assert that age is "just a number," that it's useless to assume or assign particular characteristics to anyone at any point along the lifespan, especially if they themselves don't believe that they resemble people whom society considers typical for their own chronological age.

And yet there are some generalizations we can make, not only about the process of getting older but about the social realities with which it forces us to contend.

Let's begin with this one: If you're alive, you're aging. But *how* you are aging is really the issue. We're all aware of the passage of time; however, many of us, such as some regular readers of newspaper obituaries, seem to be more preoccupied with this notion than others. Moreover, many of us can't help but compare our age to those of others. (I'm now older than every one of my several doctors.) And many, if not most of us, wish we could halt the progression of time completely, as if we could stick a cork in the middle of that eternal hourglass in order to stop its slow draining of sand.

But why do we feel this way? Why would we want to keep time at a standstill, especially if that might mean not experiencing any more adventures and learning new things? Isn't it really more about trying to stop the aging process? And if so, why do we dread it so much?

Aging confuses us. We may yearn to be considered wise elders, all the while dreading an inevitability of falling apart.

What's the real story about aging?

Before tackling this question, consider these two:

**When did you first know that you were a grown-up?** For some people, that realization occurs the first time they vote, or drive a car by themselves, or move out of their parents' house, or get their first job, or get married, or have kids. It happened to me when I was 21 and signing my very first contract, to get a credit card. As I read all of that small-print legalese, it hit me that I alone was responsible for adhering to all of the rules and responsibilities stated in that document.

The same variation of experience can also be applied to realizing when we have arrived at "older adulthood." Notice the phrase I use. It's deliberate, because I've found that while advancing in years might be equated with achieving wisdom, very few of us, no matter our age, are reluctant to admit that we have become "old." Why? Because we think it implies any number of negative characteristics, such as frailty, decay, incompetence, dependence, and irrelevance.

**How old is "old"?** An enlightening 2018 study of 502,548 people ages 10 to 89 older revealed that respondents ages 10 to 20 believe that the average person becomes old around age 60. People in their 40s and 50s assume old age occurs in the late 60s, and 80- to 90-year-olds say that the average person does not become old until 70.[1]

You may have difficulty defining "old" as it applies in your life; that's probably because you arrive at an answer based on any one of five specific paradigms:

*Chronological Age* — the number of years since you were born. This determining factor is the most common, and what we mean when we ask "How old are you?"

*Functional Age* — the age at which you are expected to independently perform basic Activities of Daily Living (ADLs), such as bathing/showering, dressing, eating, moving about, and using the toilet. It also includes performing Instrumental Activities of Daily Living (IADLs), such as housekeeping, cooking, shopping, using a phone and appliances, maintaining finances, and driving or using public transportation. This paradigm is especially problematic, discriminatory, and thus ableist because it negatively judges what a person can or can't do compared to assumed "average" behavior.

*Life-Stage Age* — the time of experiencing an event that is considered a "milestone," in this case in later life, such as retiring from a job, becoming a grandparent, or moving into an older-adult–based community.

*Policy Age* — the official age at which you first qualify for certain governmental benefits and services, such as age 65 for Medicare and ages 62 through 70 for Social Security.

*Perceived (or Subjective) Age* — the age that you may "feel" that you are, regardless of your chronological age. This less formal paradigm is highly individualistic, originating within each of us. Each of us knows how old we are chronologically, and yet most of us have trouble accepting that we are that specific number of years old. We tend to feel younger, perhaps because we associate our age with those serious-looking people in historic, sepia-toned photographs who look much older than their years. Perceived age is reflected in such statements as "Age is just a number" and "60 is the new 40." Is our reaction due to the ageist dread of getting older? Or is it because we have outdated ideas of what is admirable or even possible at our age? Can we bring ourselves to the point at which we realize that age isn't just a number but is instead an important one to cherish? To accept that 60 is really the new *60*?

I hope you can appreciate how fuzzy the concept of age can be in common interactions when one person relies on a particular paradigm while another relies on a different one, especially when it comes to functional, perceived, or life-stage age. For example, who is "older": someone aged 50 who requires round-the-clock care in a skilled nursing facility or a 90-year-old successfully living alone? Is a childless 75-year-old "younger" than a 40-something grandparent of a 20-something daughter's baby?

Because we are aging from moment to moment, it's valuable to consider what that activity is really about. In other words, what it is and what it isn't.

First of all, aging is *natural*; it's a biological progression that we're supposed to undergo. Furthermore, it's a *universal process* that happens to everyone; no one escapes it. Aging is *continuous throughout life*; there are no Pause and Restart buttons that we can hit to temporarily interrupt the action. Finally, and most importantly, the experience of aging is *complex* and *multidimensional*, involving some losses, to be sure, but also some very important gains — in experience, knowledge, abilities, and hopefully, wisdom.

As for what aging isn't, the following realities challenge widespread myths and stereotypes about getting older:

**Aging isn't a disease.** A disease is when something in our body goes wrong, beyond the parameters of what is considered normal. Aging is normal and not to be confused with actual illnesses (e.g., diabetes, arthritis, cancer, heart disease, dementia) that we are more likely to develop as we get older. No one dies of "old age."

This being said, some scientists disagree. They have identified 11 different "hallmarks" of aging that describe gradual, long-term wear-and-tear processes that they believe can be slowed down, halted, or even reversed,[2] and maybe their anti-aging research efforts will succeed. But for people who opt out of such treatments, those results will only mean that nature has been artificially modified or denied, since for them nature will take its course and result in death. Look at it this way: Humans evolved to walk upright, but today we can ride in cars and planes. That doesn't mean that walking is no longer a natural act.

**Most older adults are cognitively healthy.** One of our greatest misconceptions about age is that if we live long enough, we will inevitably get some form of dementia. This is absolutely false. According to the Population Reference Bureau, "About 3% of adults ages 70 to 74 had dementia in 2019, compared with 22% of adults ages 85 to 89 and 33% of adults ages 90 and older."[3] Moreover, a 2020 report by The Lancet Commission revealed that 40% of all dementia cases can be prevented by making certain lifestyle changes.[4]

**As a group, old people are more heterogeneous than young people.** One of the most egregious fallacies concerning age is to categorize all older adults under the umbrella label of "the elderly," as if in later life we have the exact same experiences, preferences, needs, abilities, and goals. In reality, in terms of physiology and personality development, children have more in common with one another, even when one adjusts for race, ethnicity, gender, and geographic location. That's because as we grow older, we experience different things, which lead us to make certain choices, which lead us to other paths, which expose us to further experiences, and so on. We're like the branches of a tree that divide and subdivide and spread out until our life stories increase in their uniqueness. As pro-aging advocate and author Ashton Applewhite has written, "As doctors put it, 'If you've seen one eighty-year-old, you've seen *one* eighty-year-old.'"[5]

Because of the reality of this diversity, and considering that more people are living into their 80s, 90s, and even 100s, researchers who divide their subjects into various age groups (e.g., 18–24, 25–39, 40–50) — a practice which itself should be evaluated for effectiveness — should never create as their uppermost category "over 50" or "65+."

**The vast majority of old people are open to — and capable of — change.** Another stereotype that has nothing to do with age is the notion that as we age we become stubborn, set in our ways, and cranky when faced with the need to make a change. Sure, this can be said for many older adults, but it can also be said about many children, teens, and middle-aged people. In fact, when we think about the multitude of adjustments and adaptations a person has to make in the course of a lifetime, it's the elders who have excelled in this because of their decades of existence in an ever-evolving culture.

Think about your own life: What was a telephone like when you were a kid? What is a telephone like now? If you're old enough to remember dealing with rotary phones, party lines, and tangled cords and you now use a smart phone or virtual meeting platform, you've changed…a lot. Managing all the iterations of cars, washing machines, and cameras — not to mention the evolution of air travel, medical procedures, and social media — has demanded flexibility of us all.

And let's not forget about using computers. One of the most insidious claims against older adults is that we are digitally illiterate, or at least technology averse. Sure, that's true of some elders, but they are a distinct minority compared with the rest of us. According to AARP, 90% of 50-year-olds, 88% of 60-year-olds, and 72% of people ages 70 and older own a smartphone. As for computers, laptop ownership is 68% among those in their 50s, 69% for people in their 60s, and 59% for those 70-plus. Desktop ownership is higher among elders 70-plus (58%) than among those in their 50s (51%) or 60s (52%).[6] All of these numbers show that most older adults are not tech-incompetent and, in fact, embrace developments in the digital sphere.

But increased age demands something more than flexibility alone; it demands resilience. Two of the greatest coping challenges we older people face involve 1) the gradual changes our bodies undergo in tone, strength, endurance, and often levels of pain, and 2) the physical loss and psychosocial grief of the death of peers, close friends, and partners.

Flexibility and resilience are the hallmarks of older age. Indeed, we who have reached this point in the life course are justified in considering ourselves Master Changers.

There are many other negative myths and stereotypes that need debunking, but you get the idea: Aging has gotten a bad rap for so long that it's no wonder that most of us dread experiencing what we believe are its downsides, made worse because we're not aware of its upsides.

In any experience that calls to mind our personal journey of maturing, we should ask ourselves, "What's age got to do with it?"

Sometimes the true answer is "Nothing."

But for those circumstances that honor where we've been and where we're going, we'll hopefully see that "Everything" applies instead.

# A SPIRITUAL COVENANT

I want to tell you about two old men who changed my life.

Around Christmastime of 2001, a group of friends and I made our annual trip to a Charlotte, N.C. nursing home to sing carols for and with the residents. We friends knew one another because we performed at regular communitywide gatherings in the city known as the Tosco Music Parties.

During our evening at the nursing home, we encouraged the residents to suggest songs for us to play, or for them to sing something themselves. One 69-year-old African American man named Roy slowly got up without ceremony and launched into a gospel song with such passion that it took our breath away. Immediately everyone began clapping in time to the rhythm of his powerful rendition. When he was done, we shouted and cheered. And we invited him to sing at the next Tosco Music Party.

And that he did, to a crowd of more than 700 people. And he took the roof off the place. A standing ovation, a long minute of powerful cheers, whistles, and applause. I couldn't imagine what was going through Roy's mind and heart when he walked off the stage. But later on, I got a glimpse.

That night, I had the privilege of driving him back to the nursing home. In the car, he told me a little about his life's work of 50 years as an itinerant preacher in the South during the era of Jim Crow. He also told me about the frustration, loneliness, and futility of his current situation as a nursing home resident. And my heart ached for him.

When we got to the entrance of the facility, now past midnight, Roy rang the bell, and an attendant came to let him in. She had a scowl on her face, as if our arrival were an intrusion on her otherwise quiet evening sitting in the hallway. I could see the posture of my new friend slowly change from the upright, proud stance of a preacher/gospel-singer par excellence to a stooped, repentant, prodigal son, returning home a little too late from an evening unimaginable in its emotional richness. I'll never forget the immediacy and profundity of Roy's soul-crushing transformation, which haunted me then — and haunts me still.

The other old man who changed my life was my father, Americo Leardi. Like my mother, Rosina, he influenced me in many ways throughout my life, but never more so than toward the end of his. Just as I was for my mother for more than a decade, I was his primary caregiver — in his case, for his final seven years. I saw him through several major heart surgeries, many hospitalizations, and more than one brink-of-death experience.

As different as my father was from Roy in ethnicity and personal history, they shared the experience of performing at Tosco Music Parties (my dad sang Italian songs) and receiving wild standing ovations. But my father's story ended quite differently…and happily. He was fortunate to have had the social support of many people who honored him for his talents, values, and passionate spirit. To his final day in 2003, my 85-year-old father was recognized as a vital and *viable* human being.

Roy and my father showed me both sides of the aging experience we still face today. And witnessing such a starkly contrasting picture of how older adults are treated made me decide, after a 35-year career as a freelance writer and editor, to study gerontology at the University of North Carolina at Charlotte. In 2009, I received my graduate certificate and set out to find work that would enable me to bring more of my father's experience to others like Roy whom society marginalizes and, by such treatment, are diminished.

The facts and figures I cited in this book's Introduction provide a clear picture of why we need to consider aging in realistic terms that promote the need for greater appreciation of older adults as full-fledged members of society. Unfortunately, it's our cultural perceptions about aging, and especially the insidious stereotypes we have imposed upon it, that inflict spiritual injuries of the kind of soul-crushing experiences like the one Roy had as he returned to his institutional "home."

At this point, you might be skeptical about what I'm saying. You might be thinking that society has always honored its elders and continues to do so. Unfortunately, this is a longstanding myth.

In order to talk about reverence and respect for our elders, we need to consider exactly what it is older adults as a generation possess in the greatest quantity. I can think of only three acquired things: experience, cultural memory, and, hopefully, wisdom.

Culturally, our American stereotypes of aging have been, and continue to be, negative. Few people raised in our individualistic society look forward to a future of living in a nursing home or being dependent on their own children to take care of them. Moreover, our media images have consistently emphasized the desirability of anything young, new, and improved over anything old, familiar, and dependable.

For many older adults, the prospect of living in such a future wasteland is too hard to bear. As they age, they are obsessed with maintaining an image of youth. Plastic surgery, Botox, Viagra — need I say more? Or they drive themselves to remain on the same productive economic treadmill of decades-younger workers, thinking that there are no unique spiritual fruits produced in elderhood.

But they are very wrong. And we as a society are very wrong if we believe that people's "golden years of retirement" should be spent measuring themselves against their past and coming up short or withdrawing to their own socially gated communities filled with weekly mall outings, and games of bingo, bridge, and golf.

In the insightful and highly readable book *From Age-ing to Sage-ing: A Revolutionary Approach to Growing Older,* co-author Rabbi Zalman Schachter-Shalomi, one of the founders of the Jewish Renewal movement in the late 1960s, convincingly argues that there's much spiritual work to be done in one's later years, work that can move older adults beyond their limbo of suspended time and irrelevance and into a new phase of personal — and social — fulfillment.

He considered this phase a time of harvesting,[7] of releasing oneself from the pressure to bring forth the fruits that characterize midlife achievement. He referred to this impulse to newer tasks as "spiritual eldering."[8]

While Schachter-Shalomi called for older adults to engage in greater personal contemplation in this later phase of life, this activity isn't meant to be navel-gazing. He contended, and I agree, that when older adults embrace the process, not only are they enriched, but everyone else — children, teens, young adults, and the middle-aged — reap the incredible harvest only older adults can provide.

What kind of harvest, exactly, was he talking about? He quoted the late Maggie Kuhn, founder in the 1970s of the Gray Panthers, a national alliance of older and younger adults committed to positive social change. She believed that older adults are the repositories of a culture's history and values, and they can play an important role in preserving the health of the global environment. In addition, because of their relative independence from mainstream life, elders can also be the vehicles through which society can test out new ideas and lifestyle options.[9]

How different is this call to action from the assumption by many in our society that old people should retire away from active social participation to lead quieter, more insular lives? In fact, Kuhn claimed just the opposite: Not only should older adults *not* be asked to pull back, but as simultaneous keepers of the flame of tradition and vanguards of change, they must be the ones to dare to make society healthier and more humane.[10] Roy, through his singing, preaching, and experience of surviving the pre–Civil Rights South could certainly have been enlisted to continue his spiritual roles of flame-keeper, risk-taker, and healer.

Let me be clear about this: It's more than social neglect and economic injustice we need to address in older adults' lives. We need to fill the spiritual void in their lives and in our whole society that results from not recognizing the moral contributions that elders are uniquely capable of making. For if we don't, we rob them, and ourselves, of opportunities to live more meaningful lives in all kinds of ways. All of us, no matter our age, need to create the conditions that allow older adults to make the necessary journey to higher consciousness that is their birthright, and the birthright of us all.

So where do we begin?

I say we begin with a new paradigm, which is, paradoxically, the oldest paradigm of all: that of a spiritual covenant, one made between the older adult and the rest of society. Not a promise. Not a contract. But a spiritual covenant, much like the kind in the Hebrew scriptures, that intertwines the moral values of a deity or an entire society with a person's individual sense of integrity. It's an agreement by both sides to undertake certain spiritual tasks that affirm life and promote the greatest good for all.

What are the spiritual tasks of aging? What is required of those who are growing old and of society toward them?

Let's start with individual older adults. According to Schachter-Shalomi[11] their overarching spiritual task is to become more completely who they are and who they can be by freeing themselves from years of the constraints of both social and personal expectations and limitations. To do this, they must undertake bold self-examination.

First and foremost, they must come to terms with their own impending mortality. This spiritual task is no small thing, especially if one has postponed doing it. Many people, for example, have not created a Living Will, which expresses their wishes for how they want to be treated for a serious or terminal medical condition, or designated a Health Care

Power of Attorney who will be a surrogate voice in ensuring that those wishes are followed. Similarly, many people haven't created a Last Will and Testament or named a Durable Power of Attorney to oversee their financial concerns in the event of their death.

As another way to confront one's own mortality, Schachter-Shalomi also encouraged older adults to contemplate their own funerals, thinking about the music, readings, eulogy, and other particulars they would want to have. It's not as maudlin as it sounds. In fact, it can be freeing because it's a really good way of reviewing one's own life, which is the second spiritual task.

Here's where old negative feelings and perceptions about aging can be released. Toward that end, Schachter-Shalomi suggested a three-part life review, in which older adults can take internal and external steps to 1) forgive others and themselves, 2) recast their failures as successful learning experiences, and 3) reclaim aspects of the life they have always wanted to live.[12]

If you think this practice isn't challenging, I encourage you, whatever your age, to try it by meditating, journaling, letter writing, having serious conversations, and other ways that, I guarantee you, will open you up to some fascinating and powerful insights.

The third and final spiritual task of the older adult is to make a leap into the unknown, whatever form that leap takes. In other words, to convert the first two spiritual tasks of facing mortality and reviewing one's life into an action that redefines a new self, an emerging spiritual elder that is harvesting what s/he has learned in order to now direct it toward a productive end, hopefully one that serves others as well as oneself. Each older adult needs to do this with as much support as possible from the rest of society.

So now let's consider the other side of the spiritual covenant: What are society's spiritual obligations toward older adults? Society's overarching spiritual task is to create the conditions that support spiritual eldering. This society can do in five ways.

The first way is to **dispel negative stereotypes of aging and all discriminatory practices** toward older adults. There is no place for ageism in a spiritual society.

The second way is to **encourage the creation of croning and saging rituals** that honor the passage of an adult from midlife and into elderhood and the many transitions that occur in older age. It's not enough to burn a mortgage or to give a gold watch at retirement (as if anyone does *that* anymore). Older adults' contributions to other generations should be recognized by those generations, including the very young. For when elderhood is celebrated, it becomes a time of life for everyone to aspire to rather than to dread.

Which brings me to the third way society can support spiritual eldering, and that is to **create intergenerational opportunities** for mentorship and the handing down of traditions and other forms of cultural memory. We need to listen to older adults, not ignore them or, the worst sacrilege of all, treat them as children.

The fourth way is to **provide older adults with ongoing opportunities to learn and to serve**. Think of the incredible untapped resource ("human capital" is the business term) that exists in our older population.

And finally, we should **seek constant input from older adults** about all facets of life, including policy making, urban design, and social welfare. It should be automatic that we actively include older adults in all our community and national conversations.

No member of a generous, compassionate society should be kept within artificial boundaries, relegated to second-class status. Beyond being cruel and unjust, mandating such a status quo is ultimately harmful to the very preservation and sustainability of that culture.

Therefore, I challenge all older adults to look, find, and then eagerly share the gifts within themselves. And I challenge the rest of society to eagerly encourage and accept what is shared. The spiritual covenant between elders and society can carry us to places of higher consciousness we must reach if we are to preserve the integrity of our planet…and promote meaning, purpose, and quality in our lives.

# ON THE ROAD TO AGING WELL

Not long ago, I brought in my then–33-year-old Honda Civic LX sedan for its scheduled oil and filter change. Amid the usual exchange of pleasantries and amazed questions regarding how my remarkably trusty car was doing ("Aging, like its owner," was my usual flippant reply) was the discovery that yet another part, this time the windshield wiper fluid hose, was brittle and broken. Unfortunately, as had become more common with my car, there was no way to find a new part to replace it because it was no longer being manufactured and used parts compatible with a 1990 vehicle are extremely rare. I now had to resign myself to carrying a jar of fluid to pour on the windshield to clean it.

As I drove home, disappointed but still grateful for my three-decades-plus ride, I realized that we talk about our aging selves in virtually the same way we talk about our cars: in purely physical terms. We anticipate gradually wearing out, with maintenance being a more frequent and challenging issue. And we become increasingly preoccupied with wondering how many more miles we have left to go and how easily we'll be able to get around.

But here's where we make a huge mistake in perception: Because we are organic, sentient beings, aging involves much more than the physical wear-and-tear process, known as senescence, that accompanies us through life.

In the introduction to her groundbreaking book *Ageism Unmasked: Exploring Age Bias and How to End It*, Tracey Gendron, executive director of the Virginia Center on Aging and chair of the department of gerontology at Virginia Commonwealth University, has defined the difference between senescence and aging:

- Senescence is the process of biological aging that leads to the gradual deterioration of function in cells and/or organisms.

- Aging, on the other hand, is the universal lifelong biological, social, and spiritual process of developing over time. Aging is dynamic and includes all processes, including growth, loss, maintenance, and adaptation. Aging is multidimentional and multidirectional.

Viewing the holistic and complex process of aging solely through the lens of biological senescence promotes a one-sided, decline-based view of aging....

Aging is a slow and steady process of change that ultimately leads us to becoming our unique, individual selves.[13]

If all we focus on is the singular deterioration of our body rather than on the many opportunities to experience adventure and growth, then of course it makes sense to fear and dread getting old. Let's instead change our attitudes about aging by considering the ways in which we're unique, individual selves and how over time we've matured as drivers on the journey through life.

Here's my take:

When I first learned to drive, I was so unsure about keeping my car within the lines of the lane that I focused my gaze right above the hood rather than on the road up ahead. This obviously made it challenging for me to remain aware of other cars and pedestrians, not to mention of the streets I was crossing and where I needed to turn.

However, after decades of experience, although my reaction time was slightly slower and I got tired more easily on very long trips, I and my car "became one." I was able to brake smoothly, drive defensively, and know my car's limitations so well that I easily factored them in when assessing road conditions. I became confident in getting my bearings and thus less afraid of getting lost, knowing that I could safely navigate my way around unforeseen obstacles and roadwork detours.

Most importantly, I kept traveling to new places all the time.

It's the same with how I've aged. I've had many years of experiencing change, the "growth, loss, maintenance, and adaptation" of Gendron's definition. So getting older is a far richer process than the mere, slow transformation of my body's cells. They are simply senescing, not "aging, like their owner."

However, there are two vital things we need to consider: the environment in which we travel and the road conditions it creates. Even if we do all we can to keep our senescing bodies, including our minds, in working order, the quality of our lives equally depends on how well the aging process is supported by our culture. When an ageist society, demanding that we stay young, pushes us to do whatever it takes to look, perform, and produce consistently throughout life or give up our car keys and get out of the way, it sets up roadblocks and creates dangerous potholes and slick surfaces that can cause us to lose control, veer off our course, crash...and even die.

All of us need to move our collective eyes upward from what's immediately before us and to a place farther down the road, where we're all headed. We should be creating social policies that multiply, widen, and smooth the routes so anyone can go the distance safely. And most of all, we should stop thinking that ageing involves nothing but senescence.

It's not enough to ensure that we have many miles to go. After all, of what value is the journey if the trip is a needlessly discouraging, rough, and dangerous ride?

# SUCCESSFUL AGING —
# ON WHOSE TERMS?

In 2015, I traveled to Charlotte, N.C., to visit friends in my most recent former hometown (I'm a native New Yorker). While there, I co-produced and participated in a local public radio program discussing the Age Friendly Cities and Communities movement,[14] comparing efforts in Charlotte with those in Portland, Ore., to where I subsequently moved.

It was a lively exchange among the program's host and guests as we discussed such topics as the importance of creating more affordable housing and transportation for older adults in order to reduce their social isolation and ensure their continued economic prosperity and cultural engagement. Although the discussion of these particular topics conveyed some of the challenges of aging in our culture, I was left wondering whether or not our society truly "gets it" about the need to change how we view the process of aging. Because it seems to me that how we perceive aging and the viability of older adults determines our willingness — or reluctance — to tackle social inequity, lack of access to services and opportunities, and other common challenges that elders face.

How do we know if we are aging well? What are the criteria by which we should measure our ability to function fully as older adults?

A popular way to describe what I'm talking about is the phrase *successful aging,* which is usually contrasted with "normal" or "usual" aging. One description of successful aging involves "freedom from disability and disease, high cognitive and physical functioning, and social productivity and engagement."[15] But that's only one reference. Searching the term on the Internet yields more than 285 million results, the overwhelming number of which emphasize personal lifestyle choices and behavior, such as how much and often a person chooses to exercise or whether s/he has saved enough money for retirement.

But there's an inherent problem with equating aging with the kind of success that is solely based on conscious individual achievement. For how many conscious decisions, including exercising and saving for retirement, do we really make on our own without being influenced by other, external factors?

Let's take exercise. If you belong to an athletic club, it's probably because you have the financial means to do so. If you have the time to walk, jog, or run in your neighborhood on a regular basis, perhaps it's because you don't have such obligations as being a full-time caregiver or having to work two or more jobs.

If you have enough money for retirement, perhaps it's because you worked a long time at a company that offered employees a pension, and you didn't get laid off in the 2008 recession because of your age. Or you didn't suffer a debilitating illness that drained you financially, despite having health insurance. Or you have a spouse or partner that has contributed significantly to your household income. Or you have a child who was able to attend college on an ample scholarship.

Of course, I'm not saying that personal decisions make no difference at all in how "successfully" we age. It's certainly vital that we exercise regularly, have a healthy diet, refrain from smoking, and embrace other forms of self-care, but I'm also asserting that society shouldn't attribute unsuccessful aging primarily to a lack of personal responsibility. Many obstacles can get in the way of elders' well-intentioned efforts to remain functional in mind and body, economically solvent, and socially engaged — obstacles primarily related to racism, sexism, classism, ableism, homophobia, and of course, ageism.

If the older adults in our communities aren't aging successfully, it can't be because each and every one of them has failed to live in a responsible way. Instead, it just might be that we have opted for "normal" or "usual" aging and haven't yet created a society that actively promotes and supports elders achieving the successful kind.

In short, maybe it's because *we* are failing *them.*

And thus, because of this failure, the term "successful aging" with all its attached misconceptions, is slow to die.

And I wish it would. Quickly. Here's why.

Every time we assign the sole responsibility of aging well to an individual, we disregard that person's uniqueness in a very unrealistic and unjust way. Each of us has gone through a combination of biological and socioeconomic experiences that have affected us at every turn.

Are you a male or a female? Are you a member of an ethnic or racial majority or minority? Females and minorities in general are economically disadvantaged throughout their lifespan, earning less than their white, male counterparts and subsequently receiving smaller pensions and Social Security benefits. In addition, more women than men leave the job market, becoming unpaid laborers who raise children and/or care for elder parents.

Have you spent most of your life on a farm or in the middle of a big city? Did you inherit great wealth, or have you had to earn all or most of your income? How much education were you able to afford and receive? What career paths were open to you? Have you ever experienced serious health problems that affected your ability to work? How many children, if any, do you have, and are they willing and able to help you in your later years if you need support? Do you have easy access to nearby and affordable housing, transportation, and other vital services for older adults?

Somehow questions such as these are still not factored into definitions of successful aging in most media discussions. And because these factors aren't foremost in the public's consciousness as issues to address, they are often ignored or considered irrelevant in government and private-sector policy decisions.

This situation must change. For "success" implies accomplishment within an established system. But what if that system is outmoded, disjointed, or worse, deliberately fostering social inequality? Then successful agers who have been lucky, wealthy, and in the majority are aging well *because of* our social policies and cultural norms. But agers in other categories who have managed nevertheless to age well are successful *despite* those same policies and norms. Their challenge has been far greater.

And let's not forget that there is a huge population of older adults who struggle to stay economically and physically stable as well as purposefully and socially engaged. In many cases their difficulties could be significantly eased if our society would only redefine "successful aging" in less polarizing terms.

Let's stop evaluating the level of success regarding aging as the result of either being ambitious and productive or being negligent and irresponsible.

In fact, let's totally ban the term *successful aging*. We need to replace that unproductive and discriminatory paradigm with one that is realistic, compassionate, and fair, one requiring an equal commitment between the individual *and* society.

Let's coin a new term: *empowered aging*.

Why "empowered"? Because it moves the focus away from the static goal of accomplishment and toward an ongoing process of maintaining autonomy, dignity, and self-worth through interdependence.

This bilateral commitment of the individual and society should be fostered throughout a person's life, starting from childhood. We should be raising children to appreciate every age through which they pass and to expect our cultural values to honor and support them all along the way, in their education, careers, personal relationships, and social contributions.

It's only when an individual's skills, values, aspirations, personal history, and beliefs are continuously supported by a pro-aging society's realistic expectations and common goals for all its citizens and its diverse opportunities supported by appropriate public policies, that empowerment becomes the inevitable human condition.

And isn't that the kind of success we should aim to achieve?

# ON ASKING "THE QUESTION"

"How old are you?"

I was asked this question at the end of a presentation I gave years ago called "It's All in Your Mind! How to Keep Your Brain Fit and Strong" to residents of an independent living community. The query caught me by surprise because I'm rarely asked about my age these days.

As children and teens, most of us are asked this question a lot…and are proud to answer it. That's because asking a younger person's age is usually a conversation starter, right after "What's your name?" And the exchange is a joyful one. Adults want to form a quick connection by allowing youngers to give exacting responses that show how "grown-up" they are: "I'm 6¾." "I'm almost 10." "I'll be 18 in March." But as the years pass, we become aware of the serious implications behind the inquiry.

Like questions about any other topic, the ones we ask about aging and the ways in which we choose to answer them reveal what we believe and care about.

When is it ever acceptable to ask a person's age? In other words, when is the question relevant?

As I see it, the only condition under which knowing a person's age is important is an external one, based on the need to administer a program or a law. Chronological age determines our policy age regarding the legal ability to drink alcohol, buy cigarettes, drive a car, vote, sign a contract, marry, enter military service, and qualify for Medicare and Social Security. It also determines who is considered a juvenile victim or adult perpetrator under our penal code. Administrators need cutoff points for each of these situations, otherwise there would be no other way to set practical limits by determining who qualifies and who doesn't.

But that's it. Legal programs and services aside, there's no reason why a person's chronological age should limit his or her ability to do anything. Or to be *considered* to do anything.

And yet, we constantly apply internal perceptions of chronological age as qualification standards for a range of experiences. At what age should a person retire? Stop driving? Give over his/her decision-making powers to adult children or to others? At what age is it improper to apply for a job? To go to a dance club or back to school? To wear a hoodie or miniskirt? To engage in sex? To run for President of the United States?

We get into trouble when we hold on to stereotypical ideas of what a person could or should do at a certain age and thus confuse chronological age with an individual's ability to contribute to and benefit from society. Often it's only when we ourselves reach that age and hear those limitations placed on us by others that we are caught by surprise. And then we become frustrated and maybe even angry.

All of us, no matter our age, should be having these reactions about the limitations we place on older adults.

There's only one social instance in which raising the question of age is an appropriate reaction: when we are exposed to a group that is generationally homogenous *without a good reason*. I'm not talking about meetings of a teen chess club or a hiking outing for residents of a retirement community. If, however, there are very few or no older adults at a public meeting discussing problems and solutions regarding a community's schools, transportation system, public health policy, and other issues, we need to call attention to this situation and rectify it. Older opinions should be sought and older voices heard.

Conversely, older adults should consider opening up some of their social experiences to people of younger generations. Think about the diversity of ideas, learning experiences, and friendships that can be fostered by intergenerational book clubs, neighborhood projects, café salons, and other events.

We need to be aware of a lack of age diversity in social contexts where chronological age shouldn't be a factor. By working to bring generations together, not only do we break down physical barriers but psychological ones as well. We create a fluidity of perception based on individual experience rather than on the turning of calendar pages. Thus we can make telling our age a positive — and even irrelevant — statement, no matter how old we are.

As for that age question posed to me at the independent living community, my response at the time — "I'm 64. And damn proud of it!" — caused smiles among the elders gathered to hear me talk about brain fitness. But as I spoke, I looked around the lecture hall and made a mental note to approach the activities director with a question of my own:

"How about inviting younger people in the surrounding community to join us next time?"

# THE SIX ASSETS OF AGING

I have to admit that as I get older, I get more tired. Not so much physically or mentally, although I do have my moments of fatigue. (Doesn't everyone at every age?) What I'm tired of is the ubiquitous, insidious, and rather stupid meme that considers aging to be a process of nothing but deterioration and decline. It's a handy propaganda tool for feeding the coffers of the anti-aging cosmetics, supplements, and plastic surgery industries and pressuring us older adults to remain moored to the dock of middle age rather than to cast off and sail in whatever new directions we choose.

The deterioration-decline meme originates in a narrow perception of the lifespan that is blind to the priceless assets we accrue as we add years to our lives. And this blindness stimulates our deeply entrenched societal ageism, which further limits that perception. Breaking this cycle of prejudice isn't easy, but it's possible, once we understand exactly what we gain *because of*, rather than *despite*, aging.

I've already described two important assets of older age: the **broader experience, sharper skills,** and **greater wisdom** we can acquire if we make an effort to do so. Likewise, I have explained our **greater individuation** as we age, a trait that's a good thing, because our cumulative individualities add to the diversity of humankind and to what we can share with younger generations.

These aren't the only assets we older adults possess. Here are four more:

**Closer proximity to mortality.** Yes, it's true that no matter our age, any of us can die from a terrible accident, traumatic illness, natural disaster, or cruel human act. But in the course of a life otherwise undisturbed by these events, our consciousness of mortality grows, and this increased ability gives us elders the advantage of savoring moments as the precious gifts they are.

**Different motives and life purpose.** According to developmental psychologist Erik Erikson, aging involves the evolution of individual personality. In the late 1950s, he posited the now-well-accepted paradigm of eight stages of personality development from birth through old age.[16] The last stage, above age 65, is characterized by a person's need and desire to reflect back on the life s/he has lived and to make sense of it. It's a process equivalent to what I have already described as spiritual eldering. No longer is it important to struggle for recognition or success according to society's terms. The motives of old age are to "put all the pieces together" and to find a personal sense of fulfillment. This awareness is an asset not easily acquired without first having faced and overcome other emotional challenges over a six-decades-plus lifetime.

**A different brain.** All of the above assets can be attributed to an additional asset: the experience of age-related changes that occur in the human brain. For example, a healthy human brain keeps growing new cells and new connections between existing cells throughout life. In addition, the bridge of tissue known as the corpus callosum, which connects the left and right hemispheres, doesn't fully mature until a person reaches about 50 years old, and this helps explain why older adults are able to solve problems from a greater number of perspectives: Their hemispheres operate in greater sync. Also, the ability known as crystallized intelligence, exemplified in long-term memory, grows with age and allows for better application of past experiences to help discriminate relevant from irrelevant information when problem-solving. While there are some declines in cognition that can occur with age, the fact that some major benefits also can be accrued should tell us that aging isn't the downhill trajectory we are led to believe it is.

**Strength in numbers.** This is probably the most significant asset of all, because there are so many more of us adding to the older population each day. Aside from climate change, the global aging of the population is the most significant force affecting our planet now and in years to come. How societies respond to this force will determine whether and how we will survive. With our five other assets displaying themselves in a myriad of ways, we older adults can demonstrate clearly that what many people believe is a looming disaster beginning to threaten society is actually a timely windfall full of promise, purpose, and yes, assets, waiting to be tapped and shared with future generations.

The next time you encounter someone pushing the deterioration-decline meme, feel free to explain any or all of these six great assets. Better yet, don't wait until the occasion arises. Proudly embody them every day in your words and actions.

Hopefully, in time, the people who rely on that meme will get very tired of using it.

# CHAPTER 3

# Seeing with Fresh Eyes

**WHEN I WAS IN COLLEGE** in New York City in the early 1970s, one of the requirements of freshman year was to choose a course from among the offerings in the philosophy department. So I registered for "Introduction to Ethics and Metaphysics."

The professor was brilliant not only in his scope of knowledge but also in his teaching technique. The first day of class he wrote the final-exam essay question on the blackboard. It was this. "What would you be willing to fight and die for?" He wrote the question, asked us to copy it down, and then erased it. And he said nothing more about it for the rest of the semester.

Throughout the next 13 weeks, he let our natural inductive reasoning go to work on the problem. As we covered the philosophies of Plato, Aristotle, Descartes, Pascal, John Stuart Mill, Immanuel Kant, Nietzsche, the Transcendentalists, and others, he knew that we would be looking at how each theory reflected or contradicted our own moral code. And he was right.

You might be wondering what I wrote about. Surprisingly, it didn't dawn on me to be willing to fight and die for Love or Justice or Religion or even Freedom. My answer was Beauty. At the time, I believed it subsumed all other possible ethical values.

If today, after more than 50 years of personal growth, I could take that final exam again, I'd have a different answer. I'd say Metaphors. Not *a* metaphor, mind you, but the *process of making* metaphors. Because I believe that thoughts and feelings about Love, Justice, Religion, Freedom, and even Beauty don't exist without personal meaning. And personal meaning doesn't exist without metaphors.

We don't necessarily choose to make metaphors as much as we unconsciously do so. It's an instinctive human process. According to Christian theologian John Dominic Crossan, "Humans are meaning-seeking animals…we pursue meaning the way heat-seeking missiles hunt exhaust."[1]

How's *that* for a metaphor?

It's fascinating to witness this creative process in action. If you've ever been around small children, you can probably attest to this. I remember an instance more than 40 years ago when I was lunching with a friend and her 3-year-old daughter. The child was drinking milk, and we were drinking soda. Never having had a carbonated drink before, she figured out that now was her chance, with a guest around, to cajole her mom into letting her have a taste. At her first sip, her eyes grew wide.

"Mommy!" she exclaimed. "It tastes like stars!"

No poet could have done a better job capturing the essence of that sparkling substance.

Such imagery is born from imagination, a gift most of us have in greater abundance when we're young and many of us tend to slowly lose touch with as we age, as our critical thinking skills take hold. Or maybe it's our complacency that begins to run things, convincing us to accept what others say about something rather than demand that we judge for ourselves what is true and has meaning and value based on our experience.

And maybe that's why we unconsciously buy into societal attitudes about aging. We accept others' metaphors for that process, involving shaky hands, stooped postures, and confused facial expressions, as well as stereotypical images of older adults in the form of archetypes, such as the cranky old next-door neighbor chasing kids off his lawn; the kindly, doting-but-flaky grandma who has a hard time remembering her grand-kids' names; or the out-of-touch boss who wants nothing to do with upgrading the office technology.

However vivid those metaphors are, they can actually work against our individual growth as we age, alienating us from ourselves and from our ability to feel integrated and empowered in the world. Instead of expressing timeless truths, these kinds of images reflect the narrow values of a limited society — values which may no longer apply in our own lives or which we may consciously choose to reject. Until we make such a choice, we can, nevertheless, be influenced by such counterproductive ideas.

But what if you tapped into your imagination and came up with your own truths about getting older, ones based on your own experiences? What if you can wipe off the foggy eyeglasses of your consciousness and tilt your mind just a bit to the side, or turn the landscape of aging upside down and, seeing with fresh eyes, draw a Betty Edwards picture of what is there?

It's not that hard to do, really, with just a bit of practice. To get an idea of what I mean, the following pages of this chapter contain a few examples of my own metaphor-making. Perhaps they'll resonate with you and prod you to consider the possibility that each of us has the potential skill to open portals to new ideas about aging. For me, the metaphors we create are great keys for unlocking those doors.

I believe we rely on metaphors to make our lives understandable, meaningful, endurable, and productive for ourselves and for others.

But to do so, we need to free ourselves from more mundane, status quo impulses and let our imaginations take charge.

So here's a final-exam essay question for you on the issue of aging: "What would you be willing to *grow old* for?"

I hope you'll work on coming up with a deeply satisfying answer as you begin to allow your natural inductive reasoning to reconsider and revise everything you have heard — and think you know — about aging.

# LET'S GET OVER BEING "OVER THE HILL"

How would you describe an older person, say, one who's about 75? What image comes into your mind that seems to appropriately represent what it's like to have accumulated many years of life? A stately old elm tree with huge, gnarly branches? A rock by the sea that has been eroded by the battering of countless storm-blown waves? A once-overflowing river that has dried out and been reduced to a shallow stream? A well-worn sofa that has offered years of repose and comfort to a family?

We use lots of metaphors to describe the aging process as well as someone who has experienced it for many decades. Some images may be positive, but more often than not, because our culture is mainly youth-obsessed and age-fearful, most of them reflect conditions of deterioration and decline.

The most common phrase of this sort is to describe an old person as "over the hill." That term has become so attractive that it's grown into a most pervasive — and profitable —meme of its own: over-the-hill cards as a genre of birthday greetings that rely on harmless mockery of their recipients. But even if we smile when sending or receiving such a card, the mockery isn't harmless at all, because it resonates with our subliminal fear and dread of aging...and reinforces it.

I think it's about time we analyze this particular phrase.

From the moment we're born, we experience social challenges to our survival and growth. Can we walk on our own? Can we learn to communicate to get our needs met by others? Can we make friends, succeed at school, earn a living, find a life partner, raise a family, discover our passion and purpose?

As a metaphor expressing any of those challenges, climbing a hill pretty much fits the bill. For what does it mean to negotiate steep terrain? It requires a certain amount of endurance, energy, determination, and practice. When you think about it, we "climb a hill" when we work toward reaching the goal of anything that matters to us.

To succeed in our upward treks, it helps to rely on a few important things. Training, for instance. The taller and steeper the challenge, the more it behooves and serves us to learn the ropes, so to speak, for making our way to the top. We can also benefit from having teachers who have had experience making the same trips and guides who can accompany us on our way. And, just as importantly, we need encouragement from those around us who honor our aspirations and our expectations of ourselves, who believe not only that we can achieve our dreams but also that we have the *right* to do so.

I'm not belaboring the hill metaphor by expounding on it like this. It really is the perfect way to talk about the process of living, which, if we are willing to consider it, is identical to the process of aging.

Given all of this, how did our culture determine that at some point in our lifespan there are no more challenges for any of us to face, or that it's useless to even try to meet those challenges and instead call it quits and return to ground level? When is it ever OK to describe an older person as "over the hill"?

Here's what needs to be said, to set the record straight: The longer we have lived, the more we have experienced. The more we have experienced, the more challenges we have faced. Older adults are longer-term climbers of all kinds of uphill terrain. You might even say we're the Master Climbers.

No older adult is "over the hill." S/He is at the top of a particular hill and because of this setting actually sees other hills in the distance yet to climb which couldn't be perceived from the bottom of the hill that s/he just ascended.

Let's get over being "over the hill." It's time we stop using this horrible phrase for good.

That is, for the good of us all.

# WHAT'S YOUR RELATIONSHIP WITH AGING?

As I've said before, if you're alive, you're aging. Unfortunately, many people have varying degrees of awareness of this fact. Some of us are conscious of the reality of getting older on an almost constant basis. Others of us barely give it a thought. Most of us fall somewhere in the middle.

What's more important, perhaps, isn't how often we think about aging but rather, how we feel about it when we do. Are those thoughts positive or negative ones? Do we welcome them or try to keep them from coming to mind at all? Our relationship with the aging process not only tells us important things about how we see ourselves but also about our willingness to see others of all ages as equally viable human beings.

And so, a question arises: What's your relationship with aging? I ask it in this way because living with aging is analogous to having a relationship with another person, which can be described in one of four ways.

## Aging as an "Enemy"

People who experience aging in combative terms are doing so from a place of fear. To them, getting older means becoming more vulnerable to inevitable degeneration and decline. It's a threat they struggle to defeat despite the reality that aging is a natural process of life. Nevertheless, they do all that they can to hold aging at bay for as long as possible by using such weapons as Botox, hair dye, and suspect nutritional supplements.

## Aging as a "Stranger"

People who treat aging as a stranger are basically in denial about the fact that they are getting older. Aging takes on the veneer of unfamiliarity, of being foreign to one's personal experience and moreover, something to avoid at all costs. "Who me?" they say. "No way! I'm not old." Of course, this reaction is based on the same kind of fear with which one confronts an enemy, only the tactic is more one of flight rather than fight.

## Aging as a "Neighbor"

Many people treat aging in the same way that they might tolerate an unpleasant next-door neighbor whom they occasionally feel obligated to acknowledge during brief encounters while trimming the hedges or retrieving the mail or morning paper. They are polite and try to keep the interaction short. They deal with their aches and pains as inevitable, later-years symptoms and stoically endure experiences of ageism, all the while failing to perceive any advantages to getting older.

## Aging as a "Friend"

This kind of relationship is characterized by meaningful engagement. Like any friendship, aging can sometimes be challenging and problematic but also deeply rewarding in the many experiences and insights it brings. People who treat the aging process as a valued friend mindfully seek to nurture it and will defend its honor and dignity when confronted by outsiders who threaten to diminish its importance. They stand up to ageism just as they would to a bully who is pushing their friend around. And they look forward to more years of such a fulfilling relationship.

It's easy to see that each of us not only falls somewhere along this enemy-stranger-neighbor-friend spectrum, but that during the course of our lives we often move from one type of relationship with aging to another.

Consider this: As young children, we can't wait to get older. When asked our age, we often want to make it very clear that we are "9¾" or "almost 12." Aging is not only our friend but our superhero — able to grant us newly acquired special powers at each stage of life. As teens, we can't wait to be old enough to drive, then old enough to go to college, get a job, get an apartment, and/or get married.

But somewhere along the way, say, around middle age, our youth-centric society begins to pressure us to break up with our friend and see the "reality" of the personal threat that aging poses. Then aging becomes like an "ex" whom we'd like to forget but keeps reappearing and has to be dealt with. And the relationship often grows more acrimonious with time.

But it doesn't have to be that way. Our relationship with aging can remain as a loving friendship throughout our lives when we understand that it's a cumulative experience that provides us with an ever-changing variety of psychological and spiritual gifts — if we are open to anticipating and accepting them.

So I ask again: What's *your* relationship with aging?

If you've had a falling out somewhere along the way, maybe it's time to reconcile.

# ON THE VALUE OF WEEDS

There are many negative, inaccurate ways in which our society either openly or subtly categorizes what is occasionally termed the "oldest old" people, those above age 85: They are humans who have outlived their midlife productivity. They are monolithic aliens, all of whom are alike and with whom it's difficult to identify, given our current younger ages. They are "those people" whom we dread becoming because we somehow know that if we live long enough, we will eventually be them.

Here's the thing: I believe that very old people are...weeds. And that's a good thing.

In our culture, weeds are those ubiquitous plants we either ignore or try to eradicate from the neat mental landscape of our lives, omnipresent reminders that vitality can appear anywhere and in any form. Whether or not we recognize this vitality and appreciate it is up to us. When we label something a "weed," we define it as a useless nuisance. "But," wrote an unknown author, "a weed is simply a plant that wants to grow where people want something else. In blaming nature, people mistake the culprit. Weeds are people's idea, not nature's."

To an ageist society repulsed by very old age, perpetual youth is that very desirable "something else." But if we consider the weed metaphor more closely, we might begin to better understand what we are denying ourselves as a culture when we devalue and ignore or actively marginalize those who have attained a very old age.

What are some common, positive characteristics of weeds and the oldest among us?

**They have the capacity to produce, store, and disseminate many seeds.** Think of the numerous ideas, experiences, and skills elders have accumulated throughout their lives. A significant majority of them are cognitively able to share their bounty and may want to do so but aren't given any or enough opportunities. The more determined and assertive among them share their gifts anyway, regardless of whether or not those gifts are accepted, let alone acknowledged. And those who are living with dementia have their own gifts to share, namely serving as mirrors and models of dignified aging who can teach us how to communicate and connect nonverbally and noncognitively in our cognitively obsessed world.

**They can be tenacious, subsisting in the most unsupportable and even hostile of environments.** No one survives to a very old age without having developed the ability to adapt to changes in circumstance or environment. Often weeds continue to exist and even to grow despite lack of care rather than because of it. They have been known to emerge through cracks in concrete sidewalks and brick or stone walls. Might we also imagine the impulses for passion and creativity that emerge from people living within the solid isolation of homes and the hard, inflexible institutional structures of many long-term-care facilities?

**They often take hold and populate areas very quickly.** Rapid population growth of people aged 85 and older is a major global demographic trend. But this shouldn't cause fearful, fatalistic projections if we recognize the potential abundance — rather than scarcity — that results from incorporating the untapped source of human capital the oldest people can provide in the forms of mentoring and sharing institutional memory. And those forms can vary widely. American journalist Doug Larson is right when he writes, "A weed is a plant that has mastered every survival skill except for learning how to grow in rows."[2] As you now know, the older we get, the more diverse from one another we become. Nature loves diversity and supports it within species. We should, too.

**They can provide benefits that help all of us thrive.** Just as weeds stabilize topsoil and keep it from eroding, so, too, can such longstanding social values as diligence, compassion, and responsibility held by many of the oldest among us help to prevent the erosion of our civil norms. And just as weeds can add fertility to the soil or have medicinal or economic value (think dandelions and chamomile), likewise people of all ages have the potential to fertilize social ventures with innovative ideas, add to the common revenue, and attune our cultural perspectives on an ongoing basis.

One person's weed is another's food source or flower. Instead of perceiving old age as a human condition that competes with youth for scarce resources, what if we consider the abundance of sustenance and beauty we might reap if only our society has the courage to integrate back into our communities the oldest among us? The natural resilience of many very old people can render this task quite feasible if we are willing to let a new nature take its course.

Like so many weeds whose value was unknown in the past and only later to be discovered, there is a vital crop of humanity eager to be harvested and engaged.

What are we waiting for?

# THE JACK BENNY SYNDROME

It's funny how each of us can evoke a stereotype and not even know it until it's called to our attention. And it's even more remarkable that we can easily shatter that image just by being ourselves.

That's what happened to me in 1990 when, at age 38, I moved to Charlotte, N.C. from my birthplace of New York City. To make ends meet in my new location until I found more permanent employment, I took a job as a clerk in a large store. There I met two other clerks: lovely, soft-spoken Southern ladies who had worked at that store for years. I was the first New Yorker they had ever met. They were intrigued by my outgoing, fast-talking ways and asked me all kinds of questions about life in The Big Apple.

"Is Central Park really a dangerous place?"

"No," I replied.

"How are you able to think with all that noise?"

"You really don't notice it if you're born and raised there."

And so on.

Finally, one of the women overcame her sense of propriety and blurted out, "But you're so nice and friendly for a New Yorker!" That's when it occurred to me that I was simultaneously representing and shattering a stereotype of the angry, rude Northerner from a dirty, violent city. And I was happy to oblige them.

Of course, when I first got that job, I could have decided to hide or at least downplay my New York mannerisms (although I doubt that I could have done it successfully for very long). I could have consciously attempted to blend in as much as I could. But that would have been not only futile but dishonest.

Over the years, I've thought a lot about age stereotypes and their relationship to our willingness — or reluctance — to be ourselves. This issue was brought into stronger focus for me in 2015, when I read a provocative blog post called "Lying About My Age" by then–77-year-old Warren Adler, author of *The War of the Roses* and more than 40 other novels. In it, he describes the immediate change in response by many people he encounters, merely at the mention of his age: "In a flash I have changed my status from respectful and collegial and transformed it suddenly to 'over the hill,' someone to be tolerated, politely and diplomatically endured but no longer consequential."[3]

In many ways, admitting one's age can be the equivalent of pulling the trigger on the starting gun at a track meet. You can't take back the sound once the race has begun. Depending on the circumstances, say, during a job interview, it can mean the immediate end of an opportunity. And even though age discrimination is illegal, one's appearance (*e.g.,* gray or obviously dyed hair, especially in a woman), year of college graduation (usually more than 10 years in the past), or other clues can give you away. As if any of this should matter.

But it does.

When did we, as a society, begin to assume that age was a liability? I'm not sure, but I can certainly trace it at least as far back as the career of comedian Jack Benny. Those of us who remember him from his radio and TV shows know that Benny was famous for three shticks: being a cheapskate (in real life, he was a philanthropist), playing the violin badly (actually, he was quite good), and claiming to be perpetually 39 years old. Benny milked that lying-about-his-age joke until his death at age 80 in 1974. He knew it was a ridiculous premise. We all knew it was ridiculous. But we laughed, anyway. Why?

I suspect that the laughter was derived from a sense of pity for a character who was getting older and desperately trying to deny that reality.

Perhaps we felt for him because we implicitly agreed with the assumption that getting old was something to dread. Unconsciously, we were buying into the negative stereotypes of old age.

Ironically, it was Benny's contemporary and best friend who provided the best antidote to that skewed perception. Comedian George Burns took a very different approach. For him, age was never a shtick. In fact, up until the day he died in 1996 at age 100, he flaunted it. Always with his trademark lit cigar, he practically dared his audiences to challenge his quick, sarcastic wit and impeccable timing, taking a puff before delivering each punchline. Like Benny, Burns was clear and sharp till the very end, both of whom mentored and promoted up-and-coming, much younger comedians who, in turn, admired and even tried to imitate them.

Two different takes on aging. I prefer Burns's approach.

It seems to me that the only way to begin shattering ageist stereotypes is if we older adults take the responsibility to act first, to pick up that starting gun and fire. To do this successfully, we should make our noises strategic ones. We can say no to Botox and hair-dying. We can declare our age, rather than hide or meekly admit it. We can — and must — be ourselves, proudly.

At least, that's the approach I, once having turned 70, chose.

Oh, and as for those two genteel Southern ladies, they also taught me a lesson in stereotyping. It wasn't long before I noticed that one of them would ruthlessly swoop in before any other salesperson to catch shoppers as they entered the store so that she could be the one to make the next sale and thus maximize her commission. And the other turned out to be quite a card shark, cleaning out the stockroom guys on paydays at their after-hours poker game in the back room.

In Warren Adler's words: "It is hard to reeducate people to the notion that humans are not like socks, where one size fits all."[4]

Indeed.

And so, in memory of Benny and Burns, I say: On your mark…Get set…Let the lessons begin.

# TURNING THE TIDE ON THE "SILVER TSUNAMI"

As we all know, there are those who profit from social prejudice such as racism, sexism, and homophobia and thus have a vested interest in keeping that prejudice alive. Their method of choice is to instill fear in us by insisting that our economy will suffer and our social fabric will fray if we give ourselves permission to tolerate and even welcome the dangerous "others" in our midst.

Ageism — which has certainly been around a long time — is not immune to such fearmongering. In fact, one of the most successful tactics to keep it going is the widespread use of the anxiety-provoking image of a "silver tsunami" to describe the arrival into older adulthood of the huge Baby Boomer generation of about 77 million people born between 1946 and 1964 and that cohort's destructive economic impact on society.

It is a fact that about 10,000 Boomers turn 65 each day and will do so until 2029.[5] To many Americans, this is cause for alarm because they wonder about the solvency of Social Security and Medicare. They also wonder how many people of this generation have been negatively affected by the economic crash of 2008 and are choosing not to retire primarily because they can't afford to. They see this as a threat to younger genera-tions taking their place in the workforce and moving up in it.[6]

But there's a real problem with equating the increasing growth of an older population with the effect of a tsunami. Two problems, in fact: one geological and the other gerontological.

Let's start with the geological problem. According to the National Oceanic and Atmospheric Administration, "A tsunami is a series of large waves generated by the sudden displacement of water during an earthquake, landslide, volcanic eruption, or meteorite impact."[7] The key phrase here is "sudden displacement." The earth's surface shifts without warning, triggering a disturbance of far-reaching, catastrophic proportions.

This sudden change doesn't apply to the Baby Boom generation. The American population has slowly been absorbing its 65-year-olds into elderhood since 2011. If it seems sudden, it's only because we as a society have closed our collective eyes to this gradual trend and have done little or nothing to prepare for it.

As for the gerontological problem, fearmongering is far more insidious when ageism is no longer just a numbers game in which older adults are assumed to be an economic drain. Instead, when ageism is turned into a moral crusade, it advocates that older adults (who, of course, must be needy because they are also in impending physical and cognitive decline!) be placed somewhere apart from the general younger population to be "taken care of" and that everyone else be left to engage in the productive business of life.

For the benefit of all generations, our society must rid itself of the cultural myopia that sees aging solely in terms of deficit. It's time we turn the tide on the silver tsunami myth and find a different metaphor, one that accurately reflects the huge assets older adults bring to all aspects of life.

In other words, how about a "silver reservoir"?

For what is a reservoir, anyway, but a place that stores water, an essential element of life, for the purpose of supplying it to a community? The water comes from mountain streams and rivers, usually across great distances and accumulated over time. The water is used for drinking, washing, bathing, running power sources, maintaining manufacturing processes, irrigating crops, and turning barren soil into productive farmland.

It's not a real stretch of the imagination to see how the accumulation of a large older adult population is an enormous potential resource for good in our society rather than an impending danger that threatens to wipe out everyone.

Granted, the image of a reservoir is not as sexy or exciting as that of a tsunami, but it could be. Imagine opening up to elders the floodgates of opportunity so wide that the energy and power of all that pent-up wisdom and experience would be released to inundate and irrigate society, creating new businesses that hire millions of young people; offering innovative, multiperspective solutions to longstanding social problems; and providing multitudes of volunteers for nonprofit causes.

Let's erase from our social lexicon the ageist image of a silver tsunami, gently correcting others who use it. Let's replace it with the metaphor of a vital and inexhaustible resource and offer this life-affirming — and accurate — picture of how, by transcending aging, we can transform society.

Let's turn a tidal wave of destruction into an exhilarating wave of the future all generations can ride.

# WHERE ARE THE GOLDEN YEARS?

One of my *Ageful Living* blog posts, "Dick and Jane Grow Up," (see Chapter 8) inspired some intriguing comments. One in particular gave me pause for further reflection. Here it is in its entirety:

OK, so you are an exception to the average senior. Yes, there are senior athletes, and employees working well past their designated retirement age, but please look around and take inventory of the average senior. Many have chosen a lifestyle of low activity, poor diet, and high alcohol. Dick and Jane have grown up, but they have to realize how hard it is to fight the aging process. I see it daily in my clinic, the repeated expression, 'Where are the golden years?' These are people who have lived good lives and now have bad knees, hips, need stents, hearing aids, etc. If you are in good shape, then thank you for your efforts, and please encourage others.

The commenter brings up two good points: 1) Many older adults have chosen counterproductive lifestyle behaviors that are now affecting their health, and 2) they are not working hard enough to reverse the effects of those behaviors.

But two other issues in his reaction gave me cause to reflect.

First of all, his use of the phrase "in my clinic" leads me to assume that he is a health care professional and is assessing "the average senior" based on his daily experiences with those whom he serves. And so I wonder about the sample population of older adults from which he's drawing his conclusions. After all, since the people he sees have a need for his medical services, they are a self-selecting group. We might assume that he sees very few older patients for routine checkups and many others he doesn't see at all, precisely because they are active and fairly healthy. Although the aging process does take somewhat of a toll on the human body, as a population, today's adults 65 and older are healthier than were previous generations of elders. And this should give us cause for optimism.

There's another, more important issue: how those disillusioned elders in his clinic are defining "the golden years." The phrase seems to evoke the idea of well-earned leisure, a time of rest, relaxation, and reward without cares or the obligation to maintain a level of economic productivity and the kinds of social interaction that define young and middle-aged adulthood.

But let's look more metaphorically at the word *golden*. Gold is a relatively rare and therefore precious metal not usually applied to most everyday practical uses. Pure gold is soft and malleable, sensitive to pressure and able to be manipulated easily by external forces. It is lovely to look at and never loses its shine. It is desirable to possess, mainly because it is an exceptional material and takes us out of the realm of the ordinary.

And because of these various images, I think golden is an inappropriate word to describe our later years. Many elders continually experience the pressures of social and economic marginalization and isolation. They may be treated as fragile, superfluous, and most disturbing of all, infantile. It takes powerful mental and emotional constitutions on their part to reject the stereotypical impulses of others and instead insist on contributing their time, wisdom, and talents to others and being included in everyday affairs and treated with respect. It takes a willpower that has been strengthened over a lifetime of challenges and adjustments to loss and change of all kinds. It takes guts to deal with ageism and to maintain dignity and self-esteem in the process.

In the immortal words often attributed to actor Bette Davis, "Old age ain't no place for sissies."[8]

And so I'd like to suggest that in our discussions of the later years of life we substitute the image of gold with that of another metal: steel.

Rather than being a pure and precious material, steel is an alloy that has been tempered by repeated exposure to changing environments of heat and cold. It is a substance from which everyday, useful things vital to society, such as cars, ships, planes, and skyscrapers, are built. That's how all of us should aspire to be as older adults — people of steel who are necessary to supporting and maintaining the infrastructures of culture, environment, and society.

As my blog post commenter suggests, we older adults should take responsibility for keeping ourselves as healthy and vital as possible. But I'll go a step further and say we should also take responsibility for changing social misperceptions about the "golden years" of old age and instead "steel ourselves" to forge a newer and better reality of elderhood.

Only then will we no longer need — or want — to ask, "Where are the golden years?"

# CHAPTER 4

# Aging on Our Minds

**HOPEFULLY BY NOW** you're getting used to the idea of applying a "sideways" approach to understanding aging by tilting the picture and viewing it with fresh eyes. Many of the wrong assumptions we have about growing older are based on that warped view of inevitable deterioration and decline promoted in the media by corporations interested in keeping us afraid enough to spend billions of dollars each year on products and procedures that promise to keep us young.

The reality is that while there are legitimate reasons for concern about the aging process such as a greater likelihood of living in isolation or developing age-related conditions such as cancer, heart disease, and dementia, as we ease into the realm of elderhood sometime in our late 50s, we often find the territory to be less scary and treacherous to negotiate than we first anticipated. This was illustrated in a 2022 Forbes/OnePoll survey of 2,000 U.S. adults aged 18 and older measuring their fears about getting old. The results showed that just over half of people aged 18 to 57 fear the aging process, and the percentages continue to decrease even more sharply for those aged 58 to 65 (38%), 66 to 76 (30%), and 77-plus (21%).[1]

What explains this gradual trend toward greater acceptance of growing older? In her revolutionary book *This Chair Rocks: A Manifesto Against Ageism*, Ashton Applewhite offers two anecdotes that help answer this question:

Over lunch on Manhattan's Upper East Side, I asked the eminent geriatrician Robert Butler what had surprised him about the aging process as he moved into his eighties. "The only thing, and I don't know if it's a surprise or not, is that I think you become less uneasy about death," he replied. "I'd say that in the middle years I became more conscious of it. In fact Schopenhauer said mid-life is that point in time of life when you begin to think backwards from death instead of forward from birth, which I thought was a pretty shrewd observation."[2]

It turns out that the awareness that time is short doesn't fill people with dread. It makes people spend their time more wisely. Laura Carstensen of the Stanford Longevity Center brought this point home at a seminar at the Columbia Journalism School in 2012. Her research shows that humans always set goals in a temporal context, and that those time lines change as a function of mortality. Those who perceive their time as short typically attach greater importance to finding emotional meaning and satisfaction in life, and invest fewer resources into gathering information and expanding horizons.[3]

It's therefore common for older adults to lose interest in pursuing those activities and people who don't add to — and especially detract from

— their quality of life as they define it. This been-there-done-that reflex frees them to better prioritize their needs and devote more time to them.

Of course, doing this requires maintaining autonomy, independence, and social relationships. Not surprisingly, in that same Forbes/OnePoll survey, "declining health" (63%), "losing loved ones" (52%), and "financial resources" (38%) were older adults' top three greatest fears about aging.[4]

It's also clear from that 63% figure that for most of us, maintaining our health is of greatest concern. More specifically, the survey's respondents expressed equal fear of experiencing "mobility issues (including arthritis, joint deterioration, etc.)," "cancer of any kind," and "cognitive decline (including all types of dementia)."[5]

It's obvious that we have aging on our minds. And given that fear-based health category of cognitive decline, it appears that we also fear the aging *of* our minds. So let's explore the misconceptions many of us have about what's in store for our brains in our later years.

The greatest myth about the aging brain is that in time it will likely deteriorate to a point in which it loses the ability to think. In other words, we assume that for most of us debilitating cognitive decline is our destiny. However, as I mentioned before, 4 out of 5 people in their 80s and 2 out of 3 people in their 90s and older *don't* have dementia. And the percentages drop to single-digit numbers for people in their 60s and 70s.[6] Because the overwhelming number of us don't understand how our brains work, we necessarily base this belief on what we observe all around us, plus what we read in the media. The problem is that we consciously or unconsciously give a lot more credence to what the media tell us than to what our own experiences reveal.

Think about it: Of all the old people you encounter — family members, friends, acquaintances, people in stores, coworkers, health care providers, teachers — what percentage would you estimate behave as if they are cognitively impaired? I would guess that your estimate wouldn't be anywhere as high as what the many newspaper and magazine articles would have us accept as the reality of old age. How else to explain the many public discussions about the need to establish term limits for elder politicians or mandatory retirement ages for older employees?

So why is it easier to discount our own experiences when thinking about the future of our brains?

One reason is that we are bombarded constantly by negative tropes, images, and jokes about old age in the form of advertisements, social media rants, and late-night talk-show monologues. Again, keeping us turned off to the prospect of aging meets the needs of people with agendas having little to do with our welfare.

Another likely answer is that we already experience some lapses in memory recall (*e.g.*, not remembering where we put our notebooks or car keys, wondering what we were looking for in the moment after we opened a closet door, forgetting the name of someone to whom we were just introduced) and assume such events indicate the beginning of dementia. Take heart: Those situations happen even in our childhood, teen, and young adult years.

At this point, it's a good idea to consider what is meant by the term *dementia*. It's often referred to as a disease, but it's really a syndrome, a group of symptoms that, depending on the specific disease, can include loss of memory, decreased problem-solving and language skills, personality changes, agitation, depression, and hallucinations. There are more than 100 forms of dementia, with the most common being Alzheimer's disease, vascular dementia, frontotemporal dementia, dementia with Lewy bodies, and Parkinson's disease dementia.

Serious cognitive decline defined as dementia occurs much less frequently than we think. In fact, its incidence is actually declining. According to one U.S. study, "The age-adjusted prevalence of dementia decreased from 12.2% in 2000...to 8.5% in 2016... in the 65+

population, a statistically significant decline of 3.7 percentage points or 30.1%."[7]

In addition, according to the Population Reference Bureau, "The proportion of adults ages 70 and older with dementia declined from 13% in 2011 to 10% in 2019…. The share of older people with dementia is decreasing 1% to 2.5% per year, depending on the time frame and age group examined."[8]

Let's take a moment to think about these numbers. And then let's reconsider how intensely we should fear severe cognitive decline as we age.

That's not to say that we should entirely ignore that possibility, for even a 33% incidence of dementia among people 85 and older is something that should concern us. While genetics play a role in some forms of dementia, certain negative lifestyle factors such as sleep deprivation and drug interactions can also cause dementia symptoms. However, as I explained in Chapter 2, an estimated 4 in 10 cases of dementia may be delayed or prevented. Researchers have identified "12 modifiable risk factors" for developing dementia: "less education, hypertension, hearing impairment, smoking, obesity, depression, physical inactivity, diabetes, [ ] low social contact,…. excessive alcohol consumption, traumatic brain injury, and air pollution."[9] The fact that we can do some things to mitigate or avoid getting dementia should be heartening and inspire us to adopt healthier lifestyles.

So where does this leave us in our understanding of the traits and potential of older adult brains? We're constantly told to prepare for years of inevitable decline, but in the developed countries of the world at least, the numbers don't support that warning. If the rising average life expectancy at birth in any indication, the majority of older Americans are living longer, healthier, and more active lives than ever before in history. Few of them dread becoming even older than they are, provided that they can maintain their goals of being healthy, independent, and socially engaged.

But that's just a portion of what constitutes the capacities of older minds. Surely the ability to keep learning throughout life, the potential to acquire and apply experience-based wisdom, and the prospect of further developing one's creativity are goals everyone should be able to embrace in their later years. These goals are worth exploring in greater detail.

Aging is on our minds. But it's how we think about it that counts.

# OLD DOGS, NEW TRICKS, SMART LEARNERS

"You can't teach an old dog new tricks."

If there ever was a stereotype ripe for rejection, it's this one. When older adults thrive — let alone survive — it's precisely *because* they continually adjust to changes in their bodies, relationships, environments, and economic situations.

A clear demonstration of this resilience and flexibility takes place every day in lifelong-learning settings in which people in their 50s and beyond explore intellectual interests, artistic passions, personal-growth strategies, and encore-career skills. They're learning "new tricks" all the time.

Aside from its offensive stance, why is the "old dogs" adage wrong?

"This saying is based on an assumption that all old people are the same, which of course is not a tenable proposition," says Andrea Creech, professor of music pedagogy at the Schulich School of Music at McGill University in Montreal, Quebec. "In fact, as we grow older our individual differences increase — we become more different than the same, as we age. There is much evidence now that supports the view that older adults can learn new things and want to learn new things."[10]

Thomas Kamber, founder and executive director of Older Adults Technology Services (OATS) from AARP, has attested to this view. His organizations provide free classes to people over 60 on a variety of subjects, incorporating technology-skills training in the curricula. "I've been fortunate to teach extensively at the college level and also spend thousands of hours in the classroom with older adults," he says. "For pure joy of learning and commitment to gaining new knowledge and high standards of learning, I've never encountered any group more engaged than older adults."[11]

In many ways, they are like students of any age, studying to meet their specific needs for self-development and personal growth. Just as traditional college-aged students work toward a degree or meet other occupational requirements, many of today's older learners hone their skills in order to remain in the job market and even start their own businesses. Nevertheless, their desire for self-development and personal growth can take on additional meanings with the advancement of years.

According to Tim Carpenter, founder of EngAGE, a nonprofit organization that creates vibrant centers of learning within the walls of affordable senior and multigenerational apartment communities, "The motivation for learning can change as we age.… Often older adults learn for the sake of learning, attend classes to keep their mind active, and create social connection to like-minded people."[12]

Carrie Andreoletti, professor and chair of psychological science and coordinator of gerontology at Central Connecticut State University, adds to this portrait: "Older learners are more comfortable with ambiguity and less concerned about the 'right answer,'" she explains. "They don't want to be lectured to but want to be active participants in their own learning. They ask tough questions and want to know why something is important and how it is relevant to their own lives and experience."[13]

Creech agrees that relevance is a key driver of the educational experience for older learners:

As a general framework, I use the idea that "learning" opportunities for older adults should be framed by person-centered goals (goals that are personally meaningful, and relate to the idea of "being"), fellow-centered goals (goals that are concerned with collaboration, a sense of community, and relate to the idea of "belonging"), and matter-centered goals (goals to do with development, relating to the idea of "becoming").[14]

Similarly, older adults can bring different cognitive abilities to the task of learning. Many studies have determined that the human brain changes with age, acquiring certain skills as others begin to fade.

"Research shows that older people sometimes absorb certain kinds of information more slowly, but this is offset by deeper ability to contextualize and apply new concepts," Kamber explains.[15]

Creech clarifies this distinction: "There is some evidence that as we grow older we become stronger on tasks that demand crystallized intelligence — these are tasks that depend on the capacity to reflect on acquired life experience and to apply that knowledge in problem-solving. On the other hand, some older people may decline on fluid intelligence, which involves abstract, context-free reasoning, often in the context of quick, time-limited tasks."[16]

Given this difference in mental processing, Kamber has advocated that, in addition to providing relevant content, instructors ensure safe physical spaces and allow older learners to help design the curriculum and engage in problem-solving activities in small groups.[17]

One of the most common lifelong-learning settings is among younger students in the college and university classroom. Maximizing the older-younger interaction is a mission of the Age-Friendly University, launched in Ireland in 2012, with nearly 70 participating schools in the U.S.[18] According to Andreoletti — who has continued to study the ways in which intergenerational service-learning programs reduce ageism and promote social productivity and personal well-being — the AFU's 10 Principles[19] "provide a framework for helping universities to think more broadly about how to be age inclusive and better meet the needs of learners across the lifespan."[20]

When young and old students learn together, she says, the resulting synergy can be remarkable:

I love seeing older and younger students working together in an intergenerational classroom. Today's young people are so anxious, stressed, overwhelmed, and worried about their futures. When they have the opportunity to get to know older students and hear their perspectives, they realize that it will all be OK. They see that these older adults have lived through so much, but here they are, in the college classroom, happy, having fun, and eager to learn. Age stereotypes on both sides are challenged, and younger and older students are often surprised to realize how much they have in common.[21]

When it comes to teaching old dogs new tricks, older learners' abilities make a powerful argument for abolishing that old adage. Carpenter best sums up EngAGE's view: "We have a counter-saying that I like better: 'Not only can you teach an old dog new tricks, they most likely have a few they could teach *you*, if you're open.'"[22]

# FROM "SENIOR" TO "SULLY" MOMENT

As a social gerontologist, community educator, and writer, I'm passionate about explaining how language affects, in good or bad ways, our perceptions of aging, and vice versa. Three particular phrases raise my hackles, two of which (*successful aging* and *silver tsunami*) I've already discussed.

These two terms are regularly employed by the media when covering aging issues. But we hear the third term, *senior moment*, all the time, used by practically everyone from youth to the oldest old among us. The phrase is so pervasive that it has taken on a kind of scientific validity, as if the act of forgetting familiar information is limited to the behavior of older people. It's not.

Here's the reality about senior moments: They happen to all adults decades before they reach elderhood.[23] According to University of Virginia psychology professor emeritus Timothy A. Salthouse, "some aspects of age-related cognitive decline begin in healthy educated adults when they are in their 20s and 30s."[24] Within five years after a cognitive peak around age 22, we begin to experience a gradual decline in the speed at which our brains work, as well as our ability to make quick comparisons, to think abstractly, to remember unrelated pieces of information, and to perceive patterns and relationships. And by our late 30s, problems with our memory become more apparent to us.

In short, senior moments belong to us all, although their frequency increases over time. Or as Ashton Applewhite has eloquently stated, "I used to think that those ['senior moments'] quips were self-deprecatingly cute, until it dawned on me that when I lost the car keys in high school, I didn't call it a 'junior moment.'"[25]

So instead of unrealistically attributing senior moments only to the elder experience, I'd like to offer a refreshing (and more accurate) meme for older brain activity: the "Sully moment."

Enter famed airline pilot Chesley "Sully" Sullenberger, hero of the "Miracle on the Hudson," who at age 57 made a successful 2009 emergency landing in New York's Hudson River of a U.S. Airways plane carrying 155 passengers. The inspiring story of his accomplishment can actually be explained by the brain phenomenon known as bihemispheric processing, which, as I've mentioned previously, fully develops around age 50. At this point, the older brain reaches a state that geriatric psychiatrist Gene Cohen has described as shifting from two-wheel drive to "all-wheel drive."[26] Evidence of this shift is a greater ability to approach problem-solving from many different perspectives and to detect more subtle differences in circumstances and viewpoints.

Just catch Sully's 2009 *60 Minutes* interview with Katie Couric, and you'll hear an account of all-wheel drive in action as he ticked off in succession the various factors he had to consider and computations he had to make within seconds. "I was sure I could do it," he said. "I think in many ways, as it turned out, my entire life up to that moment had been a preparation to handle that particular moment."[27]

As he also told Couric, "One way of looking at this might be that for 42 years, I've been making small, regular deposits in this bank of experience, education, and training. And on January 15, the balance was sufficient so that I could make a very large withdrawal."[28]

All of this is not to say that younger adults can't process information bihemispherically. Of course they can. It's just that they get better at it as they get older. Like much of life, we experience many things as tradeoffs. Sure, we may have more tip-of-the-tongue brain stutters, and our reaction times may get slower. On the other hand, as Salthouse has noted, our vocabulary increases, and we accumulate and retain more general knowledge at least until we reach age 60. And older adults with healthy brains continue to integrate that knowledge as they apply their skills throughout their lives.[29] Overall, when you think about it, it's not a bad deal.

I don't know about you, but I'll happily trade a "senior moment" for a "Sully moment" anytime.

# DOES ELDER WISDOM EXIST?

Is there such a thing as "elder wisdom"? Do older adults inevitably acquire a special kind of inner knowledge unavailable in their middle-aged years, or is this concept a mere stereotype and illusion?

Culturally, we tend to romanticize the notion that everyone gets smarter with age and that for this reason, age alone demands our respect. But this assumption has its pitfalls.

"I dislike the term 'elder wisdom' as it seems to have gone the way of cliché or token prize with a hefty dose of condescension," says geriatrician and University of California San Francisco professor of medicine Louise Aronson, author of *Elderhood: Redefining Aging, Transforming Medicine, Reimagining Life*. "Wisdom means using experience, knowledge, and judgment well, so there is likely something real to older adults having wisdom since they have more experience, although more of something doesn't guarantee quality, so this seems a generalization that will often fail, as most do, since one can have experience and learn little."[30]

Tim Carpenter of EngAGE apparently agrees with Aronson's views. He has asserted that "people accumulate knowledge and experience throughout their lifespan and we all, as we age, better prioritize the things we need to know and know how to apply them in our daily lives. I think wisdom is something we all aspire to, and there is a better chance of achieving it the longer we strive toward it. That said, simply becoming older doesn't make us wise. Becoming older doesn't make us anything — kinder, more giving, better people. These are things we have to work for at any age, things we must earn."[31]

"Wisdom is not an inevitable product of aging,"[32] says geriatric neuro-psychiatrist and past president of the American Psychiatric Association

Dilip Jeste. Furthermore, wisdom is more than mere knowledge passively derived from experience. It's an ability that requires conscious and careful cultivation. In an enlightening TEDMED2015 Talk, he remarks, "Wise people are intelligent, but not all intelligent people are wise."[33]

In that same lecture, Jeste asserts that throughout history as well as cross-culturally, wisdom is defined by the following traits:

- **Social decision making** — reasoning and acting in ways that consider the effects on other people
- **Emotional stability** — appropriately being able to control one's own emotions
- **Pro-social behaviors** such as compassion and altruism — not being selfish but rather helping others
- **Insight** — knowing one's own strengths and limitations
- **Decisiveness amid uncertainty** — being open to other perspectives and suggestions and yet being able to act when necessary

Of course, these abilities can be found in any adult at any age, but Jeste explains that older adults tend to exhibit more of these traits more often.

Aronson agrees: "There is evidence for greater emotional intelligence with age, for many older adults being more sanguine about life, finding it easier to prioritize and take the wider view of things, putting them into perspective."[34]

According to Jeste, human brains change throughout the lifespan, and elders engage more of their prefrontal cortex (the planning, organizing, and judging area of the brain), than do younger people. In addition, the two amygdalae of the brain, sub-organs that regulate a person's emotions, are often calmer and less skewed toward negative feelings in older adults, which explains why people usually feel happier as they get older.

Jeste believes there's a special evolutionary purpose to elder wisdom, one that rationalizes why people live decades past their ability to reproduce and past their maximum level of physical strength. Citing what is known as the "grandmother hypothesis," he explained that children who are reared with the help of infertile grandparents are more fertile when they become adults, and this helps to ensure a population's survival.[35]

Exactly what kind of help do grandparents and other elders provide? Whether or not they are involved in actual child-care duties, older adults contribute to the intellectual and moral growth of younger members of society.

When asking the question "Does 'elder wisdom' exist?", it's important to distinguish between what is (or isn't) an *inevitable fact* and what is empirically a *potential ability*. The difference is a matter of the older adult actively committing to becoming wise. Says Carpenter:

I have worked with older people for decades, and I often tell them that they shouldn't expect special treatment because they are older. We shouldn't expect respect, we should live our lives in a way that earns the respect of others. If you're looking for a handout because you're older, you've already given away your power. The best examples of elder wisdom for me have always been in people who have tried hard to learn, to grow, to be open to ideas, to listen, to live life like it's the only one they have.[36]

Perhaps the truest statement on elder wisdom is best expressed by that excerpt I previously cited in Chapter 1 from Henry Wadsworth Longfellow's poem "Morituri Salutamus":

For age is opportunity no less
Than youth itself, though in another dress,
And as the evening twilight fades away
The sky is filled with stars, invisible by day.

The key word is *opportunity*. Older adults have the potential to acquire elder wisdom if and only if they take advantage of both the opportunity and the desire to reflect on their own life, make sense of it, and apply their insight toward positive engagement with the world.

After all, those invisible stars will remain hidden unless and until elders choose to embrace the evening of their lives and let them shine.

# IF THESE WALLS COULD TALK...

Have you ever been inside a very old residence, perhaps one of historic value, and thought, "If these walls could talk, imagine what they'd say about the people who lived here and what they knew!"?

I've had that reaction while visiting such places as the Bronze Age Minoan palace of Knossos in Crete, the house of William Shakespeare, and most strongly, when I traveled more than 30 years ago to the 10th-century town of Abbateggio, Italy, to see the childhood homes of my ancestors. No doubt, the intensity I experienced within those Italian interiors was due to the connection I felt between those spaces and my own past — cultural information now lost to me and which I would have treasured.

Fortunately, my father and my maternal grandmother, both of whom are now deceased, shared with me some touching stories about their lives in that rugged town: tales of endurance, proactivity, and creativity that have helped me throughout my life to make decisions and choose new ways to grow.

That's the value of what is known as "institutional knowledge/ memory" — having access to information passed down from an older or more experienced person to someone who can benefit from that wisdom.

All too often, we incorrectly believe that achieving old age inevitably results in the loss of long-term, or crystallized, memory (actually, healthy brains retain and get better at that ability), and because of this, we rarely seek out elders' ideas and opinions when wrestling with challenges in our own lives.

In Western history, it wasn't always this way. More than 5,000 years ago, before the creation of written language, some societies revered their elders as the repositories of information vital to the survival of their clan or tribe, sharing that wisdom orally. They knew the most effective ways to hunt and gather food, which foods were safe to eat and preserve, the right times to plant crops, how to make tools and use them to build their shelters out of natural materials they found in their environment. In some ways, once such knowledge could be recorded (especially with the invention of the printing press in the 15th century) and later widely disseminated, it could be said that elders' importance began to diminish.

The value of institutional knowledge also took a great hit in the mid–19th century, during the Industrial Revolution, when younger people migrated from farms and into cities to do factory work and thus relied less on their older family members for support. Today we live in a hyper-digital world of instantaneous access to vast amounts of information. Does this devalue the content and capacity of older adults' brains? It depends on what kind of wisdom someone seeks.

Of course, we can turn to books, websites, apps, and search engines, but we also have access to personal recollections, passions, judgments, and experiences, all of which still have a value of their own. It's up to each of us to determine that worth for ourselves. In doing so, it helps to know that the brains of healthy, long-lived people contain all kinds of information, filed away in different areas of the brain according to the types of memories they contain.

Yes, there's more than one kind of memory residing in human brains, which retain two basic forms of information. **Declarative memory** is the ability to recall "things," such as names, dates, facts, and what objects look like or are used for. **Procedural memory** is the ability to recall "how to do things," such as getting dressed, traveling from one place to another, and performing a particular job — all of which require actions done in a sequence of steps.

As if this wasn't impressive enough, there are different subtypes of both declarative memory and procedural memory.

Declarative memory includes:

*Semantic memories,* which are objective facts and events (*e.g.,* what happened in 1492, the name of the current President, which foods contain vitamin C, what a hammer does).

*Episodic memories,* which are subjective, usually emotion-laden facts and events (*e.g.,* your children's names, trips you went on, how you sprained your ankle, your high school graduation day).

*Associative memories,* which form the relationship between two things or ideas (*e.g.,* being able to put a face together with a name, knowing that a lemon is sour, classifying a collie as a species of dog).

*Conceptual memories,* which consist of abstract ideas (*e.g.,* democracy, humidity, compassion) and their meanings.

*Attentive memories,* which are judgments (*e.g.,* your likes and dislikes, what makes you comfortable or uncomfortable, how you feel about a certain person).

*Prospective memories,* which contain information that you want to remember in the future (*e.g.,* tasks to do tomorrow, appointments to keep).

Procedural memory includes:

*Unconscious motor skills* (*e.g.,* waking up, breathing, balancing).

*Conscious learned tasks* (*e.g.,* driving a car, writing, speaking a language, gardening, tying your shoes, using a TV remote).

Pretty impressive, right? Now consider once again the issue of institutional memory. Can you see how older and/or experienced persons are keepers of all kinds of information that can benefit us? A grandparent who teaches you how to cook or fish or speak another language; a 30-year employee who knows the ins and outs of project management; a government diplomat with years of experience negotiating trade agreements and treaties — gleaning knowledge from such people is like accessing resources from a storehouse or treasure from a vault.

As we age, all of us increase our own reserve of knowledge, which means that our individual brains, if we keep them healthy, contain a cache of institutional memory, always at our disposal to share, should we opt to do so. Unfortunately, an ageist culture can limit such opportunities when others assume that what older adults know is outdated, at best, or trivial and wrong, at worst. Those assumptions can be counterproductive and even devastating when people lack the imagination to see how longstanding declarative and procedural memories can often be of value when analyzing current situations and seeking solutions to the problems that arise from them.

The most common examples of such disregard occur in the workplace, when the knowledge of employees who have been at the same company for many years is overlooked or undervalued. Those workers are often laid off or pressured to retire, not consulted for their input when updating old procedures or establishing new ones, or denied opportunities to be trained on newer equipment or software. Their sense of frustration as well as of loss of autonomy and dignity, can push them out the door, to the detriment of an entire business.

For what is affected when experts leave a company that doesn't conduct exit interviews or find other ways to retain their knowledge? An intriguing Harvard Business Review article[37] cited four domains that are negatively impacted when "deep smarts" are lost. First, any long-term **relationships** those people have built with customers or clients will have to be reestablished with other employees, which could take a great deal of time. Second, if the people replacing those experts aren't as capable, the company's **reputation** can suffer. Third, incoming replacements for those experts will be challenged to acquire that same knowledge, to start from scratch, repeat those efforts, and in effect, **re-work** those jobs, which cost not just lots of time but lots of money. And finally, the company's **regeneration** — the ability to create new products based on past experience and expertise — will be hugely diminished.

And such losses don't occur only when valued, long-term employees leave. Current workers can encounter the same difficulties. When businesses lack protocols that allow employees of all ages and levels of experience to share their knowledge either in person or by accessing a record of it, workers can waste time (one study estimates an average of 5.3 hours a week per employee[38]) searching for the information they need to do their jobs. And such struggles can lead to frustration, decreased job performance and satisfaction, and possibly employee turnover, which would then require hiring and training of new employees — and more time and money, often millions of dollars annually, depending on the size of the company.[39]

What a waste.

Whether we're talking about a workplace or a social space, whenever we disregard the institutional memory of older employees or of older relatives and friends, we do so to our own detriment, for we may regret the loss of their knowledge, the loss of their voices to guide us.

We may come to a point when we metaphorically think, "If these walls could talk...." and realize that the silence we encounter is because of the soundproof partitions we have built between us.

# A TALE OF TWO SCULPTORS

In 1498, when the Italian Renaissance artist Michelangelo Buonarroti was 23 years old, he received a commission from a Roman Catholic cardinal to carve a marble sculpture for the cleric's future tomb. The assignment was to show a grieving Virgin Mary holding the crucified body of her son, Jesus.

Michelangelo was familiar with that subject matter, known as a pietà, as it was a theme that was depicted in the works of other sculptors and painters before him. But he decided that his presentation was going to be radically different; he would infuse into the lofty, spiritual work a realistic portrayal of lifeless human flesh and of the quiet, mournful acceptance of death. The resulting virtuoso work completed a year later[40] and displayed in St. Peter's Basilica in Rome has been admired for more than half a millennium.

When many of us think about the human impulse to create, our minds tend to focus on people who possess that talent in its greatest amount: famous artists, musicians, writers, inventors, and scientists (e.g., Michelangelo, Beethoven, Shakespeare, Edison, Einstein) whose achievements have greatly impacted human history.

Given this tendency of ours, it's not surprising that we may discount or even deny our own abilities to be similarly creative. It's not that we think that we can't draw, paint, sculpt, compose, write, or even invent or discover things; rather, it's that we believe that the results we get are somehow vastly different from — and thus inferior to — those extremely creative efforts that make a difference. Compared to what some psychologists call "Big C" people, the rest of us are "little c" wannabes.

It's also because we don't understand what creativity is all about.

A widely accepted definition of creativity is "the ability to produce something that is novel or original and useful or adaptive."[41] What is produced can be a process, a perception, or a product — in other words, a new way of doing something, a new way of thinking about something, or a new something. This definition makes complete sense when understanding the works of Big C thinkers, but it also applies to those moments when we little c people discover shortcuts to performing mundane tasks, add new ingredients to tried-and-true recipes, or identify more efficient routes to get to where we need to go.

Since being creative is a mental process, we assume that the brains of Big C people simply work differently than ours. But that's not true. Actually, they work in *exactly the same way*. The only difference is in the level of development of that skill. According to cognitive psychologist Mark A. Runco,

> …the processes involved in personal, everyday creativity are the same as those involved in high-level achievements…. [B]oth start with the individual and his or her original and effective idea or insight. After the creative idea is produced, expertise may add to it, impression management may couch it so it is accepted, and so on, but the creative part of the process…is the same as the creativity of little c creativity.[42]

Understanding this idea should give us greater encouragement and incentive to become more creative people. In an article for The Atlantic magazine titled "Secrets of the Creative Brain," neuropsychiatrist Nancy C. Andreasen has defined these four creator-personality traits:[43]

- They are *autodidacts* who informally teach themselves, rather than merely absorb information or knowledge in typical educational environments.

- They are *polymaths* who are interested in and knowledgeable about many diverse subject areas.
- They are *persistent*; even when people are skeptical of or reject their ideas, they keep going.
- They are *adventuresome* and *exploratory*, comfortable taking risks, breaking rules, and living with ambiguity.

How many of these characteristics do you possess? And what can you do to increase your capabilities in each?

For some people, believing whether or not they can develop or improve upon these traits may be affected by their simultaneous beliefs about getting older. After all, they might think, aren't these characteristics in greater evidence when people are young and before becoming set in their ways? What's implied here is that a person is less likely to be creative, let alone be even more creative, the older s/he gets. This ageist attitude is reinforced constantly via widespread cultural messages telling us that old people have imaginations that are limited, narrow, or even stagnant. Moreover, we're supposed to be quite surprised and consider it a great exception to encounter the example of an innovative person who is well past the age of 50.

The fallacy here is assuming that there is only one form of creativity. However, researchers such as University of Chicago economics professor David W. Galenson have posited that creative approaches change over time:

Creativity is not the prerogative of the young, but can occur at any stage in the life cycle. What the psychologists failed to recognize is that there is not a single kind of creativity, but that in virtually every intellectual discipline there are two different types of creativity, each associated with a distinct pattern of discovery over the life cycle. The bold leaps of fearless and iconoclastic young *conceptual* innovators are one important form of creativity.… But there is another, very different type of creativity, in which important new discoveries emerge gradually and incrementally from the extended explorations of older *experimental* innovators.[44]

According to Galenson, conceptual creators, who are newer to their field and thus less influenced by established conventions, work more quickly and focus on expressing novel ideas or emotions. Experimental creators, on the other hand, are well-versed in a wide compendium of knowledge and work more slowly and deliberatively, focusing on integrating and further developing already existing perceptions.

Furthermore, educational researcher Sandra Kerka, citing the work of clinical psychologist Carolyn E. Adams-Price, has asserted that "the association of creativity with novelty and innovation is appropriate for the characteristics of youthful thinking, but late-life creativity reflects aspects of late-life thinking: synthesis, reflection, and wisdom."[45]

What is the significance of this distinction between two types of creativity? For one thing, it supports the immense amount of scientific evidence regarding how the human brain changes over time. The brain's bihemispheric processing ability to reach its greatest maturity in people in their 50s promotes such synthesis, reflection, and wisdom.

The reality of two types of creative thinking also supports the logical conclusion that acquiring many more years of experience enable older adults to become even better autodidacts and polymaths, as well as more persistent, adventuresome, and exploratory people.

But in a society that already denies or limits opportunities for older adults to express themselves in meaningful creative ways, being an experimental innovator requires something more, as described by geriatric psychiatrist Gene Cohen in his influential book, *The Creative Age: Awakening Human Potential in the Second Half of Life*: "An important dynamic of creativity that comes with age is courage — courage that gives permission to make a decision that may be risky, controversial, and necessary."[46]

As people continue to live longer lives, we shouldn't be surprised but rather consider ourselves fortunate that there are many more "exceptions" of older adult creators than we know who had the courage to be productive in their later years. In case you need some evidence, consider these examples:

- Ethel Percy Andrus founded the AARP at age 74.
- Jacques Cousteau was an undersea explorer until well into his 70s.
- Imogen Cunningham continued to photograph and teach photography in her 90s.
- Mary Baker Eddy founded the Christian Science Monitor at age 87.
- Benjamin Franklin helped write the Constitution of the United States when he was 81.
- Mahatma Mohandas Gandhi successfully negotiated Indian independence when he was 77.
- Martha Graham danced until she reached 75 and choreographed her last piece at age 96.
- Golda Meir was prime minister of Israel from the ages of 71 to 76.
- Mother Teresa of Calcutta continued to minister to the poor of India until her death at age 87.
- Georgia O'Keeffe, who went blind from macular degeneration, completed her last unassisted painting at age 85.
- Jeanette Rankin, the first woman in the U.S. Congress, served two terms: from the ages of 37 to 39 and 61 to 63.

- Arthur Rubenstein gave his last piano recital at age 89.
- Antonio Stradivari made violins until his death at age 93.
- Giuseppe Verdi wrote the opera *Otello* when he was 74.
- Betty White was a comedic actor until her death at age 99.
- Frank Lloyd Wright designed Pennsylvania's "Fallingwater" house when he was 69 and New York City's Guggenheim Museum when he was 91.

A pretty impressive Big C list, wouldn't you say? But it pales in length to the list we could make of the millions of little c creators who were their contemporaries.

Which brings us back to that Big C, Michelangelo. In the year 1547, when the artist was 72 and after decades of artistic accomplishments — sculpting the statue of David, painting the Sistine Chapel, supervising the building of St. Peter's Basilica, to name just a few — he began carving another pietà, but this one wasn't a commissioned work. Anticipating his own death, the sculptor created what is now known as "The Deposition" or "The Florentine Pietà."[47] It was purely his idea, for it was to be for his tomb.

The resulting piece,, which was never completed because of the artist's dissatisfaction with the quality of the stone, comprises four figures: the Virgin Mary, Mary Magdalen, and an old figure (possibly Nicodemus or Joseph of Arimathea) at the top center of the composition, supporting the lifeless body of Jesus. The work barely resembles the meticulous, confident, highly stylized piece by that 23-year-old a half-century before. The figures' positions are active and organic, as if Michelangelo were experimenting with aesthetic ideas, working out his thoughts over eight years as he chiseled away at the marble. Five decades of life experience produced a different sculptor: more circumspect and identifying with his creation, so much so that many art historians believe that the old man's face is Michelangelo's self-portrait. The piece that survives today in the

Opera del Duomo Museum in Florence, Italy displays more subtlety and depth than its more famous counterpart in the Vatican.

This kind of personal evolution is possible for all of us as we age and our bodies and minds change. For us to grow into our greatest potential and maintain a quality creative life, our culture likewise needs to evolve into one that is less ageist, less prejudiced against older adults and that supports them in whatever endeavors they choose to experience in their lives.

Creativity is available to us all, regardless of our age. Enlisting the imaginations of young and old people working together to add beauty, establish justice, and improve the quality of our environment is the surest way to transform the world.

# CHAPTER 5

# A Life of One's Own

**IN 1928, THE BRITISH WRITER** Virginia Woolf delivered two lectures on the subject of women and fiction to students at the University of Cambridge's women's colleges, Newnham and Girton. The speeches proved to be so provocative that she combined and published them the following year under the title *A Room of One's Own*. Among the many arguments she made for the right of women to pursue independent, sustainable careers as authors was this simple declaration: "[A] woman must have money and a room of her own if she is to write fiction."[1]

Today we would find Woolf's idea to be perfectly reasonable and, in fact, quite obvious. But this wasn't the case back in England's period of King George V, when in that same year women had only just achieved the right to vote and very few had independent jobs and incomes. Woolf wanted to point out the injustice of confining women to subservient roles that marginalized them and kept them from achieving their full potential to live freely on their own terms in a society that didn't — but one day might — support their goal.

To make her point, Woolf introduced a powerful hypothesis: What if Shakespeare had had a sister named Judith who was equally as intelligent, creative, competent, and passionate as her brother? Could she, like him, earn a living pursuing her craft as a writer, achieving fame, and moving with ease through society? What would have been her chances of such success?

Of course, the answer would be "Zero." She wouldn't have been sent to school, let alone live on her own, but instead would have been expected to remain in her parents' home until married off in her early teens to a lowly worker to live an untraveled, unimaginative, dreary life producing and raising as many children as she could. However, Woolf speculated that Judith the artist would not have been able endure it. The pain of such denial of opportunity would have driven the girl to end her life.

What does all of this have to do with aging?

At first it may be difficult to see the connection because Woolf was writing about sexism, just one form of discrimination that humans inflict on other humans. In this case, it starts virtually from the moment of birth when female gender is first identified. Moreover ageism, whether toward the young or the old, is different because all people experience it and do so gradually. The real similarity is found in the effects of ageism on a person's life. Like sexism, it keeps people from achieving their full potential to live freely on their own terms.

For example, young people can be denied jobs or excluded from policy-making discussions because they aren't considered mature or experienced enough. They are usually paid less than older employees based on age rather than competence and are more likely to experience financial instability when dealing with such economic conditions as the high costs of a college education and home ownership as determined by market forces set in motion during previous generations. This kind of discrimination, sometimes called *youngism*,[2] is a temporary experience, given that one ages out of it.

The more common form of ageism is directed at people who live beyond midlife (although depending on circumstances, such as working in the high-tech industry, people in their 40s and even 30s attest to being seen as "too old" [3]). It's more common because there are millions more adults above the age of, say, 50 than between the ages of 21 and 49. Given these ranges, this form of discrimination can last more than 40 years of a person's life. Not only is such ageism more common, but it can also be more harmful — and even deadly.

Yet it's not the sheer size of the older population that explains ageism's pervasiveness. Once again, we're talking about the common fear of getting old, which Gray Panthers founder Maggie Kuhn eloquently explained:

Ours is a youth-oriented country, no doubt about it…. By and large, age has been denied, glossed over. It doesn't exist. There's a fear of old people in this country. Gerontophobia is an epidemic; the fear of old people and the fear of growing old, the two are combined. It goes back, I think, to the fact that we've made a fetish of being young. We pride ourselves on being a youthful nation, and yet a growing percentage of our population has achieved a great old age. I think it goes back to our economic system, too, because we worship the bottom line — productivity, the almighty dollar. In our society you're deemed old when you can't work, they don't want you to work, or you don't want to work. Old age is just anathema in our youth-centered, acquisitive, private-centered society. In America, it is a bad scene to be old. [4]

It's a bad scene, indeed, one that's played out on a wide variety of stages: in the business world, in health care, politics, the media, social settings, one-on-one encounters, and in our own minds — known as *internalized ageism* — when we ourselves believe that being old is a bad thing.

An overwhelming proportion of older Americans report experiencing some form of age discrimination in their daily lives. I refer once again to the study I cited in the Introduction in which Julie Ober Allen and her team found that 93.4% of their subjects claimed to have encountered everyday ageism. Such discrimination was "associated with multiple indicators of poor physical and mental health.… Internalized ageism was reported by 1664 adults (81.2%), ageist messages by 1394 adults (65.2%), and interpersonal ageism by 941 adults (44.9%)."[5]

Ageism is far from being a predominantly American problem; in fact, it exists globally. A 2020 study analyzing data from a World Values Survey conducted from 2010 to 2014 reported that "[f]rom the 83,034 participants included, 44%, 32% and 24% were classified as having low, moderate and high ageist attitudes, respectively. From the 57 countries, 34 were classified as moderately or highly ageist.… At least one in every two people included in this study had moderate or high ageist attitudes."[6]

"At least one in every two people" from 57 nations having sufficient or strong ageist attitudes is more than just significant. If ageism were a disease, it would be considered a pandemic. Actually, equating ageism with disease isn't far off the mark, for the stress of coping with casual and often blatant put-downs, shaming, marginalization, abuse, and neglect can take a physical and/or mental toll on older people. As a journalist who interviewed Allen reported:

Allen said that repeatedly experiencing ageism may condition older people to expect ageist treatment, which can lead to harmful bouts of stress as they go about their daily lives. "Anticipating what other people might be thinking about them and wondering why someone is treating them a certain way acts like a fight-or-flight response. Cortisol goes up, which can damage biological systems and lead to accelerated aging, more health conditions, and premature mortality," Allen explained.[7]

One of the most startling discoveries about the impact of internalized ageism was made in 2002 by a team led by psychologist Becca Levy of the Yale School of Public Health. They found that having positive self-perceptions of aging can increase a person's longevity by about 7.5 years,[8] which conversely means that buying into negative beliefs about aging can shorten one's life by that same amount. Recognizing the implications of widespread societal ageism as a health risk, Levy concluded,

> If a previously unidentified virus was found to diminish life expectancy by over 7 years, considerable effort would probably be devoted to identifying the cause and implementing a remedy. In the present case, one of the likely causes is known: societally sanctioned denigration of the aged. A comprehensive remedy requires that the denigrating views and actions directed at elderly targets undergo delegitimization by the same society that has been generating them.[9]

Reduced longevity isn't the only byproduct of the scourge that is ageism. In another study, Levy and her team found that for people aged 60 and older who possessed the APOE ε4 gene associated with developing dementia, "those with positive age beliefs were 49.8% less likely to develop dementia than those with negative age beliefs."[10]

It turns out that both external age discrimination and internal negative age perception are the forces that conspire to deny older adults a life full of potential and self-actualization to which they are entitled. But like Shakespeare's imaginary sister, Judith, far too many elders are trapped in a culture that simultaneously keeps them from fully participating yet limits their ability to proactively expand their opportunities. Virginia Woolf reflected on gender inequity by writing: "I thought how unpleasant it is to be locked out; and I thought how it is worse perhaps to be locked in."[11] The same can be said for inequity based on age.

In order to work together to abolish ageism, we must first have a better understanding of the nature of that form of discrimination in all its complexity: where it manifests, what forms it takes, why it's so insidious, and what can be done to reduce its effects.

Our efforts should start with a simple declaration: "An older person must have a life of one's own if one is to live with autonomy, dignity, and purpose."

# LET'S FIRE AGEISM

MEMO
TO: Ageism
FROM: Management
RE: Notice of Termination


This is to notify you that, effective immediately, your services at American Society Inc. are no longer required.

During your many years of employment with us, you have displayed remarkable expertise and tenacity in fulfilling your tasks of discrimination, alienation, and isolation. However, owing to currently changing cultural perspectives and increased economic pressures that have impacted our markets, the Board of Directors has revised American Society's mission, values, and goals. As a result, it has been determined that your position in the company is now obsolete.

Yes, this is clearly a nonsense scenario. After all, a group of people can't "fire" a menacing and destructive concept. Yet I can think of no better way to entertain a fantasy that might help us get a firmer grip on reality. And the reality is that ageism lurks behind just about every challenge confronting older adults in their ongoing struggle to remain vital members of society. It is also the hidden force that is holding back our economy from achieving tremendous growth that would benefit all generations. The longer we wait to confront and abolish ageism, the harder it will be to recover from its consequences. Now is the time to launch a full-scale reorganization effort. But how?

I hereby call a Board of Directors meeting to consider our options.

First on the agenda: examining our target market. Whom are we serving? To answer this question, let's look at why we adopted ageism as a strategy in the first place. That's where the business comparison comes in. For like a company that has made a really bad decision based on a misguided mission, our society has for too long invested its capital and focused its production solely on addressing the needs and values of youth-centric consumers of *all* ages, thinking that this was a sustainable way to operate. And while these efforts have created a multibillion-dollar anti-aging industry, they have also disenfranchised a significant part of our population that ironically can contribute the most — in time, money, knowledge, and skill — to building a new nation. We need to broaden our target customers to include everyone and to help them understand and accept the value of growing old. Once we do so, we can develop a plan that takes advantage of the vast amount of human capital waiting to be productively re-engaged.

Which brings me to our next agenda item: examining our available workforce. Whom are we employing to help us in our efforts? Whether we know it or not, we're suffering from a shortage of experienced-person power. We have to make our workforce more inclusive. When it comes to assessing older talent, we shouldn't be making demographic policy decisions based on the false assumption that older adults are all alike. As a society, we need that variety of knowledge, experience, and perception to help us in our decision-making and planning. And let's not subscribe to the belief that older adults should retire from the business of living, or even assume that they want to. The overwhelming majority do not. Therefore, we should recruit older adults from and involve them in all aspects of economic and social life.

Finally, we need to examine our mission and bottom line: What is our society about, anyway, and what do we hope to gain? We need to commit ourselves to being an organized community dedicated to improving the quality of the lives of all of its citizens. Let's reallocate the time, money, and energy we've wasted on promoting and maintaining ageism and instead direct it toward this higher, more humane purpose.

Let this be the moment we fire ageism — from our thoughts, discourse, and actions. American Society Inc. owes it to its current stakeholders. And to future generations of investors.

# ADDRESSING THE CHARACTER OF AGEISM

There is a famous Hollywood story about an exchange between actors Laurence Olivier and Dustin Hoffman during the filming of the 1976 movie *Marathon Man*.

Hoffman was trained in the Actors Studio style of Method acting and thus approached his craft from the inside out, trying to draw from similar feelings and experiences in his own life to get insight into the character he was portraying. To prepare for his harrowing role, he deliberately deprived himself of sleep for three or four days in an effort to look exhausted on camera.

When he told Olivier what he had done to get ready, the renowned British actor replied, "My dear boy, why don't you just try *acting*?"[12] That's because classically trained Olivier took the opposite approach, focusing primarily on his lines and on creating an external appearance (such as getting the nose and the walk right) as the ways to develop his character.

Both styles effectively got at the truth. And because they did, they were noble endeavors.

Getting to the truth about ageism in order to abolish it is likewise a noble endeavor that requires a certain amount of conscious, and conscientious, craft. Each of us should meet this challenge in a way that suits us. Some of us may take an overt, direct approach while others may take a more subtle but equally powerful one. And any of us may switch styles depending on the circumstance. In part, our decisions may be determined by which of the two forms of ageism — prejudice or bigotry — we choose to confront at any particular moment.

Like acting, ageism can be manifested internally or externally. Prejudice, the internal kind, consists of *perception*, that is, those negative thoughts and feelings about what it means to grow or be old. Bigotry, on the other hand, consists of *practice*, of how that prejudice is outwardly expressed by means of words and actions. Addressing either type requires a different approach.

People who are prejudiced toward older adults view the aging process solely as one of biological deterioration and/or social irrelevance and fail to see and appreciate the assets of mental and spiritual growth that only aging can provide. Given this narrow perception, they rightfully fear becoming older people. In order to cease being prejudiced against aging, they first need to be able to connect on an experiential basis with that fear, and this requires developing empathy, an internal response.

Can they imagine themselves as old? If so, will they choose to identify themselves by their deficiencies or rather by their abilities? How much wiser do they expect to be due to their added years and experience? How would they want to be seen and treated by others? And what social and economic opportunities would they hope would be available and not denied to them because of their age?

If they find such imagining difficult, perhaps they can be encouraged to take another Method acting approach: to draw from their own lives any experiences they may have had of bigotry directed toward them. Were they ever denied a job, house, education, or social participation because of their gender, race, sexual orientation, geographic/ethnic origin, physical ability, or regional accent? Can they see a similarity between these destructive stereotypes and their own age-based ones?

Reaching people who are openly ageist presents an additional challenge because their prejudice has developed into bigotry. They may tell ageist jokes, use demeaning language to describe older adults, speak to or treat them as if they were children, avoid them at social gatherings, discount their opinions, or deny them access to the same services and opportunities younger generations enjoy.

For some of these people, appeals to them to develop empathy may not work. Instead, it is necessary to take the Classical approach and call direct attention to their outward behavior — gently, at first, for such behavior may be inadvertent and well intentioned. But it is important to hold them accountable for their external expressions of ageism, to help them learn more appropriate language and actions — in other words, to "focus on their lines and get the nose and the walk right." And maybe by doing this long enough, these people might change their perceptions of aging. At least, they won't be contributing to the perpetuation of ageist behavior.

Just as with sexist, racist, ableist, or homophobic discrimination, ageism won't be easily eradicated. That's because it manifests its character in so many ways in our society. It will take a concerted effort over time, but eventually, we *will* significantly reduce bias against older people.

One of the most powerful things all of us can do is to examine our own inward thoughts and outward behaviors toward aging and avoid thinking and behaving in ageist ways ourselves. We should see older adults as individuals and not caricatures. We can act in ways that serve as positive models of getting older by letting our hair turn gray, saying no to Botox, proudly disclosing our age, being actively engaged in transforming our communities, and staying as fit and interdependent as we can.

Anyone who fights ageism by working hard to understand its internal or external character is, first and foremost, the practitioner of a noble craft. Like acting, it takes experience and perseverance to hone one's skills.

In the end, no matter which approach we use, it will be worth all the effort to get at the truth.

# THE AGING EQUIVALENT OF HIGH HEELS

What's the aging equivalent of high heels?

My inquiry is inspired by having read this opening paragraph from a July 2019 Maureen Dowd op-ed in the New York Times: "After I interviewed Nancy Pelosi a few weeks ago, The HuffPost huffed that we were Dreaded Elites because we were eating chocolates and — horror of horrors — the speaker had on some good pumps."[13]

Politics and sexism aside, what caught my imagination was the reference to decorative rather than sensible footwear worn by the then Speaker of the House. As if footwear were the issue. It wasn't. It was a metaphor for questioning wearing the appropriate gear for the appropriate fight.

For the record, I haven't worn high heels since I was in my mid-20s. At that point in my emotional development, somewhere in my maturing brain arose the epiphany that I didn't have to kowtow to social norms of correct feminine attire and could instead substitute my own sensible desires to be comfortable and effective — you know, no back pain, the ability to run on demand (especially on unevenly paved streets) — and to disregard others' assessments of my worth as a human being.

It's like that with getting older, too.

That's why I ask again: What's the aging equivalent of high heels? Because, as you're most likely well aware, older adults have been handicapped for years by social assumptions of what we could — or should — be doing with our lives.

While we don't have the same culture of foot-binding that debilitated Chinese women from the 10th to the early-20th centuries, post-midlife people of any gender have been forced into equally restrictive parameters of autonomy: Be technologically savvy or get out of the way. Be young-looking or admit your repulsiveness. Be productive in middle-aged terms or accept others' charitable efforts to help you as members of a needy population.

Why should any group of people be hobbled by overwhelming social misperceptions that presume a lack of ability and therefore worth? You'd think by now that our culture has produced enough examples of long-living adults who are perfectly capable of leading vital and viable lives.

But more to the point, shouldn't any human being, regardless of circumstance or potential, be cherished and respected just because s/he is alive?

If the shoe fits....

Given the fact that an American child born today has a 50-50 chance of reaching 100 years old,[14] shouldn't we be gearing up ourselves and future generations for more compassionate, dignified, and interdependent, longer-distance journeys?

Just as I concluded about myself 45 years ago, I believe that what we older persons need now is to proudly sport our personal metaphorical footwear of choice: sandals, cleats, running shoes, thigh-high waders, combat boots — whatever will help us more comfortably and efficiently get farther down the road to social acceptance, appreciation, and especially cultural, political, and economic engagement.

We deserve that.

And longstanding fashions be damned.

# HOW TO PACK GROCERIES...
# AND UNPACK AGEISM

I get this reaction on a regular basis:

I'm at the supermarket checkout counter with my cloth shopping bags, and the cashier starts to ring up my groceries and pack them. I notice s/he is placing next to one another the couple of items that come in glass jars or bottles, and I immediately request that those bottles please be put in separate bags, of which I've brought plenty. There's a rolling of the eyes, a scowl, or a drawn-out sigh of disapproval as that person begrudgingly does what I ask.

The same exchange happens when I notice that my eggs are being placed in the bottom of a bag and are about to be covered by heavy items such as cans or a large container of detergent. Ditto when refrigerated or frozen foods are going into the same bag as cereal boxes and other paper packages that absorb moisture.

Have people like this never experienced arriving home to find their own groceries broken, crushed, or soaked? What's going on (or not) in their minds when they perform this task for others? Packing groceries isn't rocket science. It just takes some basic common sense and a concern for others' needs.

The same thing goes for unpacking ageism. And remarkably, the same rules can apply.

**Rule #1: Don't create impractical categories that defeat the experience at hand.** Why place all glass items together in the same bag? I would bet that most households don't assign separate spaces at home for "glass things," "metal things," "paper things," and "plastic things." Likewise, why continually segregate people in social or policy-making situations simply because of their age?

Which leads to **Rule #2: Create categories and policies that are meaningful.** It's more important that glass items not collide while being transported, eggs not get crushed, and cereal boxes not get soaked due to the condensation of refrigerated or frozen foods. We should consider usefulness and urgency as the criteria for our decisions. Likewise we need social policies that establish a solid foundation in order to support fragile or otherwise more particular concerns. Creating all-age-friendly communities is the basis upon which we can build economic stability, physical access, social engagement, and personal productivity for all generations. And underlying that endeavor must be an awareness of ageism as a threat to those goals.

And finally, there's **Rule #3: Be willing — and eager — to accommodate personal needs and preferences.** Maybe some people don't mind if their eggs are placed underneath that gallon of milk. But I assure you that there are others (including you, perhaps?) who do mind. It's easy for us to see how children can be quite different from one another; consider any two siblings, for example. Why is it so hard, then, for society to understand and accept the fact that older adults vary even more greatly in their experiences, abilities, and aspirations? A commitment to promoting person-centered treatment in every aspect of our culture is vital to preserving the individual autonomy, dignity, and viability of all older adults. And that commitment should be made with empathy — and enthusiasm.

Defeating ageism isn't rocket science. It's as easy as knowing which things go together and which don't.

And to have the common sense and decency to do a decent job following through.

# EMBRACING THE SPECTRUM

Red.

Cerise, maroon, raspberry, magenta, crimson, brick, fuchsia, cranberry, scarlet, rose.

Blue.

Cobalt, periwinkle, turquoise, aquamarine, navy, indigo, cerulean, azure, cyan, teal.

Our ability to describe a color depends in large part on how grossly or subtly we choose to perceive it. Is the suspicious car parked across the street gray or slate? Are your loved one's eyes brown or hazel?

The same is true regarding how we relate to the world. In recent election years, our country has been shaken to its core by the eruption of quakes whose warning tremors we have detected for an extraordinarily long time. For a sizable number of people, this eruption has created a welcome shift in the foundations of our society. For many others, it is a catastrophe. No matter which perception we may hold, one thing can be said for these campaign seasons: More broadly than any other time since the Civil War, Americans have experienced on a grand scale the human impulse to "otherize." The tenor of our discourse has morphed even further away from civility and inclusion and toward embracing "us vs. them" rhetoric.

No matter if we are discussing political affiliation, economic position, or social identity, out of our mutual fear and insecurity we have decided to opt for perceiving people at one or the other extreme end of a spectrum rather than be willing to consider every individual as occupying a distinct and often shifting position along that expansive range. We use inaccurate or offensive labels as convenient shortcuts that excuse us from the challenging task — and patriotic obligation — to do the mental heavy lifting that requires us to think about how characterizing others impacts our lives.

What's insidious about otherizing is that it's applied to all kinds of distinctions: race, ethnicity, gender, physical or cognitive ability, and sexual orientation, to name a few. And, of course, to age. We otherize members of each generation as an easy way of distancing ourselves from what we believe are the weaknesses of that stage of life. Older adults bear the brunt of ageism because most people fear a future of potential incapacity. But older adults, too, can be ageist toward successive generations, out of frustration that in their own advanced years they are no longer counted among the young in our youth-centric culture.

It's ironic that otherizing should occur so easily regarding the issue of age. After all, it's much easier to assign the label of "them" to people who are not of our own race, ethnicity, gender, ability, or sexual orientation. In these cases, "them" is a more permanent designation. But we are *all* aging. If we are fortunate and survive long enough, all of us eventually become old people. In other words, the "them" finally become the "us." Aging is a slow transformation along the chronological spectrum, and it behooves us to keep that in mind. And since as we get older our distinctions among one another increase, not decrease, it becomes more vital for us to detect the subtleties that make us individuals and to see one another in infinitely different shades of the hue we call "age."

We Americans need to take a closer look at the damage of mistrust, fear, and hostility we cause in our insistence to otherize others as we place them at the far extreme on the spectrum of existence. Racially, ethnically, ably, sexually — and generationally — we are, first and foremost, humans. And secondly, we live in a democracy and should be socially vested in the survival and prosperity of our entire nation. When we consider these two fundamental commonalities, those lesser boundaries that separate us from one another become less relevant and important.

Furthermore, it's not only more moral but also more practical to recognize and honor the diversity that is our country's greatest strength. Now more than ever, America's motto, *E Pluribus Unum* — Out of Many, One — must be transformed from a childhood-memorized slogan into a call to arms as we strive with one another to coexist and be interdependent. Let's reject red and blue, young and old, and all other facile and intellectually lazy binary categories as we sensitize our skills of perception and welcome the natural variety to be found in *any* concept, be it color, political belief, or years of living.

It's the only thing that can save us — and our nation — from our delusional, otherizing selves.

# CHAPTER 6
# Here, There, and Everywhere

**IN NEW YORK CITY IN THE LATE 1960S,** I remember my family talking about buying a new car. We agreed on a particular make and model, but the color was still up for discussion. My father expressed his preference for yellow. "I read that yellow is the safest color," he said, "because people can see it from farther away or better in the rain. Besides, it'll be easy to find in a large parking lot."

Aside from taxis, neither my parents, brother, nor I had ever remembered seeing a normal car of that color before we had that discussion. But strangely enough, once the idea was planted in our minds, we started to spot non-taxi yellow cars on a fairly regular basis. A coincidence? Not really. Actually, we were experiencing something called the Baader-Meinhof Phenomenon, also known as the "frequency illusion," in which, after learning a new piece of information, people sense that they are running across that fact more often.

There are two reasons why this effect occurs. One is *selective attention,* in which awareness, consciously or not, is focused on that new piece of information — in my family's case, the advantages of a yellow car — to the exclusion of other related ones. The second reason is *confirmation bias*. Our minds naturally seek proof that what we want or believe is true. Again, my family was looking for some proof that our color preference wasn't a farfetched one.

It's like that with ageism, too. As you are moving through this book and are becoming even more aware of the realities of the aging process and how age discrimination undermines it, it's a safe bet that you'll more likely start seeing evidence of ageism everywhere. Again, it's no coincidence. And yet, it's also no illusion, since that prejudice is ubiquitous, impacting every aspect of our lives.

A productive way to think about the environments in which age bias exists is to adopt and adapt the "ecological systems theory," first proposed in 1977 by developmental psychologist Urie Bronfenbrenner. He proposed a model for illustrating the increasingly wider environments in which a human personality develops from childhood onward.[1]

For our ageism-based purposes, imagine four concentric circles forming a kind of archery target with Circle 1, the center circle, the bull's-eye, representing each of us as an individual. Moving outward, Circle 2 involves others with whom we interact, such as family members, friends, neighbors, shopkeepers, employers, coworkers, and doctors. Circle 3 encompasses our institutional systems: business, health care, education, government, the media, entertainment, and sports. And finally, outermost Circle 4 represents the cultural tools, values, rules, and patterns of behavior that keep our society functioning: laws, social media, marketing, investing, funding, as well as organized initiatives, projects, and campaigns.

If you study each level carefully, you'll notice various expectations, judgments, and actions based on the concept of age. The evidence of ageism is too extensive and overwhelming to cover, but here are examples of a belief and a behavior in each category:

**Circle 1:** This is where *internalized ageism* lives. If we believe that it's not appropriate for us to do an activity, wear a piece of clothing, attend a social event, or apply for a job because we're "too young" or "too old" and people might reject us, we may deny ourselves opportunities for excitement, learning, or sharing our talents with others.

**Circle 2:** This is the realm of *relational ageism,* in which "an ageist thought, belief, or attitude can spread from person to person through expression and support."[2] If we accept generational stereotypes instead of understand that we're all individuals with unique lives, we might make or hear such statements as "Young people these days have no sense of responsibility," or "Old people had their chance, and now it's time to make way for the young." Being on the receiving end of such comments and believing them to be true, we might then opt to minimize our discomfort by socializing solely with people our own age rather than to expand our friendships to include other generations.

**Circle 3:** This is the ecosystem of *institutional ageism,* in which our individual needs and aspirations are considered less important than maintaining the convenience, efficiency, and sustainability of an organization, business, or government. Ageism on this level can be especially devastating, such as when it's easier or more profitable to exclude older patients from participating in clinical medical trials or to under- or over-treat them for serious conditions, or when businesses impose mandatory retirement ages on their employees.

**Circle 4:** This is the all-encompassing territory of *cultural ageism* that renders invisible or valueless the marginal, relatively powerless groups of the very young and the very old. This happens when businesses and advertisers fail to see the immense economic market to be tapped in older men and women, voters reflexively reject relatively old political candidates, or governments and health care providers ration medical supplies and triage treatment for old people on the grounds that they have already lived long enough.

By now you should be getting the idea that ageism is a social scourge that permeates every aspect of modern life. But it's even more complicated and insidious than that, mainly because age discrimination isn't a two-dimensional target of flat, concentric circles. It is a three-dimensional sphere that intersects with — and is made worse by — spheres representing other forms of prejudice, such as sexism, racism, ableism, classism, and homophobia.

Each of us is not just someone who is getting older. Every person also has a gender, a race/ethnicity, physical capacities, an economic reality, and a sexual orientation. Any of these attributes, when combined with the aging process, can make living into our later years even harder and more precarious for anyone. Here are just a few verbatim reported facts:

- Ageism is compounded by sexism, racism, homophobia, and other prejudices people are exposed to throughout their lives. In the U.S., people of color and women are more likely to work in low-wage workplace conditions that negatively impact their health. They therefore enter old age with more health problems, less savings, and fewer options for health care. People don't usually age out of inequities; these get compounded in old age.[3]

- Structural inequities unjustly set back black and brown communities in education, housing and health care, affecting both how elders of color age, and their longevity. Nearly two-thirds of black elders and 70% of Latino elders live just above the poverty line, compared to 44% of their white counterparts.... Adding a gender lens, women age into poverty at higher rates than men due to both wage disparities and caregiving responsibilities.[4]

- LGBTI older persons are at greater financial risk than their non-LGBTI counterparts. Such disparities result from the lifetime differences in earnings, employment, and opportunities to build savings as well as discriminatory access to legal and social programs that are traditionally established to support aging adults.[5]

- Ageism is often exacerbated when an older person has a disability. Think about the way you perceive an older person in a wheelchair and the assumptions you might make about their function and capabilities.… While the [Americans with Disabilities Act] doesn't protect all needs and rights of individuals with disabilities, we know that the combination of ableism and ageism can have serious effects on the livelihood and health of older adults with disabilities, including being at a higher risk for depression, obesity, smoking, heart disease and more.[6]

All of these accounts are examples of "intersectionality," first defined in 1989 by Columbia University Law School professor Kimberlé Crenshaw[7] and described by Yale University psychologist Becca Levy as the state in which "ageism combines with other forms of discrimination to exacerbate disadvantages and amplify their impact."[8]

I've said that ageism is everywhere, and it's mainly because of the other forms of prejudice that accompany it. They intersect because they are interrelated, and working to abolish one helps to abolish them all. Activist Ashton Applewhite sums up this point perfectly:

Why add another "ism" to the list when so many, racism in particular, call out for action? Here's the thing: We don't have to choose.

When we make the world a better place to grow old in, we make it a better place in which to be from somewhere else, to have a disability or be queer or non-white or non-rich. Just as different forms of oppression reinforce and compound each other … so do different forms of activism, because they chip away at the fear and ignorance that all prejudice relies upon. Ageism is the perfect target for compound advocacy because everyone experiences it. And when we show up *at all ages* for whatever cause tugs at our sleeve — save the whales, the clinic, the democracy — we not only make that effort more effective, we dismantle ageism in the process.[9]

Ironically, one reason why we are still dealing with ageism is because as a society we have insisted on maintaining a Baader-Meinhof Phenomenon of our own, namely, that we are paying selective attention to the ubiquitously drummed-in notions that getting old is a bad thing, and our resulting fears of aging form a kind of confirmation bias that makes us see its effects as dreadful everywhere we look.

It's up to us to reframe aging in realistic, holistic terms in order to open our minds to the possibility of perceiving it as the natural, life-affirming process that it is. Only when we are aware of ageism all around us can we take the right actions to dismantle it.

# WHEN "OLDER" MEANS "INVISIBLE"

The moment when many of us older adults first experience social invisibility varies. Mine hit me — and I mean literally — in my 50s, when a pair of decades-younger people in animated conversation walking down a crowded sidewalk didn't make room for an approaching me and bumped into either side of my body before I could dodge them. And although I said "Excuse me," I wasn't taken aback so much by the physical contact as I was by their lack of any recognition and apology as they continued past me.

Why do such startling encounters happen? What causes those of us who look or act old in others' estimation to be devalued and thus ignored, marginalized, and neglected?

Before I offer any answers, I should point out that age-based invisibility isn't experienced only by old people. Children, teens, and any others who aren't considered economically and/or socially contributing members of society — in other words, the powerless — are often overlooked when decisions are made and conditions are set that affect their lives.

So again, why does this old-age invisibility happen? The answer lies in the general cultural fears of scarcity, loss, and death. Believing that we share with others resources that are limited and might become scarce or that at any moment we might lose our health and/or wealth and be rendered vulnerable or nonexistent — these are the emotional triggers that set up the "us vs. them" paradigm that many of us embrace. Of course, the "us" are ourselves, no matter how old we are; the "them" are those people we otherize in order to distance ourselves from them mentally and even physically.

So who are the "them" that fit this profile? In general, three types of people are most likely to become invisible as they age.

First are those who are already physically isolated and are therefore literally out of sight, such as elders in nursing homes and memory-care centers, and those living at home who are unable to venture out for whatever reason.

The second type, as I just mentioned, are older people who are otherwise marginalized in our culture by the powerful and enfranchised. I'm referring to women, LGBTQ+ people, people of color, people with disabilities, those who are poor or work at low-paying jobs, and the homeless. Unfortunately, the invisibility resulting from ageism is usually compounded by its intersectionality with sexism, racism, ableism, classism, and homophobia.

The third type are older adults who are internally ageist and feel that with later age comes either the desire or the obligation to remove themselves from actively engaging with others. They may not know how to advocate for their dignity and autonomy or don't feel worthy of doing so because they have trouble imagining how they enrich others' lives just by being who they are. And in clinging to these beliefs, they render themselves powerless.

But the blame for the source of elder invisibility must ultimately rest on the widespread conscious or unconscious ageism perpetrated by our culture as a whole. Whether or not we become invisible as we age depends on who's doing the looking and their attitudes regarding getting older.

I'm basically talking about two types of ageists.

One group is afflicted with self-serving, or *egoistic*, ageism. They fear growing older, and so they consider older adults a repulsive population whom they must keep at a distance from themselves by seeing us as irrelevant.

Egoistic ageists tend not to pay attention to elders like me because they tell themselves, "I'm not like old people — and never will be. They don't have anything in common with me because they are useless to society and a drain on it." And so we are ignored by store clerks and restaurant wait staff, have doors shut in our faces as we approach entrances, and are ignored in group conversations of mixed ages in the workplace as well as social settings.

The other group of ageists also dread getting old, but they manifest their fear by embracing an altruistic, or *compassionate*, ageism that views elders as pathetic and needy and who must be served and protected by the obviously hale, competent, and strong. Paradoxically and sadly, some of these well-meaning people actually work in the health and social services sectors and should know better: health care providers who baby-talk to elders or who, during medical appointments, speak with an older patient's accompanying adult-child caregiver rather than directly to the patient; and long-term-care community administrators who find it more efficient to manage their residents as an amorphous group with identical preferences rather than as the widely varied individuals they are.

Compassionate ageists may or may not identify older adults as models of their own future selves; nevertheless, they also don't "see" elders as more complete individuals who yes, have needs (don't we all, at any age?) but also have the potential to contribute to, be productive in, or otherwise engage with society.

Whether older adults are subjected to discrimination by either egoistic or compassionate ageists, the results are the same: a malignant stereotyping that leads to rejection that leads to denied opportunities to be complete individuals, which is the birthright of us all.

And here's the paradox — and the irony — of it all: When people refuse to "see" old people, they are actually erasing their own reflection in the mirror of time. They are dooming themselves in coming years to the same debilitating social treatment by others.

That's the future consequence. But here's the current one: By not recognizing and accepting older adults' immense potential to contribute to society because of the acquired skills, knowledge, and experience that only grow over time, ageists are harming all of us, no matter our place in the lifespan. Ageists not only render old people powerless, but they are also depleting society itself of the power to increase in civility, equity, and economic abundance.

So what can older adults do to regain their power and make this invisibility vanish? The widespread social disempowering of the old might lead us elders to think that none of us escapes feeling entirely invisible. But that's not true.

Ironically, the people who *don't* become invisible as they age are *all of us older adults — to ourselves.* We are all too visible in our own eyes. We're well aware of how the aging process is playing out on our bodies, our lifestyles, our relationships. We can be losing some physical or cognitive abilities; losing partners, family members, and friends; and losing opportunities in the workplace. But if we're really paying attention, we're also equally aware of the many experiences we've had, the knowledge we've accumulated, and hopefully, the greater wisdom we're applying to our lives.

This awareness of our own value should inspire us to take charge of changing a society that's always slow to reform itself. After all, rarely, if ever, do the powerful voluntarily relinquish their power. Much of the responsibility of erasing our own invisibility lies with us.

So where do we start?

First of all, **we older adults need to become less ageist ourselves.** We should begin by examining our own perceptions about growing old, because in a world of egoistic and compassionate ageists, being internally ageist might be causing our own invisibility because we've bought into the idea of not being worthy to be valued by others. This lack of self-esteem is obvious when we tell ourselves we're too old to try something new or when we shy away from attending gatherings where we may be the only older person present. We develop a misplaced sense of age appropriateness and assume that some behaviors (*e.g.*, dancing in a nightclub at 2 a.m., dying one's hair shocking pink) are undignified in a person of advanced years. It goes without saying that there are activities, environments, and ways of being that are unsuitable for children, but once a person reaches the age of adulthood, there is no such thing as age appropriateness. As long as what you choose to do or how you act harms neither you nor anyone else, you should feel free to engage in it.

Taking this kind of proactive stance can be particularly problematic but necessary when dealing with compassionate ageists. For if we let them deny or do things for us that we are quite capable of doing for ourselves, we succumb to something called "learned helplessness," in which we give away much of our own power and agency to others. As a result, we get out of practice controlling our own lives, which includes asserting ourselves and being our own best advocates.

Second, **we need to internalize a more realistic picture of aging as a process of *gain* as well as loss.** We must realize that we're more than the limited beings we or others have assumed us to be. We need to reject the cultural myth that says older people can't or won't change. As I said before, we have had decades of experience adjusting to the ways our bodies change from year to year. We've relocated to different places, taken on different jobs, and handled iterations of all forms of technology (e.g., cars, phones, planes, computers). And sadly, we are also constantly adjusting to losing the people we love as they die. We are the Master Changers.

Moreover, as you've already read about aging's effect on the human mind, our brains have actually acquired certain abilities that can develop *only* with time and experience, such as being able to come at problems from many perspectives, to better regulate our emotions, to accurately detect patterns, and to store away many more pieces of learned information from which to draw and apply to new experiences. Knowing all of this can boost our own confidence in being who we are and help us encourage people of all ages to not fear the aging process.

Third, as we develop a real understanding of aging, **we should also be asserting ourselves by entering more fully into public life**. A great strategy is to look for work or volunteer for a cause that appeals to us and engages our skills. The individual brand of passion and competence we display can make us much-needed visible role models of creative, proactive aging.

An equally effective way is to engage with people of all ages. Forming intergenerational relationships is the best way all of us, regardless of age, can ensure a future that's free from ageism. With all our diversity, we can be realistic examples of elders who encourage younger people to eagerly anticipate growing old rather than to dread it.

Finally, **we must advocate for ourselves, calling out the ageist remarks and behaviors we encounter.** No one can be as convincing about the need to eradicate discrimination as the people who are on the receiving end. We can do so calmly, seriously, with empathy — and sometimes even with humor. We must be the vanguard that moves us out of the shadows and into the forefront of society. No one can do it as powerfully as we can.

I'm confident that the invisibility of older people will diminish because the issue is coming out of the closet. As the media cover more stories on age discrimination, as more men and women push to remain in the job market or start their own businesses; as more older female actors decry sex-based, or gendered, ageism; as more women are not only admitting their age but declaring it (not to mention turning down Botox and letting their hair go gray) — all of these efforts are creating a turning point in self-advocacy. More and more of us are refusing to be pushed aside or ignored. We're asserting ourselves. We're raising our hands and our voices.

And that's a sight to see, indeed.

# STATE OF THE ART FITNESS
# — FOR WHOM?

Several years ago, a new, state-of-the-art fitness center opened not far from where I live, and I thought I'd check it out. Only two weeks before, after months of convincing myself that I really needed to get in better physical shape, I joined a small, long-established athletic club in my neighborhood for a reasonable monthly fee, and since then I had been working out at least five times a week. I walked the indoor track and worked out on the strength-training machines. If I chose, I would have been able to use the pool, tennis and racquetball courts, and various cardio-exercise machines.

So imagine my curiosity when I received in the mail an invitation to attend the open-house event of a complex described as a "130,000-square-foot resort-like campus." With a monthly membership that costs 50% more than what I was currently paying, surely this place must have had lots more to offer than my club had for people like me over age 60.

Or so I thought.

The open house was packed with young families, and it didn't take me long to conclude they were the fitness center's target demographic. I should have known this from having viewed the company's website and "Welcome" video, which showed a paltry total of three model-attractive, gray-haired people in its entire marketing materials. Overwhelmingly Caucasian, dressed in stylish gym gear, packing the huge parking lot with minivans and SUVs — these young couples and their kids were the people heeding the siren song of fun, entertaining, glamorous fitness promised by the sleek, ultramodern, glass-and-chrome facility.

It was a classy place, to be sure, and as I walked through the doors, I felt like a diner entering an elegant restaurant for the first time, slightly underdressed, wondering about the prices on the menu, the size of the portions, and whether or not I'd even like the food. By the time I left, it became a place whose offerings I couldn't digest.

As an older adult, I was engaged, energetic, and enthusiastic, like the vast majority of older people I know. But in that fitness center, I was invisible. The huge, cathedral-ceiling atrium entry had no natural conversation areas. The multi-waterfall, oak-paneled women's locker room gleamed with spa-like elegance, but the lockers had combination locks with hard-to-read numbers. The cardio-fitness area was huge and industrial, and the smaller fitness classrooms blared music and were poorly soundproofed. I looked for the indoor track, which was where I imagined I'd spend most of my time as a member. There was none. No place to walk, unless it was on a treadmill among 50 other people on treadmills. About half of the entire square footage of the facility seemed to be devoted to kids: their own pools, outdoor and indoor playgrounds, eating areas, craft rooms. I couldn't help feeling that, even more than child fitness, the center was concerned with providing baby-sitting services in order to entice their parents to become members.

Maybe I was being idiosyncratic in my tastes. Maybe I was expecting too much, wanting to feel welcomed as someone past the age of midlife. In retrospect, I don't think so. After all, at my modest athletic club, older adults (people of all ages, in fact) enjoyed walking, jogging, and running on the indoor track as well as using the cardio equipment. For many of us older trackers, it was a place that addressed our need and desire for quality of experience. Being on the track provided a time of casual and familiar interaction, of quiet reflection and mindful meditation; it was a place to be away from the distracting action of rows of people running in place on machines while watching plasma TVs, and the feeling that such an atmosphere engendered of being a nameless person among a crowd of nameless others.

I learned at the open house that the center offered a book club (the promotional photos showed only people in their 30s and 40s), and a "Club for Moms." Wanting to find out about the environmental elements tailored to boomers and other older adults, I sought out the activities director, a very genial 30-something woman handing out brochures. I introduced myself and asked about design issues of concern to those like me: seating that encourages comfort and socialization, workout areas free of mindless media and distracting noise.

"Boomers? Older adults?" she replied. "Well, no…we don't have anything specifically geared for them." I pointed out the lack of an indoor track and explained that it's more than an amenity to many elders (and people of all ages with or without disabilities) seeking fitness during inclement weather; it's a necessity. She pondered: "You know, we never even thought of that in our planning."

Exactly.

Ageism is everywhere. It pervades our perceptions of who older adults are, and we have become comfortable allowing those lazy, unexercised perceptions to limit the ways we could and should move toward fairness and inclusivity regarding elders. It's ironic that none of the time, effort, and money invested in having built a 130,000-square-foot, gleaming, "resort-like campus" was spent on considering the needs of the very people who have trillions of dollars in assets[10] and spend trillions of dollars each year,[11] not to mention that 10,000 of them are turning 65 every day. It's more than ironic. It's downright financially suicidal.

Unless the developers of fitness facilities accommodate older adults, not as an afterthought or boutique population but as a core market for their services, it won't be many years before their state-of-the-art complexes won't be very fit at all.

# FROM THE CATCALL TO THE CATACOMB

I can't recall when I first saw the iconic picture "American Girl in Italy" taken by American photographer Ruth Orkin in 1951.[12] I just remember — vividly — how I felt. Maybe you've seen it, too. It shows a young American woman walking down an Italian city street, clearly disturbed by the catcalls of men standing on the corner, watching her go by.

My reaction to the photo was a visceral one combining fear, dread, and anger. As a young woman in New York City in the 1960s and '70s, I was often subjected to that same unsolicited attention. If I saw a group of male workers along my path, I'd unconsciously hunch my shoulders to minimize my chest as I passed them, staring straight ahead.

Those were the moments I could prepare for, but there were many other times I was surprised by an individual sneaking up behind me to whisper in my ear. Whatever comfortable sense of solitude I had was immediately interrupted and shattered. Violated, is how I now see it.

It's been decades since I've had such experiences, and I'm grateful for that. But there's a reason for the difference: It's not because those kinds of men are no longer around. Nor is it because they have changed. I have. I'm now in my 70s, wrinkled, 30 pounds heavier, and with gray hair. I now walk blissfully upright on my way with nary a turned head, shout, or whisper to disturb me.

Yet this experience has its dark side. As an old person, in many things that matter, I'm basically invisible to the powers that be, owing to widespread cultural ageism. And as I've said, there are subsets to ageism that incorporate racism, ableism, or homophobia.

The discrimination I'm talking about, gendered ageism, involves sexism and is based on misogyny, which considers women as inferior beings with only two uses: as sexual objects to be ogled or far worse, or as aides to serve families, businesses, and organizations. And when those in power determine that we women lose our ability to be sexual beings (which, by the way, we *never* do), then it's time to move us away from daily life, entombing us in a cultural catacomb.

Even now you'd think these were the only two inevitable experiences for women over the course of their adult lives.

In *Ageism Unmasked*, Tracey Gendron explains the strange dichotomy women experience because of gendered ageism:

Femininity is susceptible to multiple marginalizations, including ageism, sexism, lookism (appearance), sizeism, fitnessism, healthism, and sexual objectification. Ironically, the vulnerability that older women face due to these layered forms of prejudice translates into being simultaneously hyper-visible and invisible. Hyper-visibility results from the exaggerated focus on appearance promoted and enabled by media by the anti-aging industry and those who have been influenced by it. It is also fostered by the rhetoric of successful aging, which posits that aging successfully essentially translates into not aging, and that objectively looking younger provides a shield against appearance-based age shaming. For example, telling someone "You look old" is considered an insult and is tied to implications of ugliness, failure, and inadequacy. Invisibility is a counter-effect of ageism, especially in the workplace, where older women often find their contributions dismissed or ignored and are objectively less likely to get hired or promoted.[13]

An infamous example of Gendron's argument is the case of Canadian journalist and CTV National News anchor Lisa LaFlamme,[14] who in 2022 found herself suddenly terminated — "blindsided" was the word she used — for reasons that, albeit denied by her supervisors, may have been based on her gender and willingness to let her hair go gray.

Needless to say, LaFlamme's story aroused the indignation of pro-aging and feminist advocates alike, and rightfully so. It's yet again another instance, which I'm now calling "catacombing" (after the ancient Roman catacombs where early Christians hid underground to avoid persecution), of relegating to the sidelines and out of view a competent, productive woman who has consciously decided to let her personal appearance reflect her individual biological age. Interestingly, there were some surprising corporate responses, such as Dove Canada launching a #KeepTheGrey campaign[15] and the Canadian branch of Wendy's temporarily changing its namesake's hair color in its logo.[16]

Serendipitously, the LaFlamme termination occurred five days after the U.S. Supreme Court's Dobbs v. Jackson Women's Health Organization ruling that overturned the longstanding Roe v. Wade decision. The reactions to this ruling have been swift and substantial. The most surprising came from Kansas, in which voters rejected a state constitution amendment banning abortion[17] by a nearly 20-point differ-ence. Moreover, a 2022 Washington Post article[18] described a sudden huge increase in female voter registration in Kansas, Pennsylvania, and Florida, and it's likely such a trend is happening in other states as well.

The mainstream media, in its infinite myopia, has been describing this surge of dissatisfaction and determination as "the waking of a sleeping giant," as if women and their male allies have been dozing all along. Have they forgotten all those stories that ran covering the #MeToo movement? Such egregious oversight is itself a form of sexism and misogyny, which we can't seem to avoid, like a sudden close whis-per or blatant catcall confronting us along our path toward achieving women's rights.

Women have been fighting for equal rights all along, sometimes coming together in massive groups and other times acting in smaller ones or on their own. No giant has been sleeping, I assure you. But the latest tide of activism may be women's largest yet, because it now involves life-and-death situations on a national scale.

The female response to the LaFlamme and Dobbs events isn't determined solely by our gender. It also includes our age. Women like me who became adults in the 1960s and '70s, marched for women's rights, and were thrilled by the Roe decision in 1973 are not about to leave our children, grandchildren, and great-grandchildren — male as well as female — vulnerable to decisions that affect their families' health, financial security, and opportunities for self-fulfillment. We won't allow ourselves to be blindsided or sidelined at the expense of future generations.

All our lives we've played a role that defies both catcalls and catacombs. We've been — and continue to be — catalysts. Catalysts for change.

Invisibility? No way.

Hyper-visibility? You ain't seen nothin' yet.

# POWER TO THE (OLD) PEOPLE?

Today's news is filled with references to all kinds of political systems: autocracy, kleptocracy, plutocracy, theocracy, and the most relevant one of all — democracy.

Added to this list is a new one: gerontocracy, a government based on rule by old people. I suppose it's to be expected in these highly polarized times that ageism, which is really the polarization of perceptions about young vs. old, has seeped into people's assessments[19] of who is leading our government,[20] and who should lead it instead.

Those who believe that our nation is now run primarily by people much older than they are have a limited understanding of the ways in which Western governments have functioned for millennia. Furthermore, today's composition of Congress, the Supreme Court, and the Executive branch actually defy that longstanding pattern.

But that's not the only point I'd like to discuss. Even if we're currently led by a gerontocracy, let's also consider whether or not that's such a bad thing after all.

I'll start by tackling the first point: Are we really being ruled by old people?

I guess the answer depends on how old "old" is. Is someone in their 60s an old person? Given that in 2020 the average life expectancy at birth in the U.S. was 74 years for men and 80 years for women,[21] I think most people, or at least middle-aged ones, would say that to be 60-something doesn't exactly fit the bill.

So here's an eye-opening fact: According to the Library of Congress, "The average age of Members of the House at the beginning of the 117th Congress was 58.4 years; of Senators, 64.3 years."[22] And as for the average

age of Supreme Court Justices, in 2022, with Ketanji Brown Jackson replacing Stephen Breyer, the average age was 61.4 years. And the average age of the Biden Administration Cabinet[23] was 58 years. Not exactly Methuselah numbers.

But here's the thing: Throughout Western history, the men (yes, it was always men) in charge of the government were usually as old, if not older, than the average age of life expectancy at birth for their time.

In ancient Greece, for example, where life expectancy was about 28[24] years old, an Athenian man had to be 20 to be a full-fledged citizen[25] and 30 to be admitted to the council and the court jury pool;[26] in Sparta, which elected its kings, a man had to be at least 60[27] — twice the expectancy age.

In ancient Rome, where life expectancy at birth was approximately the same as in ancient Greece,[28] the earliest senators had to be at least 60;[29] the age was later dropped to 25.[30]

Even in our own early government, the average age of the members of the 1775 Continental Congress was 44, while the average life expectancy at birth was between 35 and 40 years of age.[31]

Given these examples, it appears that 21st-century American government has defied the pattern, with its groups' averages a decade or two younger than that of the current life expectancy.

Whether or not it's a bad thing to have older leaders in government is a whole other matter.

What was the driving principle behind political power historically residing in men who were old for their times? Most likely those cultures held the belief that with age usually comes the necessary acquisition of relevant experience and the kind of wisdom needed to rule. Of course, in the U.S. there have been recent exceptions (John F. Kennedy became president at age 43 and Bill Clinton and Barack Obama at age 47), and old age alone doesn't guarantee a person having either relevant experience or sufficient wisdom. But it does increase the odds.

At this point, it's important to remember that dementia is *not* an inevitable condition of old age. Of course, as with any other occupation, anyone of any age in Congress who has cognitive issues that negatively affect their job should not be serving in that capacity. But there are a far greater number of older members of Congress whose brains work unsurprisingly quite well.

This issue aside, current ageist complaints about American gerontocracy usually involve dissatisfaction with the entrenchment of political power among recent prominent members of Congress such as Nancy Pelosi, Mitch McConnell, Chuck Schumer, and Bernie Sanders. This, then, begs the question of how these people rose to their positions and have continued in them.

As in most institutions, achieving a long-term leadership position in the U.S. Congress is often based on a combination of merit, tenure, and financial backing. That means that their constituents have reelected them multiple times and their donors continue to support their campaigns. Furthermore, the members of each party in the Senate determine their leaders, while the entire membership of the House of Representatives determines who becomes the Speaker. Until recently at least, it has been rare that a relatively new member of Congress rises to power quickly; sober and responsible members usually have demanded that their leaders have a track record of demonstrating savvy political skills.

So is the gerontocracy that's seemingly built into the political system really at the heart of complaints against political entrenchment? Or rather, might a different factor be the cause? After all, it's obvious that certain much-younger members of Congress have also demonstrated their own ideological entrenchment which, when they have been given the chance to assume leadership roles, they have certainly promoted.

I suggest that what's controlling Congressional action — or lack thereof — isn't age; it's power and money, factors that have always played significant roles in American politics but have gotten more corrosive since the 2010 Supreme Court's Citizens United decision, which allowed for more unrestrained campaign contributions from corporations, wealthy donors, and special interest groups.[32] Allowing dark money to enter political campaigns has been the great age equalizer. No longer do political experience or savvy seem to determine electability. What matters now is the unaccountable, unlimited, ongoing financial sponsorship of candidates willing to push the economic, social, and religious agendas of their backers and, once they are in Congress, to obstruct those of their opponents.

Gerontocracy isn't the issue in democratic leadership; it's kleptocracy, plutocracy, theocracy, and if we're even more oblivious about the danger…autocracy.

# THE WAYS THAT AGING SUITS US

Imagine going to an elegant fashion house or haberdashery to be fitted for a handmade suit. The process would be slow, deliberate, and deferential as the tailor would take various measurements of your body, offer you a selection of tasteful materials that met your needs and preferences, create a pattern, and meticulously sew the fabric. You would be called back for several fittings and adjustments until the outfit perfectly fitted the contours of your unique body.

It turns out that the ways we grow into aging are as unique as our bodies and identities. It's a mistake for anyone to believe otherwise, but unfortunately many of us do, especially when we feel comfortable relying on one-size-fits-all ageist stereotypes that prevent us from better understanding the older adult experience in all its idiosyncrasies, complexities, and varieties. For example, we may harbor negative ageist beliefs of the compassionate kind by feeling sorry for the stooped old woman hurrying to cross a busy city street or for the lone old man sitting on a bench, squinting to read his newspaper.

Ironically, some well-meaning people creating aging products or working in aging services are inadvertently promoting compassionate ageism by designing and producing age-simulation suits that give decades-younger people the experience of navigating and moving about in older bodies. The goal of these designers is to increase the wearers' ability to understand the various possible physical challenges of bodies as they age — decreased hearing, dimmed eyesight, less flexible joints, and weakened muscles. Or, as a 2019 article on an episode of Boston public radio station WBUR's *Here and Now* program asked, "Have you ever wondered what it would be like to age 40 years in a matter of minutes?"[33] They hope that such understanding will increase wearers' empathy for what older people go through. I'll explain in a moment how their approach is ageist, but first it's important to know more about what these suits are like.

There are many models of age-simulation suits (you can view them on Google Images[34]), but all are constructed to have some basic features that restrict movement, impede balance, and interfere with the basic senses of hearing, sight, and touch.

Take, for example, one suit called AGNES ("Age Gain Now Empathy System"), designed by the Massachusetts Institute of Technology's AgeLab[35] and another called GERT ("GERonTologic simulator"), developed by the German company Produkt + Projekt Wolfgang Moll.[36] AGNES comes equipped with connective elastic bands from head to torso and from lower back to legs to restrict flexibility and range of motion, while GERT has a weighted vest that curves the spine. Both suits include padding around the elbows and knees, thick gloves, neck braces, bulky overshoes, tinted and/or cloudy goggles, and ear coverings that muffle noise.

Needless to say, younger test subjects find it a surprising and daunting challenge to walk some distance, pick up a coin, use a pen to write their name, read ingredient labels on packaged foods, listen to spoken instructions, and get in and out of a car. For a limited time, they are transformed into a seriously feeble, slow, arthritic, imbalanced, hearing- and sight-impaired population.

You get the picture. And it's a sad one, which is precisely the designers' aim. They want to send the message that non–older people should have more patience, understanding, and tolerance for others in their later years who struggle to maintain function, dignity, and independence while going about the business of living.

And in my opinion, having such a goal misses the mark…big time.

For one thing, because age-simulation suits force wearers to experience at least a half-dozen physical challenges *simultaneously*, they haven't been especially effective in increasing some test subjects' empathy or attitudes toward old people.[37] In fact, at times the overkill of those outfits even decrease those feelings by reinforcing the wearers' already existing fears of getting old. Therefore, products that were meant to evoke more realistic perceptions about aging actually achieve the opposite result.

Let's do a brief reality check regarding some of those age-simulated conditions.

- Between 2015 and 2017, only 4.6% of Americans ages 65 to 74 and 7.2% of those ages 75 and older were seriously visually impaired.[38]

- As estimated by the National Institute on Deafness and Other Communication Disorders, "Nearly 25 percent of those aged 65 to 74, and 50 percent of those who are 75 and older have disabling hearing loss."[39]

- In 2020, "Mobility limitations have been reported as increasingly prevalent in older persons, affecting about 35% of persons aged 70 and the majority of persons over 85 years."[40]

As for chronic conditions — which are, of course, serious in themselves — how many older adults are daily coping with a very large number of them at the same time?

According to the Leading Age Long-Term Services and Supports (LTSS) Center at the University of Massachusetts–Boston and the National Council on Aging, in 2018, 50.5% of Americans ages 60 and older report having two or three chronic conditions such as hypertension, diabetes, cancer, lung disease, heart disease, stroke, arthritis, Alzheimer's disease/dementia, and depression. Moreover, only 12.1% report coping with five or more.[41] If we consider the possibility that many of the people with such conditions are receiving adequate medical care, it's likely that they are also receiving adequate care regarding the mobility issues addressed by age-simulation suits.

Given these provocative statistics, age-simulation suits skew rather than accurately depict the physical reality of the majority of older adults, a population that generally enjoys greater health than previous later-years generations. The suits imply that the physical challenges they create aren't really experienced by young or middle-aged adults — an obviously distorted perception, as there are many 20-, 30-, 40-, and 50-somethings who cope with chronic limitations and pain on a daily basis. (It's also ageist — and sexist — to give those suits antiquated female names such as AGNES and GERT, which only reinforce the image of frailty.)

Finally, the idea of applying age simulation solely to a person's physical ability ties ageism to ableism. What about considering the ways in which older adults with physical challenges are also proactive members of their families and communities, engaged in a variety of satisfying personal, economic, and social endeavors? What would it require to build an interior "suit" that could incorporate the older adult cognitive abilities of problem-solving, creativity, flexibility, persistence, resilience, and emotional stability?

If we feel sorry for the stooped old woman hurrying to cross a busy city street or for the lone old man sitting on a bench, squinting to read his newspaper, our attitudes may be deceptively limited, as we have no idea about the actual people before us, individuals who have skills, interests, knowledge, and potential that we aren't able to know. After all, that scurrying woman might be on her way to the elementary school for her weekly volunteer reading session with an at-risk fourth-grader. That solitary newspaper-perusing man might be checking to see if the op-ed he wrote and was accepted by an editor has just been published. Their exteriors may belie far richer interior lives.

An aging "suit" isn't the entire person. None of us would want to be judged solely by outer appearances. And we certainly wouldn't want society to determine what those appearances are by measuring and fitting us according to ageist-based assumptions and expectations that are drab, pathetic, comical, outmoded, debilitating, or confining. Throughout our lives, including as we age, each of us deserves a suit that is the perfect fit for who we are as an individual.

It's society, not us, that needs to be tailored accordingly.

# CHAPTER 7

# Lessons from a Pandemic

**ON MAY 5, 2023,** the United Nations World Health Organization declared that the COVID-19 pandemic was no longer a Public Health Emergency of International Concern (PHEIC).[1] This statement was followed shortly after, on May 11, with a formal declaration by the Centers for Disease Control and Prevention of the termination of the Federal COVID-19 Public Health Emergency (PHE).[2]

Long before these events, many people gleefully had already decided for themselves that the pandemic was over. Gone were the masks, social distancing, and even efforts to continue getting vaccinated and boosted, even though thousands of people continued to contract the virus, be hospitalized, and die.

All these reactions currently raise the question "What, if anything, did we learn from the pandemic?"

Did we develop a greater sense of social responsibility and concern for our neighbors? Did we strengthen our public protocols to provide for more accurate disease tracking, wider production and distribution of protective materials, stricter quarantine and masking mandates, and fairer standards of medical triage?

Answering these questions would require writing an entire book. Nevertheless, it's worth discussing the pandemic as it relates to ageism, because for anyone still wondering if having negative perceptions about aging could be harmful, looking at older age through the lens of COVID should lay those doubts to rest.

Around the world, in the first two years of the pandemic, adults aged 60 and older suffered the greatest impact, comprising 80% of all COVID deaths.[3] As for the United States, a November 28, 2022 article in The Washington Post reported that "Last month, people 85 and older represented 41.4 percent of deaths, those 75 to 84 were 30 percent of deaths, and those 65 to 74 were 17.5 percent of deaths, according to a Post analysis. All told, the 65-plus age group accounted for 90 percent of covid deaths in the United States despite making up only 16 percent of the population."[4]

When any group composing 16% of a nation's total population suffers 90% of all deaths, something is very wrong. Of course, the biologically understandable conclusion is that such a high death rate is due to older adults' generally lower levels of immunity and higher chances of having multiple chronic health conditions, both of which can make COVID more serious and deadly.

But that's only half an answer. An equally important cause is the harm inflicted by the egregious systemic ageism that has existed for decades. It's as if COVID, like a huge magnifying glass, was held up to the entire globe to show all of us a reality that was hard to ignore.

Ageist presumptions by powerful decision-makers in government, business, and the medical community about the survivability of elders — not to mention the general social value of their lives — determined whether, how, and to what extent older COVID patients received treatment.

As you know, a prime ageist fallacy is to perceive all older people as alike and thus consider them as a homogenous group called "the elderly." By believing that many older adults were already living socially isolated lives and that fewer of them were employed full-time and therefore not contributing much to the economy, it became easy and acceptable to impose stricter supply quotas and quarantine mandates on them, since, according to those assumptions, doing so wouldn't make much of a difference in their lives.

But what about the many additional ways employed and unemployed older people volunteer in their communities, spend trillions of dollars purchasing goods and services, contribute to the raising of grandchildren, and provide housing and financial support to their adult children? Shouldn't all of this have been considered in the decision-making process?

Such myopia, supported and boosted by ageist politicians, health providers, and the media, resulted in the delay of the timely distribution of medicines and medical supplies to nursing homes and other long-term-care facilities, the youth-favoring rationing of ventilators and ICU beds, and the establishment of strict visitation policies denying many older residents and hospital patients access to their loved ones. All these responses contributed to elders' poorer outcomes and higher mortality rates.

The motivations behind these decisions can be traced to two basic principles of triage practice: benefits and fairness. University of Granada bioethicist Jon Rueda explains how each principle is applied:

Benefits can be measured in two ways: regarding short-term survival or long-term survival. The former seeks to save lives — basically being discharged from the hospital. The latter, conversely, seeks to save those who can have a longer life expectancy. Typically, this second type of benefit takes into account not only the number of years that can be saved, but also the quality of life of the person that has survived....[5]

The principle of fairness requires distributing the costs and bene-fits of medical services in a just manner. According to fairness, ethical relevance of age can point out two different directions. On the one hand, from an intergenerational justice perspective, individuals should have the opportunity of living a *sufficient and normal life-span*.... Fairness, on the other hand, tries also to avoid placing vulnerable social collectives on systemic disadvan-tage. Even if there are reasons to consider age in triage decisions, categorically excluding all members of a vulnerable group is blind discrimination.[6]

The problem with imposing one-size-fits-all rules on an extremely diverse population of humans of all ages is that no single rule works. Age mustn't be the only factor to consider in triage. For example, during a shortage of ICU beds, who should be provided one: a trim, athletic, and robust 80-year-old or an obese 40-year-old smoker with chronic obstruc-tive pulmonary disease? On the one hand, the older patient might have a far better chance of surviving COVID when given intense respiratory treatment. On the other hand, the 40-year-old may have another 40 years to live, while the 80-year-old would not. In this case, should age be the sole criterion in triage?

According to Rueda, "Considering age alone is inadequate because it fails to differentiate between age itself and other conditions that may have been caused by social determinants of health rather than necessarily by aging."[7]

In March 2020, Deborah Alsina, then–chief executive of the London-based nonprofit charity Independent Age, on behalf of nine aging-care service organizations in the United Kingdom, issued this joint statement on the treatment rights of older people during the pandemic:

> Any suggestion that treatment decisions can be blanket ones, based on age alone or with a person's age given undue weight as against other factors, such as their usual state of health and capacity to benefit from treatment, would be completely unacceptable. For many years we have known that chronological age is a very poor proxy for an individual's health status and resilience — something we all see among the older people in our lives. To ignore this and to revert to an approach based solely or mainly on age would be, by definition, ageist, discriminatory and morally wrong.
>
> We strongly believe that decisions about treatment should always be made on a case by case basis through honest discussion between doctors, patients and their families that factor in the risks, benefits and people's wishes. There is no reason to abandon this long-established good practice now; in fact the current health emergency makes it more critical than ever that we keep it.[8]

Just because the pandemic emergency has been deemed over, Alsina's message remains valid as a guideline to follow during not only the COVID pandemic but also any others we may face in the future.

As we prepare for the next global plague that will surely come, the key to providing treatment based on carefully considered principles of benefits and fairness must include an awareness of how ageist views can rob our decision-making of its compassion and common sense.

In a compelling New York Times opinion piece titled "'Covid-19 Kills Only Old People.' Only?" written at the start of the pandemic in

March 2020, University of California, San Francisco geriatrician Louise Aronson explained:

> But most old people are not dying. Not only are the "old" getting older, but the risk of death in the next year for a 70-year-old man is just 2 percent, and an 80-year-old woman has only a 4 percent likelihood of dying in the coming year, according to the Stanford economist John Shoven. Comments such as "They're on their way out anyway" are therefore more than colossally insensitive; they're also colossally inaccurate....
>
> When we look at people as nothing more than amalgams of age and diagnosis, we miss their humanity....
>
> We can choose to either diminish our elders or support them. When we care for them, we not only are affecting the lives of people now but also are shaping our own futures.[9]

The questions we ask about how to treat people when they are sick should be the same ones we ask when they are not. In other words, behaving toward others with compassion, respect, and good judgment should extend beyond the walls of hospitals, nursing homes, schools, workplaces, and anywhere else people interact.

Or as aging experts Jill Vitale-Aussem, Caroline Pearson, and geriatrician Bill Thomas posed in a piece for the aging housing and health care think tank Nexus Insights called "If You Hated 2020, You're Going to Despise Old Age":

> What would it take to have older people live where they wish without becoming socially isolated? What would it take for older

people to be viewed as valuable members of a society that desperately needs their lived experiences and knowledge? What would
it take for those receiving care in congregate settings to have lives
filled with purpose, meaningful relationships, and, dare we say
it, joy?[10]

What, indeed?

Our humanity is what we have in common; our individuality is what
defies generalization. If there's any great lesson we can still learn from
this horrible pandemic experience, it's that we should embrace aging as
the ongoing process of exercising our common humanity while honing
our individual uniqueness.

Ageism is the ongoing global public health emergency we must work
to end. In the spirit of intentional triage, I offer a few more, slightly
different ways to make this point.

# DO NOT GO GENTLE...

When Welsh poet Dylan Thomas wrote the poem "Do Not Go Gentle"[11] in 1947, most people would agree that the "light" he described as dying was synonymous with "life." It was a bright energy that everyone wanted to experience and enjoy for as long as possible. And so, of course, the assumption was that old people would naturally cling to it at all costs. Hence the need to "rage" against its "dying."

In May 2020, two months into a brutal pandemic, life was still a light, but one that was now casting a harsh glare into shadowy places we had long refused to acknowledge.

Before the pandemic, as I perused each morning's New York Times, I hardly ever looked at the obituaries pages, except to learn more about famous people whose lives intrigued me. But later I tended to check them daily. Here's why.

People of all ages were dying from COVID-19, and we grieved their collective loss. Not surprisingly, the deaths of babies, children, and teens from this hideous virus invariably evoked our sadness because we thought about the many more years they should have had to experience life and fulfill their potential. Moreover, the deaths of middle-agers produced their own poignancy as we acknowledged human loss in "the prime of life."

But what about the COVID deaths of individuals like me whom society lumps into that ageist category known as "the elderly"? Should collective sadness have been any less intense for us because, after all, we have already lived much of our lives and thus should have expected to die? More than that, as some people, such as the then–lieutenant governor of Texas Dan Patrick.[12] contended, should we older adults consider sacrificing ourselves to COVID so that younger people would have a greater chance at economic opportunity and therefore survival? Is the light of existence such a limited resource that we must douse our candles prematurely for others' to remain lit?

As I read the obituaries of nursing home residents,[13] Holocaust survivors,[14] World War II veterans,[15] and others in their 70s, 80s, 90s, and 100s who have succumbed to COVID, I thought, *They survived years of great challenge, only to be taken down needlessly by a tragic disease that might have been seriously mitigated, given a competent strategy.* This made me incredibly sad.

And here's where my sadness turned into rage.

The Trump Administration's obscenely botched handling of the pandemic in 2020 in a timely and effective way by 1) promoting perceptions that the virus was a hoax, 2) not establishing immediate, widespread quarantining, and 3) not providing health care and other essential workers with enough protective and emergency equipment, reliable testing, and extensive contact tracing caused an additional tens of thousands of deaths.[16] So, too, Congress' subsequent failure to promptly and adequately fund small businesses and low-wage, gig, and unemployed and underemployed workers caused economic peril and ruin. The resulting darkness in many lives was exacerbated by the intersectional effects of ageism, ableism, racism, classism, sexism, and homophobia in a pathologically unjust society.

Particularly regarding age, as all of us were constantly trying to cope with the protean realities of this virus, we were also experiencing outbreaks of ageism that had been festering all along but then had emerged more clearly from the shadows and into the light of daily life. And while we were asking such questions as "Should I wear a mask?" and "How close is too close?", we should also have been asking "What is a human life worth?", "Are some lives worth more than others?", and "Is it moral to calculate such worth?"

Every person's life has equal value. No one is dispensable or disposable.[17] No one can determine the potential of one human being — be it a baby or a centenarian — to positively affect one or more fellow humans. And no one should have the authority to do it.

The amazing thing about a lit candle is that it can share its flame by lighting an infinite number of other candles without itself becoming dimmer or being extinguished. What this pandemic should have been teaching us was how to build a more equitable society that provides the chance for every one of us to keep our personal flame ablaze as brightly and enduringly as we can.

Yes, we should make our peace with dying. After all, that time will come to all of us. But for now, even today while we're alive, let's not go gentle into accepting and perpetuating the nightmares of discrimination that keep others in darkness and may hasten their death. Instead, let's burn and rave for moral solutions to the shadows of inequity.

Let's rage, rage against the *denying* of the light.

# HOW MANY "AT BATS" SHOULD WE GET?

As with all other crises, the 2020 start of the COVID-19 pandemic in America sparked discussions that employed our nation's two favorite metaphors: war and sports. We were "waging a fierce battle" against the virus, "fighting for our lives" while researchers and pharmaceutical companies were "racing" to find a vaccine and "jumping over hurdles" to get their discoveries and products "over the finish line."

Given such tendencies, it shouldn't be surprising that, at a time when America's major league sports were struggling to start, restart, or continue their seasons, discussions about the possible need for health care rationing naturally included athletic references — more specifically, to those of our National Pastime, baseball.

In a post for The New York Times' The New Old Age blog titled "Should Youth Come First in Coronavirus Care?", columnist Paula Span cited the opinion of retired bioethicist Larry Churchill, who "…subscribes to a 'life span approach' to ethics, sometimes called the 'fair innings' approach: He has had his turns at bat. Younger people have had less time to experience life's opportunities and pleasures."[18]

In comparing the death of a 40-year-old to his own, 75-year-old Churchill considered the former "tragic" because of that person's "unfulfilled potential" as opposed to his own demise, which would be merely "sad."

In all fairness, wrote Span, Churchill didn't claim that everyone else should subscribe to his view, which he felt was appropriate only for himself. Each of us older adults should make up our own minds about whether to forego hospitalization, ventilation, or other means of care in order that a younger person could benefit from it.

But let's look deeper into the validity of making such a comparison at all.

In the newer National Pastime called "surviving the pandemic," our testing, tracking, and treatment resources were scarce and disproportionately distributed. Because of this situation — and unlike in a baseball game — any of us may have been limited to the number of "at bats" we could get for treatment.

And so health care providers as well as the rest of us were being forced to consider two painful questions: 1) Who gets to decide which patients are admitted to the ICU, offered available drugs, and, if need be, put on a ventilator? and 2) On what should those decisions be based?

By citing the criterion of "potential," Churchill reflected an ageist position that assumes that the passing of years naturally reduces a person's chances to be productive, engaged, or contributory, however he defined them. For him, potential was based solely on one's place on the lifespan timeline. But who can draw such a blanket conclusion?

Given ageism's intersectionality with systemic racism, sexism, ableism, classism, and homophobia in our culture, that 40-year-old's potential could be significantly stifled or even quashed just by living life as a female, an immigrant, poor, gay, or a minority; or living with a disability, in a rural area without Internet accessibility, or in a neighborhood with inadequately funded public schools. Let's remember that institutionalized discrimination is often the main cause of someone's "unfulfilled potential."

Acknowledging this intersectionality is vital when dealing with the effects of COVID-19 on older adults. Toward this end, the American Geriatrics Society released a position statement[19] that said, in part:

A just healthcare system should treat similarly situated people equally, as much as possible. There is something particularly unjust about membership in a class, such as an age group, determining whether a person receives health care[20].... When assessing comorbidities, the disparate impact of social determinants of health including culture, ethnicity, socioeconomic status, and other factors should be considered.[21]

As Span pointed out: "The statement also opposes criteria like 'life-years saved' and long-term life expectancy, which similarly disadvantage the older population. Instead, it recommends treating patients based on the likelihood of being discharged from the hospital and surviving for six months."[22]

In a lethal wargame against a plague, we should recognize ageism as the global social pandemic it is and inoculate ourselves against our own internalized ageism as well as the prejudice and bigotry of others. That's the "full season" strategy.

In the meantime, while COVID-19 rages across the globe, governments and health care systems need to abandon longstanding tribal rules that pit two "teams" — Youngsters and Oldsters — against each other. The real deadly contest is between the members of all leagues (based on age, socioeconomic status, race, gender, geographic location, and physical ability) vs. the virus itself. Everyone, regardless of individual situation or condition, deserves unlimited at-bats.

Now and in the future, anyone in charge of allocating resources, directing research, or caring for the sick should stop focusing on a rationing strategy that determines who will live and who will die based on broad parameters. Instead, they must fully commit all their efforts and resources to maximizing the speedy, accurate diagnosis and effective, *individualized* treatment of anyone who gets the virus.

To win against COVID-19 and any future pandemic disease, they shouldn't eject anyone from the field. Instead, they need to immediately create, distribute, and follow a robust, organized, universal playbook outlining four directives:

Get in the game. Step up to the plate. Swing for the fences.

And knock it out of the park.

# OUR SURVIVAL AND SAFETY ARE AT A CROSSROADS

In the 2020 election during a global pandemic, racial unrest, climate change, and unsettling politics, we stood in a crossroads of two distinct paths our nation could take. Each of us chose a direction reflecting our own needs and experiences based on our individual identity, social situation, and economic needs.

But are we really that separate and different? No. The truth is, whether we know it or not, we are interdependent because our lives intersect. Maskless crowds refusing to follow pandemic safety guidelines soon overwhelmed hospitals with more COVID-19 patients, which further delayed school openings and shut down more workplaces. The violence perpetrated by police against people of color and the destruction of property by extremist groups continued to hit cities economically in the forms of lost tourism and shuttered small businesses. Massive raging wildfires in the West and hurricanes in the East caused by our refusal to address global warming destroyed hundreds of thousands of homes and millions of square miles of land, and displaced millions of people at a cost of billions of dollars.

Today we are still suffering global illness and social hostility based on our inability to appreciate the ways in which our lives are inextricably bound.

Have we reached an apocalypse? Not yet. But we *are* at a crossroads. Our individual challenge is to start by finding a personal connection with the struggles of a group of people with whom we don't comfortably identify.

For example, from the confines of my then–nine-month self-quarantine in a Portland, Ore. apartment with windows sealed against the overwhelming toxic smoke of Northwest wildfires, I watched on TV how daily down-town peaceful protests turned into nightly violence. These acts shocked and disheartened me and left me wishing I could join the peaceful marches to promote social justice for people of color. But at age 68 and medically at high risk for contracting COVID-19, I remained indoors.

Nevertheless, I empathized with their cause because I also belong to an often marginalized and disenfranchised group: older adults. Like racism, ageism carries its own forms of injustice. Older adults, too, are "otherized" by most of society as people whom no one wants to be, or to be around.

Like racism, ageism manifests in particular ways. Although most of us are not feared or demonized, neither are we embraced or respected. Rather than being viewed with suspicion, we're looked upon with disgust. And while we're not treated with overt cruelty, we're often patronized, pitied, or not treated at all.

I've already discussed how nursing homes suffered from a lack of adequate medical supplies to defend against COVID-19[23] and how some political officials considered us expendable. It's also important to note that people aged 65 and older were excluded from more than half of all COVID-19 vaccine and treatment clinical trials even though at that time they comprised more than 80% of all COVID deaths.[24] We older adults were, and still are, invisible and neglected.

The health care situation is often worse if you're an older person of color, and even worse for an older woman of color, or in a wheelchair, or gay. For example, one 2021 study reported that

> high-minority nursing homes had 61% greater COVID-19 deaths compared to those with no minorities....

These findings are consistent with prior studies showing that that Black and Hispanic nursing home residents are more likely than their White peers to reside in nursing homes characterized by inadequate resources, less staffing, higher deficiencies, poorer performance, and worse quality of care…

 One of the most telling findings was the issue of resource availability; nursing homes with higher levels of minorities were located in poorer, urban communities.[25]

When any combination of race, gender, age, physical ability, and sexual orientation intersect, the impact of unjust social policies that lead to a lack of access to adequate, affordable health care, education, housing, jobs, and lifetime income is intensified.

By living in conceptual bubbles defined by our own self-interests, we do untold damage to others, which then does untold damage to us. The cure for this condition is to understand just how circumstantial and fluid are our personal identities — and interpersonal ties.

I'm convinced that only by accepting that our lives interconnect will we be able to enact laws and develop programs that will make all our lives healthier and more secure.

The choice is ours to turn our inertia into action. We can remain motionless on our own experiential street corners, carrying our own ideological protest signs. Or we can recognize our interdependence. To survive this pandemic and others in the future, and to heal our cultural wounds, each of us must take that first step into a crosswalk leading to greater understanding of another, different, population by including its members in our efforts and by joining theirs.

And maybe, just maybe, we might be able to proceed to the very conceptual middle of all intersections, where everyone's desires for economic equity, physical safety, social stability, and global health unite, in that central place where we can create a society based on these shared needs and goals.

Only then will we be able to live — safely and peacefully — on common ground.

# THE EPIDEMIOLOGY OF AGEISM

If there's anything that the last several years have taught us, it's that a pandemic can't easily be ignored, even by those who steadfastly seek to deny its existence. By now, whether we subscribe to any of the basic guidelines or not, most of us know about masking, social distancing, using therapeutics, and most important of all, getting vaccinated and boosted.

But COVID isn't what I want to address. While I'm thoroughly committed to following safety measures to avoid getting or spreading that virus, it's another dangerous illness that continues to haunt me.

As it turns out, ageism is proving to be a social disease that has a lot in common with COVID. It's widespread, easily transmissible, and once it takes hold, tenacious and pernicious.

Just how widespread is it? According to the 2022 University of Michigan's National Poll on Healthy Aging,[26] which reported the responses of adults aged 50 to 80:

- 82% experienced one or more forms of everyday ageism in their daily lives.
- 65% were exposed to ageist messages.
- 45% experienced ageism in interpersonal interactions.
- 36% expressed internalized ageism.

Any other "disease" that afflicted 82% of Americans would be a national catastrophe and cause for immediate, unquestionable, nationwide emergency action. Not even COVID comes close.

So what can we do about it?

Here's an idea: What if we treat the plague of ageism the same way we treat COVID? What if we take those same pandemic protection/prevention protocols of which we now are so conscious and adapt them for this other scourge, which has been around not just for two years but for centuries? Maybe we should set up a special CDC (Centers for Discrimination Control and Prevention) of our own and create a few guideline strategies for everyone to follow.

**Guideline Strategy #1: Self-educating.** Let's learn from reputable experts such as gerontologists and psychologists about what this ageism virus is, how it's contracted and spread, the serious harms it causes, and how to eradicate it and prevent its reemergence. There are plenty of great resources such as books, articles, videos, blogs, podcasts, and campaigns to help us understand these issues.

**Guideline Strategy #2: Masking.** Understanding that we can inadvertently spread to others the age biases we may have, we should be mindful of "masking up" by refraining from using ageist language and behaving in ageist ways toward others.

**Guideline Strategy #3: Social distancing.** Just as we don't want to transmit age prejudice, we should likewise be mindful about exposing ourselves to those people, media outlets, marketers, and businesses that promote the fear-based messages of ageism. Let's boycott them and their products and activities, which deny or demean the aging process by excluding, belittling, or otherwise marginalizing people because of their age. And let's call out such purveyors of discrimination and spread the word about who they are.

**Guideline Strategy #4: Using therapeutics.** If and when we speak or behave in an ageist manner (and we all do, from time to time), we should take the responsibility to stop those actions from turning into habits. An effective way to do this is to identify the false stereotype upon which we're basing our judgment and replace it with a therapeutic perspective: the realistic view that each person is an individual rather than a representative of a homogeneous group that doesn't actually exist.

**Guideline Strategy #5: Vaccinating and boosting.** The best inoculation against the future spread of the scourge of ageism is to boost our interpersonal immunity by forming strong, positive relationships with people of all different ages from toddlers to the oldest old. Doing so ensures that ageism — which can infect children as young as 3 years old — doesn't take hold and perpetuate indefinitely.

As a society, we're slowly managing to get stronger control of a potentially deadly virus that affects us all. I'm referring, of course, to COVID.

Let's waste no time being able to say the same thing about ageism.

# COULD APPRECIATION OF OLD AGE GO VIRAL?

In a March 18, 2020 opinion piece for Forbes titled "COVID-19: Now We All Know What It's Like To Be Old & Alone," Joseph Coughlin, director of the Massachusetts Institute of Technology AgeLab, argued compellingly that in the time of pandemic, people who were not yet considered "old" were now experiencing some of the longtime daily challenges endured by their elders:

In the span of a few short days, millions of Americans of all ages have gone from our often-harried daily routines to living and working at home. Many of us are experiencing this change not as a liberating day off or a snow day, but as an anxiety producing semi- or full isolation. There is one silver lining to such an experience, however: It can serve as an exercise in empathy (albeit an imperfect one), permitting younger people to appreciate some of what many older adults go through every day — even on a good day, in the absence of pandemic disease.[27]

He made a legitimate point, and one that should be raised more often, given our culture's pervasive ageism that underestimates, marginalizes, and even vilifies older adults for living longer and for wanting those additional years to be quality ones.

That being said, I think we should also consider an intriguing flip side to our new coronavirus reality: One significant impact of this pandemic might just be a gradual integration of the positive qualities of elderhood into the rest of society.

In short, as we modify our behaviors, COVID-19 may be pushing many of us toward more empowered aging though a greater appreciation of the assets of old age.

There's no doubt that the beginning days of extreme fear and uncertainty magnified the longstanding view that a person's later years involve solely processes of deterioration and decline. Overwhelmed, overstressed, and undersupplied doctors, nurses, and other hospital personnel were having to make and carry out gut-wrenching decisions as to which critical patients would receive lifesaving treatment and which would die. Unfortunately, even today many people believe that a patient's age rather than his or her medical condition should be the deciding factor in those circumstances.

That belief not only currently delegitimizes the right to grow old; it also endangers that right for future generations.

If we instead consider the unexpected *positive* ways in which our lives are having to change because of this insidious virus, we'll see the benefits of embracing the values, skills, and attitudes most older adults already possess, and we'll want to incorporate them into our own lives.

What are those benefits, exactly?

For one thing, we began to **appreciate the value of in-person and tactile communication**, those everyday methods (in addition to postal mail and the telephone) that were more commonly used during the formative years of older generations before the development of computer technology. Although most older adults are now online and using the Internet and smart phones regularly,[28] in general they are also the most socially adept at in-person conversations than are younger generations, who may now begin to experience the emotional downside of physical distancing in ways all too familiar to their parents and grandparents.

Also, as shuttering ourselves in the same environment over the course of weeks (and most likely months) began to get to us, increasing our levels of frustration, anxiety, and depression, we had **become more aware of the need to regulate our emotions** so that we wouldn't succumb to negativity. Believe it or not, this skill most commonly found in the older adult brain is due to a natural physiological change[29] that occurs over the process of many decades of living.

Another important characteristic of old age is **a growing comfort with being in the present moment rather than preoccupying oneself with a lot of tasks**. Because many of those tasks had been removed from our lives through a loss of work and/or the cancellation of social activities, many of us found ourselves uncomfortable just sitting around doing nothing. But the kind of "being" I'm referring to is internally active: It's the search for greater meaning and authenticity in one's life. It's the kind of life review that mid–20th-century developmental psychologist Erik Erikson called *integrity* (as in integration) — the fitting together of the parts of one's life into a coherent whole.[30] The need to do this self-examination becomes more powerful as people approach the last years of their lives. People who are not yet at that stage now had an unusual opportunity to take advantage of their physical inactivity to ask themselves what their lives have meant and who they'd like to be once this pandemic crisis is over.

The physical distance that COVID-19 demanded of us became a real and visceral phenomenon that engaged people of every age, socioeconomic status, gender, race, ethnicity, and physical ability. And because today all of us continue to be susceptible to getting the virus, we're all in this together, which means that our traditionally divisive negative stereotypes are becoming less valid. And becoming less valid, they may one day become irrelevant.

In the meantime, I'm hoping that through their own direct experience of the kinds of conditions regularly experienced by many older adults, those who are in midlife and younger may start to appreciate some of the psychological traits of elderhood and, by extension, appreciate even more the people who best possess them.

Let's hope that it's *this* condition, and not COVID-19, that will go increasingly viral.

# Sending the Right Messages

**HAVE YOU EVER PLAYED** a large-group game called Telephone? That's the one in which a person quickly whispers a sentence into someone else's ear, who then quickly whispers that same sentence into the ear of a second person, and the process is repeated until the last person, after hearing the sentence, says it aloud. What makes the game entertaining is when the resulting distorted final sentence is compared with its original version. For example, in a group of several dozen people, what starts out as "The shy elephant repressed its infatuation with the pleasing dog" may turn into "The sly elephant confessed its fat situation to the sneezing frog."

The physical causes of the hilarious distortion can be traced to three factors: the number of people playing the game, the speed with which each sentence is whispered, and the volume of the whisper compared with the ambient noise in the room. But psychological factors can also play a role. For example, some participants may be distracted or otherwise not be paying close attention. Others might not be familiar with one or more of the words (such as "repressed" or "infatuation"). Still others might unconsciously mishear and transform a word toward which they have a fear or otherwise negative bias (such as changing "dog" to "frog").

Sending the right messages about age is like participating in a multitude of simultaneous, widespread social games of Telephone. Except that they're not games. They are vital chances to educate the public in order to improve the quality of life for people of all ages. What is said, received, interpreted, and acted upon by individuals with different capacities, experiences, and biases can affect the ways in which others are treated, whether and what kind of opportunities and support are available or extended to them, and even how long they live.

What must we do to ensure that our communication regarding age-related issues is clear, accurate, and effective in promoting a more equitable and enriching society for the young, old, and everyone in between?

Not surprisingly, the same kinds of Telephone-based factors also distort our perceptions regarding age.

Take inattention, for instance. If we're not aware of the ways in which ethnicity, race, gender, physical ability, geographic location, and levels of education and income — together known as "the social determinants of health" — influence a struggling older person's ability to age well, we will be oblivious to the impacts of ageism and thus wrongfully blame that individual for totally lacking a sense of responsibility or diligence. Or we may come to the same conclusion if we're not familiar with ageism because we haven't (yet) personally experienced it, and thus don't consider that form of discrimination to be a problem at all. Or lastly, we may have our own fear or negative bias toward getting older, and will convert any accurate, pro-aging messages entering our minds into more negative ones that conform to and confirm our biased perceptions.

Fortunately, a nonprofit research organization called the FrameWorks Institute has considered these issues and come up with effective strategies to tackle public misperceptions about aging. In addition to the factors I've already described, the institute has identified six basic misunderstandings[1] held by the public that need to be addressed and corrected:

**Ideal vs. Real:** Public perceptions seem to veer between an ideal vision of aging ("self-sufficiency, staying active, participating in leisure activities, and building intimacy with family and friends") and a warped "real" vision ("a process of deterioration, dependency, reduced potential, family dispersal, and digital decline"). They don't envision an accurate picture that moderates these two extremes and allows for the many variations of how we age.

**Us vs. Them:** This conscious polarity, which I've previously described, otherizes elders and leads to the zero-sum belief that public policies supporting them threaten the general economy by leaving fewer resources available to "the rest of us."

**Individualism:** This assumption places on each older person all the responsibility of making wise decisions to maintain their physical, financial, and social health without considering the public's shared obligation to provide supportive environments, initiatives, and laws that will help them do so.

**Inefficient Government:** As exemplified by a general belief that the future of Social Security is precarious at best, this misperception reflects the idea that government isn't capable of sustaining and managing any and all shared resources that are to be distributed equitably.

**Fatalism:** The general dread of getting older plus any concerns about the potential insecurity of living well in our later years can inspire the belief that any actions to cope with the "problem" of aging are futile, as there isn't much that can be done to forestall the inevitable.

**Ignorance of Demographic Trends:** Generally, the American public isn't aware of how diverse the older population is, how quickly it's growing, and how it will not only require more economic and medical support but can also contribute economically and culturally to our society — if given greater opportunities to do so. It's this last point that isn't on the public's radar at all.

So what can and should we do to communicate the right messages that will 1) change people's minds about aging by dispelling their fears and 2) inspire them to envision and support solutions to the challenges older adults face today? Whatever we do, we'd better be sufficiently loud and clear so that those messages don't get distorted in either their transmission or reception.

Before we go any further, let's consider the many different places where messages about aging appear, if they appear at all. Think about it: How often are older people included in everyday online, print, and film media — in articles, photographs, movies, TV shows, and advertisements? And when they do appear, how realistically are they depicted?

For starters, let's consider photos that accompany online and print articles. In "How Photos Showing Older Adult Hands Reveal Cultural Bias," a 2022 article I wrote for Next Avenue, an online digital publication for people aged 50 and older, I bemoaned the widespread phenomenon of showing close-up photos of wrinkly hands in articles about older adults. Just posed, wrinkly hands. Doing nothing.

> Older adults aren't isolated body parts, but human beings doing things in the course of living life. The problem with a wrinkly hands shortcut is that it's commonly used in articles about aging. But general hand close-ups are hardly ever used in articles about people of other ages.

> Other generations are always depicted in a context, be it a home, nursery, preschool, school, workplace, entertainment venue or vacation site. This discrepancy turns a wrinkly hands photo into

an ageist icon that may discourage visitors from reading the article it illustrates.[2]

That same year, I wrote another Next Avenue article, "Selling the Idea of Pro-Aging Advertisements," about how older adults in video advertisements are often shown to be comical, clueless, and/or incompetent and how to create more realistic depictions. I offered, with explanations, the following six tips:

- Tell us a story that makes us care and with which we can identify.
- Depict us as the complex individuals that we are.
- Address the reality of our challenges as well as our willingness and ability to overcome them.
- Use humor in ways that build us up, not tear us down.
- Show us having affirming, productive relationships with others, especially those of younger ages.
- Include us older adults on your marketing teams.[3]

In other words, show us as autonomous human beings, worthy of dignity and respect.

Fortunately, I'm not alone in my concerns. Many others are pushing to change widespread societal misrepresentations of aging. Here are some findings from a September 2019 AARP Research analysis[4] of online media images of older adults (defined as people aged 50-plus):

- Nearly half (46%) of Americans are older adults, yet they appear in only 15% of images.
- Moreover, 28% of the time, those images are negative portrayals, compared with 4% of negative portrayals for people younger than 50.

- By 2030, American older adults will spend more than $84 billion on tech products, but currently, only 5% of images in which they appear show them using technology.
- One-third of U.S. workers are older adults, yet they appear in only 13% of photos depicting a work setting.

The numbers aren't any better for movies and television programs. In December 2021, an interesting survey was conducted by Ontario-based Amica Senior Lifestyles, a Canadian company providing private-pay retirement residences for older adults. The company described its methodology this way:

We reviewed the top 50 movies of 2021, 2010, and 2000 ranked by domestic box office figures as stated by IMDB's Box Office Mojo. We counted the number of senior actors (aged 60+ upon movie's release) in the main and supporting cast and analyzed what kind of characters they played in these movies. Movies in the analysis were chosen in December 2021.[5]

Here's some of what the researchers found:

- Only 2% of the top movies of 2021 have seniors as the lead actor.
- Seniors are more likely to play parental figures in movies than any other type of character.
- The top 3 jobs seniors play in movies are politicians, monarchs, and high-ranking military officials.
- In the top films of 2021, the vast majority (79.49%) of senior characters were played by white actors.

- The frequency of seniors in the main cast (including lead actors) of Hollywood movies has increased 30% since 2000.
- While positions of authority portray strength, it's interesting to note that 60.8% of senior characters were villains in top 2021 movies, compared to only 39.2% heroes.[6]

While there continues to be some progress in including more older adult characters in movies, much more needs to be done.

As for older adult presence in television programs, a 2020 study found that "of 112 episodes of popular American television series aired between 2004 and 2018…6.6 per cent of characters [were] aged 65 and older — a slight improvement to the values reported in previous studies…. Further, the typical older character was young-old, male, Caucasian, middle-class, able-bodied and straight — if his sexuality was referenced."[7]

So here's the basic situation we face when it comes to recognizing and incorporating older adults into the panorama of our culture: If we see them at all, it's through foggy glasses of negative bias, and therefore what we think we perceive is actually a distorted picture that can harm those very people — and younger others who will one day be old.

Telling the truth about getting older shouldn't be so difficult. Again, the FrameWorks Institute has shown us the way by offering some practical, effective tips:[8]

- Tell stories that are complete, which include the positives as well as the negatives about the aging process.
- Reframe crises about the growing older population as opportunities for society to reap the benefits of older adult empowerment and engagement.
- Always connect any problem or challenge to the implementation of a concrete protocol or other solution.

- Show how applying effective social policies can directly affect the ability of older adults to age successfully.

When it comes to a perpetual, age-based social activity of Telephone, those limited, biased ideas already stored in the organ that resides between our ears block us from hearing different, more accurate messages that can inspire us to understand aging in a life-affirming way.

Instead, let's imagine a world in which our universal Telephone network transmits one basic message: "We honor and support people of all ages."

And that the message gets through…continuously and unchanged.

# AGING'S BIG PR PROBLEM

Years ago, I attended a New York University course on health care public relations. It was shortly after the time of the big Tylenol incident. Perhaps you remember the event. In 1982, seven people in the Chicago area died from cyanide poisoning because of tampered Tylenol Extra-Strength capsules. While parent company Johnson & Johnson had nothing to do with this criminal act, which occurred post-shipment, it took full responsibility to remedy the situation.

Because its priority was to save the lives of its consumers before saving the life of its product, it 1) immediately recalled and eventually ceased production of all Tylenol capsules, 2) created new tamper-resistant caplets and packaging, 3) offered consumer discounts on Tylenol products, and 4) educated the medical community about its public-safety efforts in order to restore trust in the company. In public relations courses everywhere, the Johnson & Johnson response was hailed as the gold standard in crisis management: Name the problem, tell the truth about it, and work quickly and diligently to solve it.

In some ways, the concept of aging has had major PR problems of its own for an exceptionally long time. It's gotten a horrible reputation as a process of inevitable and irrevocable decline. Widespread ignorance about the physiology of aging has led to culturally accepted negative stereotypes that not only are false but engender fear. And with increased talk about "silver tsunamis" and endangered "entitlements" such as Social Security and Medicare, it's accurate to say that the PR problem is now slouching toward the level of PR crisis.

There is nothing wrong with people getting older. The process is a natural part of life. Just as we don't consider childhood, adolescence, and adulthood as lifespan aberrations that must be halted or corrected, neither should we feel the same way about elderhood. Each life stage has its problems and challenges, but it also has its benefits and rewards. That's why it's important to identify the huge PR predicament we face concerning aging. It is up to all of us to name the real social problem (ageism), tell the truth about it (it's human-made and preventable), and work hard to solve it as soon as possible.

All of us have a stake in handling this problem, but none more so than the professionals who work in aging services — businesses, educational institutions, government departments, and nonprofit organizations — whose mission is to serve the needs and aspirations of older adults.

Ironically, many people in this field manage to contribute more to worsening the PR problem than to solving it. They do so unintentionally through their compassionate ageism by continuing to define elders as a basically needy, in-decline population and emphasizing individual responsibility as the sole requirement for aging successfully. By not giving equal time and energy in the course of their work to raising awareness of older adults' capacity to be economically and socially productive and of the intersection of the various social factors that limit this capacity, these professionals undercut their efforts to improve the lives of the people they serve.

When it comes to aging's PR problem, we need to adopt our own gold standard of crisis-management response. We should 1) immediately challenge ageist views and work to remove them from public discourse, 2) replace those views with tamper-resistant perspectives of aging that are based on science rather than on fear, 3) offer meaningful opportunities for elders to engage with their community in more comprehensive ways, and 4) educate all generations about the challenges and benefits of the aging process at every stage of life.

Today, people have no reservations about taking Tylenol. Who knows? If we can lick our ageism-based PR problem, perhaps someday soon we might be able to say the same thing about growing older.

# LET'S TEACH THESE ABCS, TOO

At some point in a school year, many lower-elementary-school classes celebrate the 100th day of school with a "Dress as a 100-Year-Old Person Day."[9] The educational justification is to teach the value of 100 as a quantity.

Which leads me to ask: What is the value of any number, really, except in its comparison to another number? Given this assumption, there are many ways to teach number value. However, aligning it with a person's age — or rather, with the common cultural *perception* of how a person of that age looks and behaves — has become an appealing strategy. So young children come to school wearing made-up facial wrinkles; sporting gray wigs; dressing in shabby, unfitting, unfashionable clothes; using canes or walkers; and being encouraged to walk slowly with stooped postures and to speak in shaky voices.

Really.

There's a basic problem with teaching the value of 100 in this way. As a number increases, so does its cumulative value, which means that something fundamental about it is gained, not lost. After all, isn't it more desirable to have $100 than $1? Or to have read 100 books instead of 1? Or to have traveled to 100 places in the world than to have visited just 1? While it's true that some old people use walkers, canes, and wheelchairs (as do some much younger people), having young children dress up and act as "cutely" decrepit old people sends the message that what is accumulated is simply and solely more deterioration and decline. It would be like asserting that 100 is less valuable than 1 because it's further away from 0.

We're all aware of the deterioration-decline narrative about aging that we fully embrace as a society. But this is not the whole truth about aging. In fact, it's not even half of the real story. For the sake of our future selves, and those of our kids, grandkids, and all generations that follow, in addition to teaching children the possible deficits of the aging process, we need to teach them its potential assets. And we need to do so right now. Why? Because ageism is a bias that can be internalized as early as age 3.

In a groundbreaking study published in 2020,[10] researchers found that young children's attitudes toward older adults were determined by direct interactions, such as having an ongoing relationship with a grandparent, and aligned according to the quality of those experiences, which tended to be described as neutral or positive. In most cases, children aged 3 to 6 thought of older adults in warm terms (*kind, loving, sweet, gives hugs, plays with me*) and were simultaneously aware of physical conditions (*slow, has wrinkles, wears glasses*). However, between ages 7 and 9, children start to perceive aging in ways that may be influenced by unconsciously ageist parents, their views taking on negative overtones that reflect dependence, loneliness, sadness, and disease. Such parental influences, combined with ubiquitous ageist media messages, reinforce and strengthen children's negative biases as time passes.

And thus, ageism perpetuates within another generation.

Since this kind of education is the cause, it must also be the remedy. Intergenerational programs that expose young children — especially those who don't have regular, supportive contact with grandparents — to positive role models of aging can add balance to their perceptions. Locating a preschool within the site of a long-term-care community and holding daily interactivities[11] is one solution. Another is to pair older adult volunteers with at-risk lower-elementary students for tutoring and companionship.[12]

While these initiatives tend to reduce age bias subtly and indirectly, we can and should do better. Why not bring discussions about aging out in the open and into kindergarten through 6th-grade classrooms, to tackle ageism at every level of student comprehension?

I propose the following:

Let's create a nationwide "ABC" curriculum for public and private elementary schools that pair and train a 20- or 30-something adult with a person aged 50-plus (the older the better) to go into each classroom and hold an informal but substantive conversation about aging that answers kids' questions, addresses their fears, and educates them about the basic realities of getting older as well as the benefits and *fun* of sharing experiences with people of very different ages. Those conversations and the curriculum topics covered will be tailored to the students' grade level.

Such an initiative would teach these ABCs:

**Aging.** Children need to know that aging isn't a disease but rather a natural process that all living things undergo (and yes, death should be discussed). Every stage of a person's life from infancy to old age has its challenges and benefits that depend on individual experience and the ways in which the body and especially the brain develop. The younger-older teaching pair can model a mutual appreciation for each other's skills, talents, and accomplishments and encourage students to describe their own abilities and interests.

**Belonging.** All humans need to feel connected to and accepted by the people around them. To communicate the fact that ageism affects people of all generations, the teaching pair can describe their own experiences of being misjudged and excluded solely based on assumptions about their age. This can include discussions about stereotypes and the unreliability of first impressions of an individual's physical and personality traits.

**Community.** All humans also need to be productive and to lead meaningful lives. The teaching pair can talk about ways in which they have contributed to their community as well as benefited from the contributions of others. They can focus on the special roles an older person can play throughout life so that old age doesn't equate with neediness and uselessness. Students must learn that society shouldn't deny older adults opportunities to keep growing, learning, and sharing their experiential wisdom with others.

Because increased longevity in our population is resulting in many more people living to be centenarians, maybe we should rethink the whole approach to teaching the value of 100 that enhances rather than detracts from the achievement of reaching old age. Surely we owe it to future generations to employ better ways[13] to communicate acceptance and appreciation of growing older. We can do it, you know. It's not that hard.

In fact, it's as easy as ABC.

# DICK AND JANE GROW UP

*See Spot run. Run, Spot, run!*

If you were in elementary school in the 1930s through '70s, these words probably evoke memories of sitting quietly at desks in neat rows and reading books such as *Fun with Dick and Jane*, whose main (white) characters reflected gender-constrained norms. My strongest memory of a Dick and Jane story involved Jane in the kitchen with Mother, wearing dresses and tidy aprons and making an apple pie, while Dick was in the backyard with Father building a doghouse for Spot.

As a child, I was bothered by that story. Sure, I liked cooking and baking, but I also liked building things, and somehow this plot line, which didn't include Dick and Jane participating together in both activities, seemed to tell me that I could choose only the one assigned to females. I'm sure I wasn't alone in my frustration. There must have been lots of budding female architects and male chefs — of all ethnicities and races — who felt the same way.

So maybe it was more than coincidental that in the 1970s I became a writer of educational materials for children. In those burgeoning Women's Liberation and Civil Rights days, elementary school textbooks deliberately began chipping away at traditionally monolithic gender and racial roles. We writers were creating multiethnic, multiracial stories about female airplane pilots and male nurses. The pedagogical theory driving our work was that educational materials should not only reflect the reality of the times but also help promote positive changes to that reality. Our approach was to mold young minds by offering them plots, characters, and attitudes we wanted to see incorporated into everyday life. Slowly, the barriers to what was possible for a girl or boy to be or do began to fall. New paradigms were created for working and living in community.

Dick and Jane were growing up.

Now Dick and Jane have reached elderhood. What scenarios are they living or want to live? In what ways are they being held back by the restrictive stories that society insists on telling about them? And how can we revise those stories in order to change social attitudes and expectations about aging?

First, we must deal with language, because the words we choose define the who, what, where, when, why, and how of any story.

*Look, Jane, look. You can look.*

*Dick can play. See Dick play.*

I don't know about you, but I've never heard young children express themselves using such stilted, oversimplified syntax. Perhaps the same is true of the stilted, outdated language used to describe older adults. We can't even agree on terms that depict aging status. *Senior citizens*? *The elderly*? Most older adults reject these terms as ageist and patronizing. And what about describing active older adults as *spry*? Just like calling a young woman *perky* or a young man *bold*, applying such a term trivializes age by implying that a proactive, engaged person in his or her later years is an exception and not the more realistic rule.

If we can't agree on language that describes aging, can we at least agree on the kinds of activities older adults can and should be encouraged and expected to do? Just as I bristled at the implication that I shouldn't be allowed to build a doghouse, I reject the premise that as an older adult I shouldn't be allowed to work as long as I want to at any job I am capable of doing, that my opinion shouldn't be sought on matters of civic policy, and that my time as a volunteer and my knowledge acquired from experience aren't as valuable as are those of persons decades younger.

I bristle, too, that as an older adult, I am assumed to be needy (don't we all, at every age, need things from society?) but not also assumed to be a source for providing for the needs of others of all generations.

Whether our culture accepts it or not, the reality is that older people are here to stay — for a lot longer than did previous elder generations — and that we still have much to contribute to all aspects of our economic, political, and cultural experience.

*See Dick lead a county arts commission.*

*See Jane create a small business.*

*See Dick and Jane take part in all aspects of life.*

And thanks to them, *see our society thrive.*

# A IS FOR AGEISM, B IS FOR BIGOTRY

In 1949, when Oscar Hammerstein II and Richard Rodgers wrote the song "You've Got to Be Carefully Taught" for the musical *South Pacific,*[14] both men knew that they were opening a Pandora's box of unprecedented self-scrutiny in American culture regarding the issue of racism.

Today, American society is still struggling to come to terms with ongoing racial strife, which explains the endurance of this song. But these lyrics also reflect the childhood root of other forms of discrimination: sexism, ableism, classism, homophobia, transphobia, xenophobia…and, yes, ageism.

Like all forms of discrimination, ageism starts in the mind with faulty, fear-based perceptions. When these prejudicial thoughts aren't checked, they can soon turn outward into bigoted behaviors that harm the lives of the people victimized by those perceptions.

No child is born being ageist. Like all prejudices, ageism is an acquired belief, and as you know, it can begin to take root in children as young as 3.

There are many ways in which this can happen.

To begin with, the first influence on any child's life **starts within the family**. When a young child's parents and other relatives and caregivers exhibit ageist behavior in the forms of showing negative facial expressions, using negative words, or even physically moving a child away from an old person, that child picks up those unconscious messages. Researchers have even found that many young children prefer to see pictures of younger adults over those of much older ones.[15]

Another factor is whether a child has **regular, positive contact with an old person**, such as a grandparent. In fact, as one study remarked, "… children's views of older people did not correlate with their parent's (sic) views but were significantly more positive in children who spontaneously evoked their grandparents when asked to think of an old person."[16]

Unfortunately, in our society, many children don't have access to such realistic and positive role models because they lack grandparents either through death or through a physical or emotional distance created or supported by their parents. And that's where a third factor comes into play: **the cultural indoctrination of ageism via fairy tales, TV shows, movies, and commercial ads**. Think about it: How many of us were exposed as kids to picture-book stories and TV cartoons about mean, dangerous — and old — wicked witches and evil kings? Today's children also watch movies and TV shows that mock old characters who are feeble, clueless, cranky, and/or stubborn.

And there's one final ageist influence on young children, coming from a place where one would assume this should never happen: **the classroom**. As I've noted, many schools participate in that rather barbaric activity "Dress as a 100-Year-Old Person Day," meant to celebrate the 100th day of the school year. There's nothing like asking young children to draw wrinkles on their faces, don gray wigs, dress in baggy or frumpy clothes, and use walkers and canes to reinforce in their minds that these physical attributes should be the first (and often only) associations they should have with the concept of aging.

In addition to my "ABC curriculum" strategies for instilling an appreciation of older age, here's another one: **exposing young children to pro-aging books**. According to children's book author Lindsey McDivitt, creating such books is an uphill struggle:

I believe ageism in young children often manifests as the belief that older adults are less competent than others. Unfortunately, modern books for children go beyond witches to reinforce this belief by showing the child's character as the active one generally helping the older character in some way. A child protagonist is what publishers prefer, and a story that tugs at the heartstrings. Many age stereotypes rear their ugly heads: old and sick, old and forgetful, old and lonely, old and grumpy, and so on. Of course the authors and illustrators have long been inundated by these images via other media, and kids are, too.[17]

McDivitt's website, A is for Aging, B is for Books…,[18] aims to help adults prevent ageist attitudes in their children by offering pro-aging alternatives for young readers. She has found certain strategies to be effective in embedding in children's minds more realistic perceptions of what it means to get older:

Children's books that show creative olders enjoying life through a great variety of activities beyond knitting and gardening and fishing. There are amazing older artists, adults continuing careers and beginning new ones, people traveling and sharing skills by volunteering, for instance. A far greater diversity of older characters is needed. Older adults are actually more different from each other than young people because of their long life experience.

It's definitely important that the messages shared include possibilities for late life that children may not be aware of, but balanced with the fact that not everyone can start running marathons in their 70s. Also, we should impart the truth: that people are often happier in later life despite nearing life's end, and happiness doesn't require extreme pursuits or success.

I particularly celebrate picture book biographies for kids that highlight long lives well lived, a recent and growing genre. They are included in schools quite frequently when focused on science. However, most teachers and librarians remain unaware of the importance of showing kids a diversity of older characters and talking about late life. Even the word "aging" is generally avoided in children's literature and still equated with illness, dementia, and decline.[19]

Whether it be through books, school activities, or direct interaction with older family members or other adults, exposing young minds to the myriad ways in which people experience their later years is incredibly important if we are to abolish ageism for good.

Since children can absorb messages promoting fear and hate, it logically follows that they can also be exposed to the true ways to think about aging.

All of us must become the teachers they so desperately need.

# IN OTHER WORDS: FINDING NEW TERMS FOR OLD AGE

As the current longevity economy regularly adjusts to an increasingly larger older population, there is a growing need to find words that more accurately describe those consumers' experiences. Some traditional terms that once reflected what it means to be older are now demanding updating to reflect today's post-midlifers and how they live.

The big issue is how to do this in the most effective way. To get an answer to this question, I sought out two experts for their ideas. I started with gerontologist Tracey Gendron.

"In order to develop a more realistic and accurate vocabulary to describe this population we have to start by acknowledging that older age is in and of itself a developmental stage of life," she explained. "Presently, we have a variety of terms to describe different stages of life: *infancy, childhood, adolescence, emerging adulthood,* and *adulthood.* But it stops there. That means that we are in one stage of development, adulthood, that can last 80 years!"[20]

For some reason, finding the right age-based words stymies individuals, organizations, and businesses. Too often, what's acceptable for one person is taboo for another. Take the term *the elderly,* for example. What used to be a common label for a group of people in late life has become offensive to many older adults for two reasons: 1) It conjures up the ageist image of a feeble, passive population, which they don't feel they represent, and 2) It categorizes them as one homogenous cohort, when, as we know, the reality is that as people age they become more diverse in their experiences, preferences, and skills. Many aging-services professionals — as well as the public — agree with the more neutral terms preferred by American Geriatrics Society:[21] *older adults* or *older people.*

Another expert, Julie Sweetland, sociolinguist and senior advisor at the FrameWorks Institute, has emphasized the importance of the meaning of words we rely on to describe elderhood:

> If we talk about *battling* old age, then it's clear that aging is a bad thing. We say people are *older but wiser,* with the contrast of *but* implying that one is good and one is bad. The message that aging is bad is repeated and reinforced daily through subtle cues like these. So it's no wonder that few Americans want to identify as "aging" — and in turn, no surprise that we don't have a robust policy conversation about what we need to do to create communities that support us all as we age.[22]

Ageism is sustained by the words people use. Will changing the vocabulary of age help to change minds about the value of people in their later years?

According to Gendron, "the fight to end ageism begins with an acknowledgement that there is more after adulthood — more growth, more opportunities, different roles, different milestones and different markers. To this end, we need a term that accounts for this and embraces the growth, maintenance, adaptation, and decline that we all experience as we age. I believe the term *elderhood* fits the bill."[23]

Substituting one term for another is one option; however, there may be a tendency to use euphemisms, which can defeat the purpose. Reclaiming and redefining currently negative terms may be a better solution. Added Gendron,

> I think that simply changing the terms that we use is like putting a band-aid on a gaping wound. For example, if we use the terms

*vintage, experienced,* or *mature* to cover up the word *old,* we are ultimately still saying that being old is undesirable — so let's give it another name to make it feel better. What would happen if instead we took words like *old* and *elderly* back and used them in such a way that conveyed desirability and value? Rather than avoiding these terms, we embrace them.[24]

It's not just words describing old people that need updating. Ageist vocabulary used by the medical, long-term-care, and other industries also needs to change. Some examples (and their preferred substitutions) are *geriatric* (older patient),[25] *facility* (an independent or assisted living community),[26] *senile* (a person with dementia),[27] and *Grandma/Grandpa, Sweetie, Honey,* and *Old-Timer* (the older person's name).[28]

It's incumbent on professionals as well as the public to adjust aging-related vocabulary so that it reflects a growing understanding of the realities, including the positive ones, regarding getting older. To add to Gendron's and Sweetland's suggestions, I've got a few of my own: four word-transforming strategies that can make a substantial difference in our communications:

**Let's retire some words and phrases permanently**, such as *cranky, grumpy, doddering, feeble,* and *over the hill.* If we wouldn't consider using these terms to describe decades-younger people, we shouldn't use them for older people either.

**We should find other, non-loaded words as substitutes for ageist terms**. For example, instead of referring to *the elderly,* we can say *olders, elders, older people,* or *older adults.*

**We can opt to embrace and neutralize toxic terms by redefining them**. The word *crone* doesn't have to conjure up images of a warty, ugly, hag-like woman; instead, we can recognize it as an original synonym for *wise woman.* I, for one, would like to reclaim the word *senior* and its association with cumulative accomplishment. After all, doesn't being a high school or college senior denote an achievement of academic longevity? Doesn't the senior vice president of a company supervise the other vice presidents? Don't get me wrong: Merely being old doesn't make someone more valuable than anyone younger. But there is something to honor about surviving and hopefully thriving in one's later years. Personally, I wouldn't mind being considered a "senior vice president of life."

And finally, **let's reject what geriatrician Bill Thomas calls the "tyranny of 'still'"** (as in "My grandma is 96 and she *still* drives!"):

> The word "still" is intended as praise but actually serves to wound and diminish older people. The prominent place it holds in our lexicon, reminds us that, when it comes to people living in the latter decades of life, success is defined by the absence of "change, interruption, or cessation." It is a peculiar conception of human life that equates "success" with a lack of change. Our use of the word "still" reveals an ordinarily unstated assumption: In contemporary American society, any deviation from the parameters of vigorous adulthood, by definition, carries the stigma of failure.[29]

Keeping appropriate language current is a challenge in a culture of widespread social media, which, according to Gendron, "can both help and hinder the efforts to combat ageism,"[30] but it's not impossible.

Because print, television, and radio news organizations have huge social media presences and are major arbiters of linguistic style, Sweetland asserted, "It's a good rule of thumb to revisit a style guide at least every other year — and to pay special attention to the organizational policies on terms of reference."[31]

Gendron has offered other tips:

Given that age discrimination in the workplace is rampant, businesses should look at their marketing, advertising, policies, and procedures for hidden — or not so hidden — ageist language and practices. Think about terms that might perpetuate age discrimination (e.g., *digital native, recent graduate*).... businesses and organizations should use caution and avoid phrases and words that "other" people. It's essential to remember that aging isn't an "us vs. them" proposition. We are all aging every day of our lives. It is just about us.[32]

"People sometimes dismiss intentional efforts to change language as superficial or artificial," explained Sweetland. "I think of the stories we tell about social issues and social groups as dress rehearsals for the policies our society will endorse. It matters that we get our lines right."[33]

In other words, let's rethink — and rephrase — how we talk about getting older.

# CHAPTER 9

# Talkin' 'Bout Our Generations

**SOMETIME IN THE 4TH CENTURY B.C.E.,** the Greek philosopher Aristotle wrote:

> In terms of their character, the young are prone to desires and inclined to do whatever they desire. Of the desires of the body, they are most inclined to pursue that relating to sex, and they are powerless against this. They are changeable and fickle in desires, and though they intensely lust, they are quickly satisfied; for their wants, like the thirst and hunger of the sick, are sharp rather than massive. And they are impulsive and quick-tempered and inclined to follow up their anger [by action].[1]

Nearly two millennia later, around the year 1599, William Shakespeare described the seven ages of man, ending with the qualities of old age:

> Last scene of all,
> That ends this strange eventful history,
> Is second childishness and mere oblivion;
> Sans teeth, sans eyes, sans taste, sans everything.[2]

And in 1965, singer-songwriter Pete Townshend of The Who penned the lyrics to "My Generation," a song that became the manifesto for a cohort bemoaning the intolerance and callousness of older generations and reflecting a desire to never live long enough to become like them.[3]

Spanning 2,300 years, these three commentaries — by an ancient Greek, a 45-year-old playwright, and a 20-year-old rocker — are amazingly similar in two important ways: They stereotype members of a cohort that isn't their own, and those stereotypes are negative.

'Twas ever thus.

It seems that we can't refrain from making judgments — usually false ones (more about that later) — about people who don't share our own approximate age. But we shouldn't find this surprising. We do the same thing about people who don't share our race, ethnicity, religion, social class, geographic home, or personal values. We do so from an instinctive need to identify with a group, create our own tribe, and locate ourselves in a segment of time that becomes a psychic home from within which we can function.

The problem with this impulse is that while it may provide us with a kind of false sense of security, it denies us the opportunity to identify and empathize with as well as learn from others who are much older or younger than we are, responses which, in their own way, provide for a different kind of security: the comfort of seeing ourselves not as *apart* from the whole of humanity but rather as *a part* of it.

Because of this dilemma, some people entirely reject the notion of applying generational labels. In a 2021 Washington Post op-ed,

"Generational labels mean nothing. It's time to retire them," University of Maryland, College Park sociology professor Philip N. Cohen wrote

> The supposed boundaries between generations are no more meaningful than the names they've been given. There's no research identifying the appropriate boundaries between generations, and there is no empirical basis for imposing the sweeping character traits that are believed to define them. Generation descriptors are either embarrassing stereotypes or caricatures with astrology-level vagueness....
>
> Worse than irrelevant, such baseless categories drive people toward stereotyping and rash character judgment. This is disappointing, because measuring and describing social change is essential, and it can be useful to analyze the historical period in which people were born and raised. People *should* write books and articles on these topics. But drawing arbitrary lines between birth years and slapping names on them isn't helping.[4]

According to Michael Dimock, president of the nonpartisan Pew Research Center, depicting people according to generational categories is unrealistic and counterproductive for the following reasons:[5]

For one thing, **there is no definitive way of determining the year in which one generation ends and another begins**, and any one of the many variations can make individuals uncomfortable and resentful to be assigned under one label, let's say as a Baby Boomer, rather than as a Gen Xer.

Secondly, **such labeling often results in stereotyping and oversimplifying.** There are no hard-and-fast traits that adequately describe all or even most of the individuals that are born within a certain range of years.

Moreover, **generational labels encourage comparisons to other generations according to their differences rather than their similarities.** If we really thought about it, each of us likely shares quite a few values (*e.g.,* compassion, integrity, honesty, devotion to family) with others who belong to younger or older generations.

In addition, **generational assumptions are often based on upper-class experiences.** Assuming that all young people are self-indulgent or that all old people are greedy geezers belies the experience of many people who are not urban, affluent, highly educated, or materialistically driven.

And finally, **as people get older, they change.** The attitudes and behaviors they embrace in their later years may differ substantially from those of their teenage and young adult years. By age 80, a former 20-year-old rocker might have a different take on the so-called terrible things that mature adults do; conversely, an aged person most likely will have forgotten the many times s/he obeyed those "bodily desires of sensual pleasure" that were so hard to control.

All these caveats raise the question of whether it's ever valuable to refer to generations when describing human experience. In his insightful book, *The Generation Myth: Why When You're Born Matters Less Than You Think,* Bobby Duffy, professor of public policy and director of the Policy Institute at King's College London, has concluded that it is, indeed, valuable:

My argument is that although it is possible to learn something invaluable about ourselves by studying generational dynamics, we will not learn these lessons from a mixture of manufactured conflicts and tiresome clichés. Instead, we need to carefully unpack the forces that shape us as individuals and societies; the generation we were born into is merely one important part of the story, alongside the extraordinary influence of individual life cycles and the impact of historical events.[6]

What Duffy means by this is that people whose ages generally fall within the range of the same particular generation may tend to experience any huge cultural or historical event in a similar way, partly because they are viewing it through their cognitive lens as children or teens or midlifers or older adults, depending on which stage of the lifespan they're in when the event happens.

For example, people labelled Millennials, having experienced the events of September 11, 2001 as young children, may have one general type of reaction to and understanding of what occurred compared to what their Boomer parents felt (themselves having previously experienced the national tragedies of the assassinations of John and Bobby Kennedy and Martin Luther King Jr.). And those Greatest and Silent generation grandparents probably had a different take on the attack, given their own experiences of having lived through the 1940 to 1941 London Blitz or the 1942 attack on Pearl Harbor.

Duffy acknowledges these differences by referring to what he calls "[O]ne of the fathers of generational thinking, the Hungarian sociologist Karl Mannheim...":[7]

> For Mannheim, generations are not just a group of people born at the same time; they have a social identity formed by common, and often traumatic, experiences. His insight was that major events have a stronger effect on those who come of age during them, because we tend to form our value systems and behaviors during late childhood and early adulthood.[8]

I agree with Duffy and Mannheim. Generations are different, not because members of one generation differ from those of another as biological human beings, but rather because of the events and external pressures each group experienced in their formative childhood and teen years and the ways in which most of them adapted to such influences.

For example, my parents were members of the Greatest Generation. The most influential events of their formative years were the Great Depression and World War II. As a result, in general they and their peers coped with their circumstances by embracing frugality, intense patriotism, responsibility to community, commitment to marriage and family, a strong religious faith and work ethic, and optimism about the future.

As you know, I'm a Boomer. My generation grew up in an affluent America of the 1950s through '70s. We were the first children to be the recipients of direct marketing (*e.g.,* Saturday morning TV cartoons, superhero lunchboxes and toys) and to be the center of social attention. Our general response was to believe in an unbridled future of possibilities such as space travel and the Peace Corps, and in ourselves as the movers, shakers, and reformers of social values at every stage in our lifespan: during the Vietnam War, the rise of national feminism, the sexual revolution, environmentalism, and the expansion of the Civil Rights movement. To this day, many of us continue to carry with us our impulses toward equality and personal growth as we redefine aging as an asset rather than as a process of total decline.

The Gen Xers? They grew up during Watergate, the energy crisis, the end of the Cold War, increased incidence of divorce, and economic downsizing and layoffs. As the first "latchkey" generation of single or two working parents, many of them learned early on how to take care of themselves and to distrust the effectiveness of social structures to provide for them. Their overall generational behaviors have reflected independence, entrepreneurism, pragmatism, and skepticism.

Millennials are the first social media digital natives who have had to negotiate their way through a nanosecond world of global communications, terrorist attacks, overscheduled lives, and helicopter parents. Growing up in the wake of the September 11 attacks, many of them have been self-confidently striving to rebalance society in more spiritual, tolerant, humane, and interdependent ways.

Gen Zers are coming of age in a time of crises caused by global warming, the rise of global autocracies, intense social polarization, threats to democracy and to personal rights and safety, and the skepticism and denial of scientific facts. How they are adjusting to these factors is yet to be determined.

As for Gen Alphas, they are just getting started.

Now of course, as Dimock has pointed out, when speaking about members of any generation, it shouldn't be said that all people in that cohort respond in all — or any — such characteristic ways. Nevertheless, an overwhelming pattern can be detected when examining their lives as a group.

However, there are two important caveats to keep in mind: First of all, populating every generation is a substantial number of people who live in poverty and/or are subjected to racial, ethnic, sexual, or other discrimination that marginalizes them and reduces their chances of fully integrating into society as members of their generation. We must never forget this intersection of social biases and individuals' lives. Secondly, there are members of every generation who, independently of poverty or discrimination, are outliers in their idiosyncratic responses to the events and external influences in their lives. After all, we are, and remain throughout our lives, individuals.

As you can see, generational analysis is complicated but valuable in its own limited way. As Duffy attests, "...true generational thinking can be a powerful tool that helps us understand the changes and challenges of our day. This starts by recognizing an underappreciated fact: there are just three explanations for how *all* attitudes, beliefs, and behaviors change over time — period, life-cycle, and cohort effects."[9]

How does Duffy define these common sociological factors?

*Period effects* refer to the way people of different generations can react to an event in the same way, regardless of their age. A case in point is the immediate wave of patriotism that swept the United States in the days right after September 11. American flags were placed in windows and hoisted on poles on porches and in front yards. Stadium games included tributes to the armed forces. Many Americans felt united through a renewed sense of national pride and resolve.

*Life-cycle effects* are evident in the patterns of behavior that reflect the process of sexual and social maturity we undergo as we move from childhood to adolescence to adulthood. These behaviors include seeking and choosing a life partner; engaging in study, employment, and leisure; and raising children.

*Cohort effects* are determined by the way in which members of a generation are impacted by the social pressures of their time, for example, that Baby Boomers were the focus of marketers from the time they were children resulted in instilling in them a sense of agency and promise.

Again, to avoid overgeneralization, it's important to keep in mind those caveats of 1) the uniqueness of any individual's will and 2) the impact of social bias on limiting that individual's opportunities and capabilities.

And as if all these aforementioned factors aren't enough to complicate generational understanding, Duffy presents us with what he calls the "global phenomena"[10] of generational differences among nations. It's not hard to understand how Greatest Generation Americans experienced World War II differently from their cohorts in Europe, especially those in nations directly affected by wartime atrocities and destruction.

"'Country before cohort' will still be a regular message in this book," Duffy writes; "even now, where you are born often remains more important than *when*. The true value of the international study of generations isn't in identifying global generational groups; looking at generations across countries reveals when and why generational difference is important."[11]

After being introduced to these various key factors, I find myself in the don't-reject-generational-discussions camp. I'm not ready to throw out the baby with the bathwater.

Apparently, neither is the Pew Research Center. In 2023, after a yearlong process of reevaluating its generational research methods, the organization determined the following guidelines (with explanations) for moving forward:

- We'll only do generational analysis when we have historical data that allows us to compare generations at similar stages of life.
- Even when we have historical data, we will attempt to control for other factors beyond age in making generational comparisons.
- When we can't do generational analysis, we still see value in looking at differences by age and will do so where it makes sense.
- When we do have the data to study groups of similarly aged people over time, we won't always default to using the standard generational definitions and labels.[12]

I highly recommend reading the article by Pew Research Center's director of social trends research, Kim Parker, that describes these guidelines in greater detail (see Notes). I believe it's a responsible decision that other researchers can and should adopt.

The rest of us involved in the media, education, advocacy, aging services, business, health care, government, as well as the general public, should think twice about ever reducing any generation to a caricature, stereotype, or other simplistic meme or trope, all for the purpose of pushing an agenda that doesn't serve the general good.

As we continue to talk about our generations, let's be sure to do so accurately, fairly, and within the appropriate context, lest we reinforce those natural tendencies of ours to confirm our biases by tribalizing ourselves as we alienate or marginalize others.

If Aristotle, Shakespeare, and Townshend were around today, on this I'd like to think they'd agree.

# A FOREST OF GENERATIONS

As humans with complex brains, we're born with the instinctive ability to find or create meanings for everything we experience. A huge part of this ability is the tendency to categorize things, mainly because naming something or putting it in a particular box allows us to feel a sense of security, stability, and control over it.

Obviously, people are not things. We're far more diverse and complex and tend to defy any labels that others want to assign to us. However, it's as if we can't help categorizing one another by race, gender, ability, ethnicity, nationality, sexual orientation, socioeconomic level, or political affiliation…and age. And that last trait involves defining each of us according to our generation.

Those needs for security, stability, and control often intersect with our fear and dread of getting older, making us reluctant to mingle with younger or older cohorts and envious or suspicious of what we assume to be their greater ambition or their greater wealth at the expense of our own. When we give into those zero-sum assumptions, the convenience of embracing generational definitions takes on a darker purpose as corporations in the billion-dollar industries of age-restricted retirement villages, high technology, and anti-aging products/services play on our views and promote generational warfare.

When, if at all, is it accurate and therefore acceptable to generalize about generations? Are attributing stereotypes to their experiences, preferences, and behavior valid, or does this instead promote misunderstanding, polarization, and ageism?

I've been wrestling with these questions for a long time, and I think I've arrived at an analogy that provides some good answers.

All of us of any age are like trees growing in the same forest: old trees, midlife trees, saplings, seedlings, evergreen, deciduous, tall, short, wide-trunked, narrow-trunked, of many varied species. Some trees needing more sunlight or water than others. Some trees pushing their roots deep into the soil and others spreading their roots wider and closer to the surface. You get the picture.

Now consider two other scenes. Instead of a huge, diverse forest, picture a Christmas tree farm and an apple orchard. Within both places grow trees of the same variety and roughly the same age and tendencies, coexisting together with no other arboreal species around.

The farm and orchard surely have their limited purposes and advantages. They yield considerable amounts of a specific crop and are easy to manage. I'm not saying that they shouldn't exist. But such plantings aren't natural. Their lack of diversity erodes the soil and depletes it of nutrients that must be deliberately and continually supplemented. They are less able to fight off diseases and pests. For these reasons, such artificially constructed monocultures shouldn't be the norm but rather the exception.

We have likewise created a society of monocultures that experience extraordinarily little intergenerational interaction. A retirement village of residents aged 50 and older that discourages young families may meet the needs of some older adults, but how socially fertile, really, is that environment? The same can be said for high-tech workplaces that discourage the hiring and retention of older adults. In such companies, how nutrient-rich is the soil of much-needed innovative ideas and processes? And those businesses that push plastic surgery, Botox, and other anti-aging remedies provide the fuel that keeps the engines of those other industries chugging away.

We can't see the forest for the trees.

It seems to me that the only valid thing to say about generations (keeping in mind that the age ranges assigned to them are arbitrary and vary depending on who's doing the defining) is that we are existing together, sharing the same soil and the same oxygenated atmosphere of culture, events, and time, yet are enduring and reacting in our own ways to natural and human-made catastrophes that impact us all.

Just like individual trees of the same age or species, we are nevertheless individuals who are affected differently by those events, based on other factors. Some, such as our gender, race, ethnicity, and geographic location, are more widely socially determined. Others, such as our personal history, preferences, level of education, economic status, and family dynamics, are not. All these differences make it problematic to speak constantly and consistently of ourselves in broad generational terms.

So maybe we should stop placing such great importance on identifying ourselves according to generational categories. Instead, let's value, protect, and enrich the ecosystem we inhabit together.

How well we care for our shared environment will determine the extent to which we all survive and thrive in it — in the many growing seasons to come.

# GRAINS OF TRUTH

Imagine this: Two cups, one containing sugar and the other containing sand. You pour the sugar into a large bowl. Then you carefully pour the sand on top. Next, you take tweezers and pick up each grain, separating the sand and sugar back into their respective cups. How long do you think it would take you to complete the task?

A very long time, I would suspect.

Now imagine a second scenario: Same two cups of the same ingredients, poured into the same bowl, except this time you stir the ingredients together very aggressively. Then you try to separate the grains of sand and sugar using those same tweezers. How long do you think it would take you to complete this unfathomably arduous task?

An interminably long time.

This metaphor can be applied to tackling the insidious injustice of ageism. Here's how.

Let's consider those two types of grains — sugar and sand — as two specific populations. There are the "productive" young adults and middle-agers, and there are the presumed "unproductive" children, teens, and older adults. By maintaining cultural ageist attitudes toward these latter three groups, we keep them from fully integrating into the rest of society. And like those grains of sand sitting atop the granules of sugar, they are easier to identify and remove from our policymaking, civic engagement, and even public discourse.

But what if we adopt the realistic idea that someone's age should have very little to do with accessing opportunities to participate and grow? What if we re-examine how we define productivity and evaluate age-appropriate behaviors and we actively "stir up" our collective culture to allow greater integration of different ages in common activities? What if we purposely foster intergenerational communication and relationships in our schools, workplaces, recreation areas, and long-term-care settings?

Once populations of all ages are interspersed and exposed to one another on a more regular and widespread basis — working together on business teams, enjoying all-age-friendly recreation parks and centers, enrolling in higher-education classrooms, living in mixed-age residential communities — it will be next to impossible for us to go back to embracing our discriminatory beliefs and practices. No tweezers of time would be able to separate us, each a grain embodying our own truth while living in an interdependent, age-affirming society.

Stirring things up in this way is a task well worth the effort — no matter how long it takes.

# THE "WOW" FACTOR

"Wow!"

That's the word I'm hearing us adults say most often these days regarding the wave of activism led by many decades-younger people in their efforts to impact social and political policy. We're highly impressed by their passion, integrity, and organizational skills — in short, with their *maturity.*

But what do we really mean when we say "Wow!"? Aren't we actually assuming that the mature behavior these younger cohorts display is exceptional rather than typical? And is that because we have a very narrow view of the capabilities of a young person?

It's funny, but people use the same word when reacting to older adults who do what they consider to be exceptionally youthful (or at least middle-aged) things, such as run a marathon, sky-dive, bungee-jump, or climb a mountain. "Wow!"

There's a strange pattern here. We're surprised by young people who display what we consider to be the kind of sophistication and wisdom that we associate only with experience and age, as well as by elders who display the physical stamina, prowess, and productivity of people decades younger. It's as if to be young means only to be strong and to be old means only to be wise. (At this point, it's worth stating the obvious: that not all young people have the same physical strength and not all old people are equally wise.)

In geriatrician Bill Thomas' consideration of that particularly insidious word *still* (as in "My grandpa is 98 and he *still* lives on his own!") — which, while it is usually used to praise active older adults, actually diminishes the concept of aging in its entirety — he wrote, "We live in an age when older people are deemed worthy only to the degree that, in their thoughts and actions, they resemble young people. This ethos is very rigidly applied and we all know what happens to older people who can't still do the things that adults are supposed to do. They disappear."[13]

Let's consider this disappearing act that our culture imposes on the old. It's based on two fears.

The first is the fear of death, for which old age is the most common precursor.

The second is the collective fear of an inevitable, cumulative state of deterioration that we mistakenly attribute to aging. When we wrongly believe that all older adults are destined to have stooped postures, cognitive decline, poor eyesight or hearing, and slower reaction times, we assume that fate for ourselves and fear it. Thus needing to ease our minds, we resort to a number of strategies to avoid identifying with our future selves and thus seek to distance ourselves from that scenario. We tell ageist jokes, we avert our gaze as we pass elders on the street, we don't think of including old people in our social activities or policy making efforts. We erase older adults from our social landscape.

What we lack because of this second fear is a more complete, realistic understanding of what it is to grow old. By now you know that aging results in increased life experience and several significant positive changes in the brain; they actually help improve older adults' emotional well-being and can promote greater flexibility, resilience, and a more sophisticated perspective on life. Whenever we apply a "Wow!" factor to older adults based on our assessment of how closely they resemble much younger people, we fail to appreciate the complexity and richness of many others who may not be able, or may not choose, to run a marathon, climb a mountain, work full-time, or even physically resemble someone 40 years younger.

We commit a great social injustice by failing to recognize and accept the variety of ways to be a child, or a teen, or a middle-aged adult...or an old person.

Of course, we should always be excited by and supportive of the efforts of others. But to do this in a realistic and fair way, we need to see one another as individuals rather than as examples of a successful or unsuccessful way to live out a certain age. We must remove the factor of age out of any equation expressing the achievements of a human being.

For me, it's a matter of having a simple hope. I dream that someday we'll be living in a pro-aging society that understands that all kinds of people at all kinds of ages do (or not do) all kinds of things, a society that promotes their right to live however they choose to live. Maybe someday our "Wow" responses will be replaced by "Ho-hum" ones.

And wow, wouldn't *that* be something to achieve?

# AGEISM: THE NEXT GENERATION

The now famous "OK, Boomer" meme that went viral in 2019 is just another example of an ongoing tense dialogue between the two generations most prominently covered in the media. Articles exploring ageism usually cite the cultural experiences of Millennials and Boomers while overlooking the cohort between them.

What about the members of Generation X? What do today's 40- and 50-somethings know about ageism? How does it affect their lives? And how can they change the social, economic, and political trajectory of its course?

Addressing these questions once again raises the basic issue of how valid it is to discuss generations as discrete groups.

According to Eunice Lin Nichols, a Gen Xer and co-CEO of the nonprofit CoGenerate, which promotes intergenerational cooperation for solving social problems,

We like to talk about large numbers of people born between specific years as if they have a predefined set of characteristics, but there's incredible diversity within generations. That diversity — in outlook, values, and life choices — is shaped as much by other factors as by exposure to a set of shared events over a discrete period of time…. I'm much more interested in looking at the relationship of one generation to another through the lens of life stage and life experience.[14]

As it turns out, those life experiences cover a wide range of cultural circumstances. Sociology professor emeritus Stephen Katz of the Trent

Centre for Aging and Society at Trent University has described Gen Xers' age-based challenges as "a) being in the 'shadow' of the much larger and affluent population of their parents, b) experiencing a more volatile and precarious labor market, c) growing up in both a retro-Conservative political culture and dissolution of the Cold War, d) relating to the world through new digital technologies, e) coping with the consequences of greater divorce rates."[15]

That's a lot of change to adjust to, in addition to the realities of growing older among an aging global population. Moreover, Gen Xers are now experiencing the pressures of sandwich-generation caregiving and workplace ageism more than ever before.

A 2019 National Alliance for Caregiving report revealed that while 19% of Baby Boomers and 31% of Millennials were simultaneously caregiving for both children and parents, Gen Xers were most likely to do so — at 49%.[16]

Furthermore, according to a 2018 AARP survey, 54% of older workers believed that age discrimination at work begins in one's 50s[17] (although, according to a British survey, in some industries such as technology, it is occurring for 30-something workers[18]).

What adjustments in perspective about getting older are Gen Xers making in response to their current lives?

"For Gen Xers, age is a state of mind," said Candace Steele Flippin, executive research fellow at the Weatherhead School of Management at Case Western Reserve University. "They do not have to 'grow old gracefully.' They can have a second act, reinvent themselves, and have new adventures."[19]

Katz would agree. He explained that

while the Boomer generation may be obsessed with retaining their youth and catering to a commercialized anti-aging "positive" culture of exercise, diet, wellness, brain-training and active lifestyles, Gen Xers will know better, since their youth was not similarly idealized and their acceptance of more diverse identities and bodies is part of their generational identity…. They understand ageism as not just as an "attitude" but as a central question of social change.[20]

One major social-change strategy Gen Xers are using to counter ageism is to promote intergenerational cooperation in all social endeavors.

"Right now," said Nichols, "we are the true midlifers, with a unique vantage point and influence as we transition out of early careers and child rearing toward our encores…. As we navigate midlife, sandwiched between aging parents and our own children, we have an opportunity to live, work, and play across generational lines, to create a different, more age-integrated reality for everyone."[21]

Added Steele Flippin: "Gen Xers are sandwiched between Baby Boomers and Millennials and can serve as an intergenerational bridge. They can mute the stigma associated with ageism by adding their viewpoint and voice to this issue. By modeling constructive behaviors, they can also take action to remove ageism barriers for themselves and Millennials."[22]

She predicted that "Gen Xers will be more optimistic and pragmatic about managing life as [they] age."[23] And why not? Gen Xers will have greater advantages than their Boomer predecessors at fighting ageism.

Steele Flippin pointed out that "technology and social media will benefit Gen Xers greatly when dealing with typical age-related challenges. Some of these challenges include social isolation, physical health, financial, and transportation issues. Gen Xers will have more tools, access to information, and resources available to help them better navigate."[24]

Katz summed it up in this way:

Gen Xers are also, of course, parents; they are no longer "the next generation," but their children (and their children) are such. Thus they are moving into becoming "seniors" themselves and face the challenges of socializing their own children in terms of the intergenerational legacies they wish to pass on. So as Gen Xers are learning about growing older themselves, we can all learn along with them new meanings about aging.[25]

If they are successful, those new meanings will further disrupt ageism — for the benefit of generations to come.

# CAVEAT MENTOR

Here's part of a conversation I once overheard at my local gym between an older woman (in her 40s) and a younger woman (in her 20s) — working out together:

Older Woman: Just so you know: The more you wash your hair, the faster it turns gray.

Younger Woman: Really?

Older Woman: It's a fact.

Younger Woman *(sighing):* Shoot!

Aside from the obvious ageism that underlies this conversation (why is it so dreadful to have gray hair?), there's a problem with Older Woman's sage advice: It's not accurate. In itself, the process of hair-washing doesn't cause gray hair. In fact, the act of regularly massaging hair follicles stimulates blood flow and helps keep them healthy. Rather, it's the basic aging process of the death of pigment cells in the scalp, as well as the quality of the water (namely the amount of chlorine in it) that plays a role by changing the chemical composition of hair and stripping away its melanin pigmentation.

The point here is that in her attempt to mentor Younger Woman, Older Woman fell short. Which has me thinking about the process of mentoring and the mentor's role in it. As someone who has been mentored both wisely and unwisely at various points in my life, I've come to some conclusions about the qualities I seek in such a person. And as someone who has been a mentor, those same conclusions have guided me as ideals to attain. Maybe they will resonate with you, too:

**The mentor is, first and foremost, a guide.** And by "guide" I mean someone who creates a safe intellectual and emotional space in which the mentee can explore ideas, possibilities, and opportunities to fulfill his/her own dreams.

**The mentor listens deeply.** A person who constantly interrupts or puts pressure on the mentee to "get to the point" isn't listening deeply. Deep listening involves slowing down and paying attention not just to the words being said but also to body language, facial expression, tone of voice, and most especially, the hesitations and silences between words.

**The mentor knows his/her own limits.** When someone looks to a mentor for information and advice, it behooves the mentor to know what s/he is talking about, as well as to be willing to admit a lack of knowledge and help locate or verify the information. Humility and curiosity are essential in a mentor.

**The mentor defers to the mentee.** Mentoring isn't about the person giving guidance but about the one seeking it. The best mentors in my life have been those who took their cues from me and respected my choices about how and when I should take my next steps. They let me make necessary mistakes and didn't give I-told-you-so gloating responses. Great mentors aren't judgmental; they are compassionate.

**The mentor provokes.** I've found it valuable when a mentor lets questions, not assertions, guide our interaction. When someone whose experience I value poses provocative questions to me rather than tells me what the answers should be, I am empowered to reach my own conclusions and to develop better critical thinking and emotional skills that will serve me in the future.

**The mentor describes, not prescribes or proscribes.** My skeptical antennae go up whenever the word *should* or *shouldn't* enters a mentoring conversation. I've found that it's far more effective for a mentor to offer examples from personal experience to see if they might likewise apply to my issues.

**The mentor is careful about the type of information shared.** On a few occasions, I've experienced mentors relaying gossip or warning me away from So-and-so because it could harm my projects or career. While I can understand why a caring mentor might consider such information relevant and important, I've also been burned by following the advice, only to find out that the mentor misunderstood or had limited knowledge of the background situation.

**The mentor has no vested emotional interest in the mentee's choices.** It's counterproductive, not to mention unethical, when a mentor's ego is enmeshed in the process. Occasionally, I was slow to realize when a mentor tried to make our relationship a kind of power struggle, patronizing me or intimidating me with his/her "greater" understanding, expecting from me a kind of worshipful stance. I consider it major progress that as I matured I became better at terminating such relationships early in the process.

There's no doubt that being a mentor carries responsibilities. But so, too, does being a mentee. As a person seeking guidance, I also understand that mentors are fallible beings. I always try to measure the information and advice I receive against the reality of my own experience. If I hear something that gives me pause, it's my responsibility to check it out and share my findings. Great mentors, like great physicians, are always willing to hear second opinions.

One other thing: It's been wonderful when on the rare occasion a mentor of mine eventually became my peer because I grew in understanding and/or because my mentor came to recognize and solicit a particular kind of wisdom I could share that would enrich his/her life. But those times have been few, and rightfully so, as I never expected those transformations to happen.

In my 70s, I'm lucky to have experienced mentorship from both perspectives. And I must say that it's especially refreshing to be mentored by younger people. The reversal of traditional roles only proves that all of us can learn — and teach — something at any age. All of us are potential mentors.

If and when we assume the role, it's important to do so with purpose and integrity. I look forward to my next experience as a mentor or mentee. Until that time, you'll find me nonchalantly and regularly washing my gray hair.

# A CASE FOR "RE-GENERATION"

The Chinese calendar characterizes years according to the traits of certain iconic creatures. For instance, 2024 was the Year of the Dragon.

For me, 2015 was the Year of Boomeritis.

If you've never heard of the term, it was first coined in 1999 by Nicholas A. DiNubile,[26] at the time an orthopedic surgeon at the Hospital of the University of Pennsylvania, who defined it as any injury incurred by a Baby Boomer, usually in the course of doing some kind of physical activity such as exercising or playing a sport. But I prefer to define it more broadly as a cognitive condition in which many of us Boomers mistakenly assume that we are the same people physically, mentally, emotionally, and spiritually as we were decades earlier. And act like it.

So imagine my rude awakening at the gym when I believed I could handle the same vigorous weight-training regimen I performed in my 30s. Wrong. I tore muscles in my right shoulder and pulled a ligament in my left wrist, which together required a year of physical therapy to heal.

Now lest it appear that I'm being ageist here, I assure you I'm not. Ageism is the unfair misperception and discrimination that result from attributing something to aging that has nothing to do with it. But there is truth to the physical manifestation of Boomeritis. Physiologically, most of us will undergo some deterioration as we get older. Of course, one should never assume that every older adult suffers Boomeritis, as there are many in my generation and older who are more physically fit now than they ever were in their 20s or 30s, probably because they have shed bad habits and taken greater care of their bodies. But I suspect most physicians would say that these people, given more time, will also likely feel some physical changes.

Nevertheless — and here is where Boomeritis itself promotes ageism — if we have been living a life of vitality and purpose, we *can't possibly be* the same people physically, mentally, emotionally, and spiritually as we were decades earlier. Nor should we want to be. Believing that we can and should halt time is an ageist attitude that does us a disservice. Human development urges us to evolve into beings with greater experience, wider perceptions, newer capabilities, and fresher possibilities for regeneration.

Or "re-generation."

A surprising benefit from my bout with Boomeritis was the chance to get to know a genial, highly competent physical therapist named Matt. A Millennial, Matt was in the fortunate position of working with older adults every day, getting to know and appreciate us as the complex, interesting people we are. Conversely, as he helped ease our pain and heal our injuries, he shared his interesting complexity with us.

Similarly, during visits to my local bank, I have thoroughly enjoyed all-too-short, eye-opening conversations with the tellers and managers (all Millennials and Gen Xers) on various social topics. I have surprised them and they have surprised me as we mutually disproved the many false stereotypes of age. And I began to develop a genuine appreciation for this intergenerational interaction.

In the course of a typical day (and apart from encounters with immediate family), I and many other older adults who are retired or live in generationally segregated communities or work and socialize only with others our age have very few personal interactions with younger people. And I'm convinced that we are the lesser for it. When nonrelated individuals of different generations are artificially separated, either by necessity or choice, what often results are an ignorance and intolerance of one another's special insights that could otherwise be mutually enlightening and beneficial.

Fortunately, enjoying opportunities for intergenerational activity is becoming more common. Nonprofit organizations such as CoGenerate,[27]

Generations United,[28] and national programs such as the federal government's AmeriCorps Seniors[29] and AARP's Experience Corps[30] offer a variety of enjoyable, engaging volunteer opportunities that bring older and younger generations together to learn and work on social issues. Other organizations such as Sages & Seekers[31] promote in-person and virtual conversational visits between younger and older adults. All these efforts can effectively break down the false generational stereotypes we have internalized and help us to appreciate the wide variety of personalities that exist among all age groups.

Multigenerational, intergenerational solutions to our age-based cultural segregation abound, and we have only to look around to discover them. Actually, only looking around isn't enough. We must also agree that we need such solutions, appreciate what they can do, and have the will to put them into practice or create others of our own. A valuable resource for inspiration is the ongoing series of essays, "Meeting the Multigenerational Moment," compiled and published by the Stanford Social Innovation Review.[32]

For my part, I'll be eagerly seeking more chances to mingle with decades-younger and -older people and, if I'm lucky, to establish friendships with them. I want to keep learning from them and in turn share my life-based wisdom. As I see it, if we want to thrive, no matter our age, we need to find cultural ways to increase intergenerational communication, activity, and relationship. Precisely because we're in different places in the lifespan physically, mentally, emotionally, and spiritually, we can enrich our own lives and those of others by helping one another to grow.

And maybe in the process, we can create a social environment that stimulates "re-generation" of all kinds and keeps people like me from falling prey to the cognitive condition of Boomeritis.

# CHAPTER 10

# Growing Older Your Way

**AT THIS POINT** in our "sideways" investigation into aging, I've described older adults as weeds, reservoirs, and people of steel rather than gold. I've talked about generations as grains of sand and sugar, as well as diverse trees in the same forest. I've compared the process of getting older to climbing hills, taking batting turns at home plate, and being in an enriching relationship. And I've pointed out how ageism constricts us in ill-fitting footwear and suits, otherizes us, and renders us invisible. I've presented all of these ideas from a "we" perspective — of us in it together.

But what about you as *you*? How are *you* aging? How do *you* want to grow older?

Notice that I didn't ask "How do you want to *get* older?" That's because I'm about to request that you tilt your mind sideways once again to ponder another perspective on aging. Yes, this book's subtitle is "Changing Our Perspectives on Getting Older," but that's just the starting point. Getting older is something that automatically happens to you as the years pass. But growing older is another thing. It demands that you take a more conscious and proactive part in your development as a current or eventual old person.

Hopefully by now you've been assessing your own assumptions about living a long life and whether or not you're looking forward to doing so. Since we are individuals, we age in unique ways. To a great extent those ways depend on how we function in daily life. So it's wise to think about the many identities you have and things you currently do, whether they engage and satisfy you, and how they might change — or you might want to change them — in the years to come.

In the 1960s, American psychologist David Bakan asserted that the tasks we perform can be described according to two modalities: agency and communion.[1] Northwestern University psychology professor Dan P. McAdams describes these modalities in this way:

> Agency refers to the individual's striving to separate from others, to master the environment, to assert, protect, and expand the self. The aim is to become a powerful and autonomous "agent," a force to be reckoned with. By contrast, communion refers to the individual's striving to lose his or her own individuality by merging with others, participating in something that is larger than the self, and relating to other selves in warm, close, intimate, and loving ways.[2]

Here's how agency and communion manifest themselves and compare with each other:

In performing a task of agency, a person acts alone, with a goal of achieving some kind of power or mastery, is energized by the ambition to succeed, possibly being driven by a sense of competition with someone else. Any decisions are made by that person, who assumes all responsibility for the task and directly derives a reward from it.

In performing a task of communion, a person acts in relationship with others, with a goal of achieving some kind of equity, is energized by the impulse of empathy, being driven by desire to establish a sense of cooperation. Any decisions are made through the majority vote or consensus of a group who share the responsibilities for the task and the rewards it provides.

The difference between these two modalities may tempt us to believe that one modality is more masculine and the other more feminine, but that's not the case. Men as well as women move from one modality to another and are often involved with both. Modalities are not gender specific.

In addition, single tasks or occupations often involve switching back and forth between agency and communion. Let me give you two examples.

You might think that being a teacher falls under the modality of communion, and certainly in the classroom a teacher is acting in relationship with the students. But when that teacher is creating lesson plans or evaluating homework, those are tasks of agency performed in isolation. On the other hand, an architect may spend hundreds of hours alone at a drafting table designing a structure, but when it comes to working with subcontractors and clients, those are clearly times of communion.

Now think of some of the roles you play or jobs you do. Which ones do you think primarily involve agency and which ones primarily involve communion? Are there any that fall equally into both categories?

What do these two modalities have to do with aging your way? Whether you act with agency or communion is often determined by social biases and pressures, especially when they involve ageism.

For example, if you work with others, how encouraged are you to take the initiative in solving a problem if you are seen as too young to assume responsibility or too old to be considered relevant for the task or project at hand? In such a situation, your agency is blocked by your supervisor's assumption of you as solely in communion with a pool of others working under the direction of someone else. Conversely, have you ever been denied the opportunity to manage a team of coworkers? In this situation, your opportunity for communion is blocked by the limited assessment of you as a mere agent of simple tasks.

Or if you live in a retirement community whose administration provides residents with nothing more than bland, unchallenging social activities and doesn't offer ways to actively engage with other generations or with the greater surrounding neighborhood through mentoring or other volunteer projects, both your agency and your communion are being severely limited.

In your everyday life, where and when might you be finding your powers of agency and communion stifled, thwarted, or demeaned by family, friends, coworkers, acquaintances, health care providers, marketers, or others because of your age?

Keeping in mind your potential for participating in various kinds of agency and communion, what are some ways in which to more easily grow older your way? Consider these strategies:

**Examine your own reactions to aging, including any ageist views you may hold.** Remember Max Planck's words: "When you change the way you look at things, the things you look at change."

**Step out and engage others by sharing your story, your time, and your talents.** If you think about it, there's probably something you know or a skill or interest you have that someone else might like to learn. And don't be surprised if someone decades younger than you is eager to hear about your life.

**Know your value and potential to make a difference and communicate them to others.** By now you're aware of the assets of the older brain and the ways that older adults can contribute to workplace productivity, the education of children, and the general improvement of our environment and society.

**Start declaring your age,** which is something to be grateful for and proud of.

**Be open to surprise and to surprising others.** Show up in places where older adults aren't expected to be. Follow your urges to learn new things and activities, travel to new places, and meet new people.

**Demand that society reality checks its expectations of you.** As I've said, consider the fact that once we become adults, there's no such thing as "age appropriateness." If someone questions your values, desires, or actions based on your age, ask why that's a concern. Engage in a dialogue to promote greater understanding.

**Openly question any situation that makes age an issue.** I'm not talking about infiltrating a high school Ecology Club meeting or a young mothers weekly breakfast at the local café, but rather those occasions and gatherings having nothing to do with age, such as public government or school board meetings.

**Actively enlist and involve allies,** not only those who resemble you but also — and especially — those who are different from you in gender, race, physical ability, socioeconomic class, and, yes, generation. There are plenty of them out there, and they can have a different credibility in the estimation of others who resemble them and can help change attitudes toward aging in ways that you alone might not.

**Take the initiative to challenge ageism whenever you encounter it.**

It's time to flex your muscles by enlisting those sideways skills of evading obstacles, rejecting or redefining terms that don't apply to you, looking peripherally to find other options, and remaining open to unexpected opportunities.

It's time to begin growing older — *your* way.

# ROOTS, SHOOTS, AND FRUITS

In the workshops I facilitate on journaling, memoir writing, stress management, caregiver support, and ethical-will creation, one particular exercise resonates quite deeply with participants. Based on the organic structure of a tree (which is a great metaphor for life itself), the activity is a fun and revealing way to explore the influences and inspirations in one's life and how they are transformed into meaningful passions and productive actions. I call it Roots, Shoots, and Fruits.

Here's how to do the exercise:

1. On a piece of paper, draw the trunk of a tree. The trunk represents you.

2. Now think about the people, experiences, and things that influence and/or nurture you in your life. For example, your faith, family members, and friends each might be a source of support. Perhaps you are greatly influenced by your experiences of travel, work, periods of crisis, or time in the military. You get the idea. Downward from the base of the trunk, draw and label a root that represents each such aspect in your life.

3. Next, consider your passions and actions. Toward what activities do you direct your energies and spend your time? For example, you might focus some of your energy on volunteer work. And it's highly likely that you spend time doing things for and/or with your partner and/or children. You might also enjoy a particular hobby or play a certain sport. Each of these channels of your energy is a "shoot," or branch, of your tree. Upward from the top part of the trunk, draw these shoots and label each one accordingly.

4.  Finally, look at each shoot on your tree. Ask yourself: "In what particular way am I living out this passion?" or "What specifically am I contributing to the world as a result of this effort?" In other words, what is the "fruit" of each labor? For example, if volunteering is one of your shoots, a fruit might be "tutoring a child," "working at the food bank," or "making quilts for shut-ins." At the end of each shoot, draw and label one or more fruits that describe the results or end-products of your actions.

By now you may realize that a root (such as "my partner") can also be a shoot. Or a shoot (such as "photography") may also be a root because the activity nurtures you. Or a fruit (such as your child) can be a root because of the love s/he provides in your life. That's great. It indicates full-circle aspects to your life.

As I said, this exercise is always a hit with my workshop participants. It provides a way for them to take stock of their lives and to recognize and appreciate the connections that help define who they are in the world. But the exercise has an additional benefit, one that has to do with proportion and balance.

Some people have greater difficulty identifying their roots rather than their shoots/fruits. They are clearly able to name their passions as well as the many things that they do. But they can't seem to cite specific people or events or values that provide stability and inspiration in their lives. For others, it's just the opposite. They have no trouble acknowledging the influences in their lives, but they aren't clear about the ways in which they contribute to the world through their actions or gifts.

Another interesting effect occurs when someone recognizes a root, shoot, or fruit that has been withering for some time due to lack of attention or appreciation, and s/he resolves to invest more time and energy into nurturing that aspect back to life. Or perhaps a root, shoot, or fruit no longer provides positive energy in that person's life and must be pruned away.

Over the years, I've done this exercise in many workshops with participants of all ages. What is particularly remarkable is how much easier this activity tends to be for older adults than for young adults and middle-agers. Perhaps it's because of the greater perspective elders have about their own lives and the longer amount of time they've had to develop it. And the trees of elders who are not isolated or depressed tend to be balanced between downward and upward entries.

I've noticed, too, that the trees of young adults often have more roots than shoots/fruits. This is to be expected, since they are still evolving as individuals and discovering the ways they can contribute to the world. Middle-aged adults, on the other hand, sometimes have more top-heavy trees. They can label many shoots and fruits, but they tend to lose awareness of their roots, influences, and sources of support. And maybe that's a symptom of the drive to achieve that often preoccupies people in mid-career.

But here's what I've found most valuable about introducing my participants to Roots, Shoots, and Fruits. Since I began noticing these generational differences, I have encouraged my students to take this exercise beyond the classroom and do it again with family members of different ages. How, for example, might grandparents help their grandchildren to identify their gifts? How might they help their middle-aged children restore themselves by tapping into their root influences? And how might grandkids and their parents better appreciate and aspire to grow the sturdier, more balanced tree of an engaged elder? And how different might a person's own tree look as s/he repeats the exercise from time to time throughout life?

Try this exercise, and pay attention to what it teaches you about yourself. I hope you'll agree that if more of us spend time thinking about our Roots, Shoots, and Fruits (and encourage others to do the same), we will begin to cultivate a lush new forest of personal and social growth.

243

# THE POWER OF ONE

When I turned 70, I was particularly excited about reaching that milestone. That's right. You read me correctly. Not fearful or depressed, but excited.

However, it was more than arriving at that age that elated me. That's because I received one of the most meaningful birthday cards I could ever have imagined. Instead of being a dreadful over-the-hill one (you know, the kind of ageist, black-balloon sentiment that's meant to be funny in its snarky acknowledgment of the fear of getting older that pervades our culture), it actually celebrated my age as a *positive* achievement. Unheard of, in my experience.

Three years before that, a different friend sent me an over-the-hill card, which I took in a good-natured way. But something clicked — or rather, snapped — in me, and that's when I decided to do something about it.

Before telling you what I did, I need to explain that as a longtime journalist and editor, I've learned that when seeking a source of information, always start at the top, such as a CEO, president, or chair of the board. Of course, you might get kicked down a few rungs to someone lower on the hierarchical ladder, but sometimes you actually get the attention of the person in charge.

So I looked at the back of that over-the-hill card and saw that a major greeting card company produced it. I looked up its website, found the name of its CEO and the address of its headquarters. Rather than call or email him, I decided to include his company's product in my communication. I whited out the signature of my friend on the birthday card and wrote a long note to the CEO.

I said that I was a 67-year-old gerontologist and explained why the card and others like it are offensive and ageist. I posited that his company wouldn't consider creating a card that was racist, sexist, ableist, or homophobic and that advanced age is nothing to belittle and mock because age discrimination seriously harms people's lives in many ways.

I put the card in a different envelope and mailed it to the CEO at the headquarters. I didn't really expect anything to come of my effort; I was simply glad to vent my frustration.

A month later, I received a letter from that company's director of corporate communications. "Thank you," she began, "for taking the time to write our CEO to share your thoughts on the recent birthday card you received. Your letter was passed along to me, and I wanted to take the opportunity to respond to your specific concerns."

Not surprisingly, she rationalized that their cards are meant to address a large number of customers with a range of tastes. But then I was startled at how she closed the letter: "I have…shared…your feedback with our creative teams for them to take into consideration for the planning of future lines."

Often we feel that as individuals we have little power on our own to change the status quo, especially when it has been shaped by large groups of people in power. "I'm only one person," we tell ourselves, "and there's nothing I can do about it."

Well, think again. What happened to me wasn't a fluke experience; that's because it happened again, in another context.

For a long time, I've been annoyed by the close-up photographs of wrinkled hands that accompany many articles about older people. It's as if we are a group of pathetic, passive victims who do nothing but sit and let life happen. Not even our faces — which would identify us as individuals — are shown.

So in 2022, I wrote that article for Next Avenue I mentioned in Chapter 8 called "How Photos Showing Older Adult Hands Reveal Cultural Bias."[3] Once it appeared online, I then referred to it each time I saw posted on social media an article using a hands-only photograph. I requested that the publisher find a different photograph showing an older adult as a whole human being in a vital, person-centered context. And it has helped change the practices of writers, editors, educators, and marketers at national organizations, major medical schools, and online media companies.

I keep calling out ageist transgressions of all kinds every time I encounter them, in the hope that my efforts will continue to make a difference.

As an older adult consumer, I'm not unusual. I know lots of others who feel the same way about wanting to change the way society views us. I used to tell myself that I had no such power on my own. But I was wrong. And you're wrong if you feel that way, too. Take a chance and try going directly to the source of your dissatisfaction. You might be surprised at the outcome.

As surprised as I was to get that lovely 70th birthday card. You see, it was created by *that same card company* to whose CEO I wrote. While the business still produces the over-the-hill, black-balloon variety of greetings, it has now added more pro-aging cards to its repertoire. The last line of my card said, "You've mastered the art…of being young at heart."

"Young at heart"? Yeah, I know. That phrasing needs work, and they've got a long way to go. But it's a beginning — an effort that company might never have made, were it not for the Power of One.

## SIX WAYS TO BE A SMARTER PATIENT

Anyone who has followed the news since 2020 knows that the risk of serious illness from contracting COVID-19 rises with age. Therefore, older adults like me need to be particularly vigilant, protecting ourselves by adhering to the well-known safety precautions of wearing masks, getting vaccinated and boosted, frequently handwashing, and physically distancing.

For us especially, contracting the virus may result in hospitalization, ICU confinement, and being put on a ventilator, all the while being separated from loved ones. No matter our age, being smarter patients and better advocating for ourselves can make a dramatic difference in the likelihood of completely recovering, avoiding long COVID, or better yet, in preventing getting the virus at all.

Think of all the acute and chronic illnesses that can afflict us, no matter our age. Given this, ageism can play a role in whether our health concerns are addressed or dismissed. So for anyone, I propose six basic ways to be a smarter patient and your own best advocate. I call them "H.E.A.L.T.H." strategies:

Hire your team.
Enlist a care partner.
Ask effective questions.
Learn about your body.
Take charge and control.
Have vital plans in place.

Let's consider each one.

**Hire your team.** The basic thing you as a smarter patient can do is to see yourself as the central point of your own care and thus "hiring" trusted people to work with you to keep you healthy. Are your doctors and other providers compassionate, competent, confident, and candid? Do they collaborate well not only with you but also with one another? You should never feel intimidated, confused, or neglected when seeking care. You have the right to change practitioners if your needs go unmet. It helps to think of yourself as a consumer seeking satisfaction rather than a victim seeking rescue.

**Enlist a care partner.** Even if you believe you can manage things on your own, it can be helpful and even vital to have a relative or friend with you when you go to see your doctor or if you are hospitalized. That trusted person can serve as another pair of ears and eyes during or after in-person contact or televisits with your doctor to make sure you understand and remember what's being said and to help prevent medical errors that can arise. However, sometimes having someone accompany you may not be possible. With your individual doctor, you might consider recording your discussion to play back later when you need a handy reminder or have more time to absorb all of the information covered in such a short time. If you're alone in the hospital, know that most hospitals have patient advocates on staff who can serve as liaisons for you.

**Ask effective questions.** Your providers rely not only on what they see when they examine you, but on what you tell them about your condition. Be as specific as you can when describing your symptoms, and prepare two or three questions that get directly to the point about what concerns you. Be ready to report anything that doesn't seem quite right, even if you don't think it's related to your condition. (Your doctor might see a connection that you don't.) If any test or lab work was done in advance of your appointment, check ahead of time with your provider's office to make sure that those results have been received and are ready to be discussed during your appointment. It's also important to ask about the purpose, risks, and costs of any newly prescribed medications or treatments.

**Learn about your body.** Regardless of how well your doctor knows you as a patient, you are still the person who best understands how you move, feel, and react on a moment-to-moment basis. Your health care providers rely on you to be aware of the changes in your body and health status and to let them know in a timely manner. A big way to help your team is to work with them to keep the following measurements in check: HDL and LDL cholesterols, triglycerides, blood pressure, blood glucose (sugar), hemoglobin A1c, and body-mass index (BMI).

**Take charge and control.** As a smarter patient, this is the most important thing you can do. Be proactive about the care you receive. Always feel free to ask your provider to: 1) listen attentively to what you have to say without interrupting, 2) speak directly to you rather than, or in addition to, whoever accompanies you, 3) slow down, repeat, and/or use simpler language when speaking to you, and 4) give you enough time to read and sign consent forms.

Being in control also means being a responsible patient. Know your rights as a patient[4] as outlined by your doctor's practice and local hospital, share your concerns, follow agreed-upon instructions, and track your progress. Sign on to your provider's online portal system and contact your doctor in a timely way if you experience side effects to medications. Seek additional help if you need it. This includes getting a second opinion, to which no competent and confident doctor should object.

**Have vital plans in place.** Now, more than ever, it's important to have "that conversation" with loved ones and your doctor concerning the kinds of emergency and end-of-life care you want. Make sure you have an Advance Directive (Living Will)[5] in place and have appointed a Health Care Power of Attorney.[6] Also know the purposes of the Physician

Orders for Life-Sustaining Treatment (POLST)[7] and Do Not Resuscitate (DNR)[8] forms.

Remember: The quality of care we receive as patients is within our control. As older adults, let's apply the wisdom we've acquired over years of experience by being informed and engaged patients while adhering to those scientific protocols supported by reputable medical experts. And let's continue to be role models of self-advocacy for all generations, keeping H.E.A.L.T.H. always in mind.

# WHAT'S YOUR "AND"?

In 2010, at a Philadelphia conference on aging issues, I witnessed an extraordinary performance by an intergenerational improvisational comedy troupe called Second Circle. A dozen people ranging from teens to nonagenarians put on a dazzling, fast-paced, one-hour tour de force highlighting the challenges experienced by different generations as they interact in fictional workplace settings.

In addition to being impressed by the players' wit and spontaneity, I was fascinated by the seamless way they worked together. Their mutual respect was clear. Little did I realize that I was reacting to a basic principle of improvisation known as "Yes And."

In his insightful book on science-communication skills, *If I Understood You, Would I Have This Look on My Face?*, actor Alan Alda — himself highly trained in improv — explained the principle:

For improvisers, Yes And means you accept what the other player presents you with, without blocking it or denying it, and then you react constructively to it. You add to it. As an example, [scientist] Uri [Alon] says, "If one player says, 'Look at all that water down there,' and the other player completely blocks it by saying, 'That's not water, that's the stage,' then the scene is over. But if the player follows the principle of Yes And, he can accept what's been handed to him and add to it. 'Wow, what a lot of water. Let's jump in. Let's grab onto that whale.'" And they're off and swimming.[9]

The Second Circle players said "Yes And" not only to the audience's often hilarious scene suggestions, but also "Yes And" to one another's instantaneous specific words and actions. The result was a marvelous example for us conference attendees of how all generations might cast aside stereotypical notions of age and accept the "Yes And" of any individual's more complex personal reality.

Since that event, I've also come to appreciate the improv principle in a whole other way. "Yes And" requires the two-step approach of acceptance and addition: accepting an idea or belief and then further extending that idea or belief by elaborating on what it can mean. However, when it comes to ideas and beliefs about aging, people often take the first step without following it with the second one. Here's what I mean.

When older adults perceive aging as solely a process of deterioration and decline, they often freely acknowledge the negative aspects of growing older: "My eyesight is getting worse," "I wish I weren't slowing down when I walk," "I don't want to end up in a nursing home." These statements comprise the "Yes" of their later years. We older adults are all too aware of the many physical and social challenges that confront us with each passing year — ageism being the biggest one of all.

But what if we adopted a more improvisational, pro-aging stance toward getting older? What if we move beyond our "Yes" beliefs by taking a "Yes And" approach? "My eyesight is getting worse," a person might think, and then immediately follow it with "...AND I intend to find better ways to enjoy more books than ever before." Or "I wish I weren't slowing down when I walk...AND yet my pace allows me to enjoy more fully my daily stroll around the neighborhood." Or "I don't want to end up in a nursing home...AND I'm doing all that I can to remain active and engaged in my home and community."

There are so many vital ways to apply "Yes And" thinking as we age. We can and should acknowledge any limitations we may be experiencing as our bodies and personal circumstances change, because awareness leads to finding solutions. But to stop there and not take the next step does a disservice to our autonomy, dignity, and value as society's elders. Each of us needs to be equally aware of our "And." We are not a compendium of downsides. We all have valuable skills, experiences, and insights to share.

For example, I can say, "Yes, my eyesight and hearing are not as good as they used to be…AND I am a better writer AND more insightful editor AND more effective teacher than I've ever been in my life." Whenever we share an "And" with as much conviction as we express a "Yes," we are modeling a truly realistic and productive way of being in the world as old people. And our society desperately needs positive role models.

I invite you to join me in improvising our way through these later years. It's easier than you think. All you have to do is answer this very simple question:

What's *your* "And"?

# OLD PERSON — NO LONGER IN TRAINING

If we're lucky, someday we'll become old. But many of us don't know how to make peace with this fact and, in fact, don't want to admit that it *is* a fact. We know we're aging, we want to keep living in the best ways we can, and yet…

Once again, Ashton Applewhite offers an insight, this time in the form of a job description that can help us "integrate the real and the aspirational":

In 2008 I heard geriatrician Joanne Lynn describe herself as an old person in training, and I've been one ever since. I know I'm not young. I don't see myself as old. I know a lot of people feel the same way. They're in the grips of a cruel paradox: They aspire to grow old yet dread the prospect. They spend a lot of energy sustaining the illusion that the old are somehow not us. Becoming an Old Person in Training bridges the us/them divide, and loosens the grip of that exhausting illusion.

Becoming an Old Person in Training acknowledges the inevitability of oldness while relegating it to the future, albeit at an ever-smaller remove. It swaps purpose and intent for dread and denial. It connects us empathetically with our future selves.[10]

In 2023, as I turned 71, the time felt right to greet my future self and assume its identity. I've taken off the training wheels and now consider myself an Old Person. And the job title suits me.

I've not always been comfortable with the aging process. True, during the first three decades of my life I couldn't wait to be old enough to cross the street by myself, then get a driver's license, then go to college, get a job and my own apartment. But sometime in my 30s, I became aware of the cultural swampland of ageism that mires us and pulls us back from those exciting feelings of anticipation and aspiration. I entered a phase of what I now realize was a decades-long unconscious apprenticeship experiencing the increasingly toxic pitfalls of being considered unattractive, uncool, irrelevant, and finally, burdensome.

The dysfunctional attitudes of our society toward the idea of growing older don't allow us to see that becoming an old person is not only natural but a requirement, if longevity is our goal. That's because there seems to be no social value in being old. No job description. No inherent reward.

And therefore, no training.

It's as if our culture demands that once we reach the position of middle age, it's a job we should be expected to hold forever and perform in that same way until we die. But then, paradoxically and ironically, society inevitably fires us from that position when it deems us to be unproductive and unable to contribute anything new and valuable to the social contract.

And so I slowly had to come to terms with my increasing age. It was in my 50s that I assumed an internship of sorts by beginning to call myself an "older adult." (Not coincidentally, it's also when I went back to graduate school to study gerontology, mainly to understand why we get the concept of aging so wrong and what to do about it.)

Our workplace is Life. We sign a contract when we're born and renew it repeatedly throughout the many stages of our growth. When to consider oneself an old person is a decision that varies with each individual. When anyone makes that decision is entirely up to that person; nevertheless, it's one that we all have to make if we're lucky enough to live many decades.

In ways too nebulous to describe, I felt that 2023 was the right time for me. In Applewhite's terms, for the past 20 years I've been replacing dread and denial with purpose and intent. And now I feel ready to explore what's next.

I'm officially an Old Person, on the job and excited to embrace a new "future self" by assuming different responsibilities and enjoying the perks (and as you well know by now, there *are* perks) of the current position.

If and whenever I'm asked, I'm also ready to train others.

# MAKING THINGS ANEW

The object of a New Year is not that we should have a new year. It is that we should have a new soul and a new nose; new feet, a new backbone, new ears, and new eyes.... Unless a man starts afresh about things, he will certainly do nothing effective.

— G.K. Chesterton
"New Year's Day"
from *A Chesterton Calendar*

Regardless of how we feel about our lives during the course of a previous year, the arrival of a new one has the potential to inspire us with hope and a desire for change, in ourselves and in the world around us. What forms these changes take and how we implement them depend on our willingness to examine our current beliefs and behaviors, and to make things anew. British writer and philosopher G.K. Chesterton was on to something when he described the breadth of those changes as including not only the physical body but the soul.

As we age and approach the ends of our lives, too often do we focus on the inevitable deterioration of our bodies, as trillions of our cells stop replicating themselves, or senescing, while not acknowledging the fact that trillions of other cells still continue to multiply and thrive. Given that we keep on going, that we still have noses, feet, backbones, ears, and eyes, what then should we say about our souls?

Like our cells, our younger concepts of reality can, with time, undergo a senescence of sorts. We may reject old beliefs and ways of acting in the world as we acquire — and learn from — greater experience. Whether or not we replace those old perceptions and behaviors with newer ones by using the particular kind of wisdom that comes with age is up to us. Should we choose to do it, we can renew our souls.

But how?

By remaining open to personal growth, we can develop a "new nose" for sniffing out fresh truths amid the stench of hackneyed and cynical ideas that surround us. We can exercise "new feet" that take us in previously unexplored directions. We can replace our "backbone," curved from the frustrating burden of coping with ageism, with a straighter, more supportive one of strength and determination. We can better listen with "new ears" and more keenly observe with "new eyes."

Personal growth shouldn't be our only goal in a new year. We can resolve to be more effective catalysts for change all around us as well. As we renew ourselves, we become better able to renew the world around us. After all, our culture is like an organic body that constantly replenishes itself while simultaneously undergoing its own form of cellular senescence. As various civil rights groups of determined individuals organize and act, they cause social tipping points that challenge old perceptions, trends, and injustices — and bring about change.

Today, the issue of aging is on the verge of a social tipping point, too. More people are becoming sensitized to anti-aging language and agendas and are embracing pro-aging attitudes. For example, it's inspiring to witness the speed and number of many social media replies that challenge ageist attitudes calling for older people to "act their age" or not run for political office.

One particular milestone was established in 2017, when Allure magazine editors decided to abandon the use of the term "anti-aging."[11] Here is what the magazine's then–editor in chief, Michelle Lee, wrote in 2018:

A little more than a year ago, we banned the term "anti-aging" from *Allure*'s vernacular. It got people talking. A lot. All around the world. It spawned many a think piece on aging and language and the language of aging. Within minutes of the story going live, brands, individuals, and organizations reached out to say they wanted to join us in the movement. Some, like AARP, acted fast and issued statements of solidarity. A few skin-care companies cheered us on in private calls but admitted they weren't quite ready to change their own messaging.[12]

It's not just the messaging that's changing. Now more than ever, generations are working together to stop the ongoing replication of ageist propaganda and to boost our social immunity to ageism by creating innovative programs that honor and support people of all ages. As I've mentioned, the work of such organizations as CoGenerate, Generations United, and Sages & Seekers attest to this fact. Each of us can become more engaged in this movement.

Chesterton was right. It's obvious that, unless we start afresh about things, we will certainly do nothing effective. The arrival of each January gives us yet further opportunities to make over our body politic and restore our collective soul.

Let's keep wishing one another a Happy "Anew" Year.

# CHAPTER 11

# Empowering Aging

**BY NOW IT SHOULD BE CLEAR** that there are a lot of things you can do as an individual to grow older your own way. You can examine your life to better understand your influences, preferences, talents, and values as well as how your actions have defined you and impacted others. You can advocate for yourself when seeking new opportunities and better health care. You can accept aging as a process of personal growth and renewal and then choose additional roles to play that can improve the lives of others. Doing these things as you age can keep you energized and increase your resilience, a quality absolutely necessary for living throughout your life in an empowered way.

In Chapter 2, I introduced the term *empowered aging* as a contrast to the "successful" kind. As I argued, empowered aging involves an interaction between society and the individual that moves the focus away from the static goal of accomplishment and toward an ongoing process of maintaining autonomy, dignity, and self-worth through inter-dependence. It isn't enough to forge ahead on our own, no matter how determined we are; society must create for us new paths as well as clear or smooth out existing ones.

What does empowerment involve?

One way to understand it is to consider the way an electromagnet works. Perhaps at some point back in your school days you made a simple one in science class. It consists of four simple materials: a D-size battery, an iron nail, copper wire, and tape. The wire is coiled multiple times around the nail, and each end of the wire is then taped to each end of the battery. The electrical circuit that's created transforms the nail into a magnet that can then pick up paperclips and certain other metallic objects.

Think of an older person as the battery storing potential energy waiting to be released. Think of society as the nail that provides a structure through which that energy can flow. And think of the wire and tape as forming the bridge or relationship permitting the interaction between the person and society.

These days, if elders are empowered at all, it's probably because they have managed to retain those vestiges of power (retirement pension, long-term investments, home equity, occupational prestige) they began to acquire years before in midlife. Unfortunately for many older adults, those vestiges have vanished or never even existed.

Moreover, what *new* powers does society bestow on people in their later years? If anything, widespread ageism toward older adults is the circuit breaker that disconnects the two-way relationship, blocking older adult opportunities for new employment, greater financial security, further social engagement, and improved health. These effects deplete elders' intensity of motivation, feeling of optimism, and ultimately, their desire to engage with others.

That's not providing energy to power their resilience; it's pulling the plug.

A truly empowering society increases older adults' resilience by providing them with the physical, financial, cultural, and spiritual conditions that promote autonomy, enrichment, and engagement. It enables them to access every part of culture; to benefit from equity in the workplace and in health care; to be strong, positive role models for younger generations; to freely make decisions based on their personal values; and so much more.

Older people will start to gain greater empowerment only as society begins to do the following:

**Recognize intersectionality.** As you already understand, no one matures simply by living longer. Nor do we get older in identical ways. Each of us is impacted by our race, gender, ethnicity, sexual orientation, socioeconomic level, marital and family status, spiritual beliefs, educational experiences, and where we live and work. Social policies and programs need to be tailored as much as possible to serve various individual needs and goals rather than administered in boilerplate and cookie-cutter ways.

**Encourage bottom-up decision-making.** To shift the focus more appropriately to the individual who is aging, it makes sense for anyone working with or serving an elder to seek that person's direct opinions and choices about the best way to define and achieve a high-quality life. The operative motto of older adults must be "Nothing for us without us," as top-down directives only encourage the stereotyping that leads to discrimination, marginalization, and neglect — three effects guaranteed to debilitate one's spirit rather than energize it.

**Establish "therapeutic communities" wherever possible.** Originally referred to regarding group therapy for treating people who are incarcerated or addicted, the term has expanded to include gatherings that promote greater understanding and healing of those who have been socially stigmatized and marginalized. Therefore, aging-based therapeutic communities would include workplaces, hospitals and long-term-care facilities, recreational settings, government programs, media portrayals, and advertising campaigns. In this case, empowering older adults would also empower society in a more holistic way, as our culture itself greatly needs rehabilitation when it comes to widespread action based on how elders are perceived and treated.

In these broader terms, the structural "iron nail" of society, fed by elders' "battery" of stockpiled energy of experiences, knowledge, skills, and sense of purpose, is transformed. It becomes a magnet, gaining a new kind of power it didn't — and couldn't — previously possess without them.

When older adults are empowered, the rest of society is, too.

# ANALOG AGING IN A DIGITAL WORLD

There was a time not too long ago when, if you stopped a stranger on the street to ask for the time, that person might reach into a pocket or purse, pull out a smart phone, and give you the answer. Unless s/he was wearing an old-fashioned wristwatch. In that case, it required only a glance at the wrist to access the answer.

In those days, I tended to feel a little smug for being a watch wearer who could relay the time so quickly without having to use my hands to dig for a device. But soon many people began wearing their smart phones like additional appendages, gazing into them, texting, playing games, checking out apps, all while walking down the street, driving, or riding public transportation. My time-telling edge was gone, since they already had the answer literally at their fingertips. But my hands were still free.

This phenomenon has led me to think about the benefits of adhering to a few analog ways of aging in the world, despite all the digital progress that's been made. Don't get me wrong: Like the vast majority of older adults, I'm not against embracing technology — a malicious and false stereotype applied to us, although we overwhelmingly continue to adapt to constant challenge and change all around us, including becoming highly proficient in using social media and the latest computer software. What I *am* advocating is that we become much more discriminating about which current trends we follow and which we reject. While digital advances are meant to save us time and/or the inconvenience of effort, it seems that as a society we keep throwing out the traditional baby with the bathwater every time a new cultural development occurs, just because it's new.

Here are three examples of analog values relating directly to aging that we should retain:

**Considering older adults as individuals rather than as memes or caricatures.** Our reliance on time- and effort-saving high technologies has trained us to look for and accept the quickest and most expedient solutions to problems, regardless of whether those solutions are effective or even realistic. Our culture has become more comfortable creating and buying into stereotypes of aging and assigning cookie-cutter characteristics to extremely diverse older adults. It takes much more time and effort to see each elder as a unique person rather than as a greedy geezer, an old codger, a spry exception, or a needy soul marking time until death. Taking shortcuts may be quite handy, but it doesn't always reflect what's real.

**Accepting aging as a natural process.** All of us are aging. The only question is whether and how we are acknowledging that fact. Rebelling against the notion that our bodies will eventually wear out leads many of us to seek out certain products and services created and foisted on us by the multi-billion-dollar anti-aging industry. Often these options resemble software upgrades that cause more problems than they solve. That's not to say that longevity research shouldn't be done. No doubt, scientists will find more ways of extending our lives, perhaps by several decades, and that's a good thing only if those extended years are filled with quality and meaning. Meanwhile, we do ourselves an injustice to perceive aging — and yes, death — as inherently evil processes to be avoided at all costs.

**Serving elders by using a person-centered rather than institutionalized approach.** For centuries before the establishment of long-term-care communities, hospitals, and medical schools, older adults were often served on a one-on-one basis by their families and friends who, if they were devoted and mindful, considered each elder's specific needs, experiences, assets, and values. Granted, standardized institutional care has enabled the sharing of information and skills that has drastically reduced infections, illnesses, and mortality, but in the process, much of an individual's autonomy and quality of life have been lost. The "one size fits all" approach that makes running a hospital, clinic, or nursing home easier instead demands that "all fit one size" and that the people being served adjust their preferences and behaviors to follow an administration's rules. This then turns the paradigm into "one size fits none." Fortunately, more physicians, nurses, and other health care professionals are being retrained to serve their patients using an individual, holistic approach.

And ironically, thanks to today's digital solutions, there's more good news on the aging front. As older adults are demanding greater personalized care, including more options to age in place, technology is being applied toward these purposes. More companies are designing hardware such as robot assistants and software such as medicine-dose alert reminders that monitor an elder's safety and health at home.

Analog needs are driving the digital world, which is how it should be for all people, regardless of age or circumstance. Take your smart watch. You can tell time (and do a whole lot more) just by gazing once again at your wrist. No digging around for a device, no clutching another appendage. Progress best serves us when it's aligned with an essential, humane, common sense purpose. Many of us are beginning to get the point. It's about time.

But there's a bit more to be said about the benefits of taking analog approaches, especially while a person is young, years before entering older adulthood. Because everyone is aging, it's smart to want to maintain a productive, quality life as long as possible and to accumulate the kind of social wisdom that comes with experience and a perspective that is honed over many years.

For these reasons, everyone should aspire to be an "elder in training" and to anticipate that time of life by developing the following analog habits early on:

**Appreciating silence.** Our world is becoming increasingly crowded with aural and visual noise: blaring music, ubiquitous advertisements, cross-conversation interruptions, and superficial and/or strident cable and social media chatter. While these modern, digital situations are designed to convey information quickly, we often forget to question the necessity, quality, and tone of that information. Moreover, it seems as though we are losing the ability and desire to be comfortable with silence, to turn off our electronic devices and simply be in our environments, to really listen to someone else before speaking and to evaluate the level of truth of what we hear and say. Besides seeking freedom from distractions when focusing on tasks, older adults often take great pleasure in savoring experiences for their intrinsic value, placing them in proper perspective. Not bad skills for elders-in-training to hone.

**Setting personal boundaries of information sharing.** One of the potential gifts of elderhood is the ability to be more discriminating, to know what is important and appropriate and what is not in any given situation. While there have always been people of all ages who lack personal boundaries and have a compulsion to tell everything about themselves or others, there's a growing ease bordering on recklessness regarding the desire to focus on self-important details and to constantly share those details with others. Selfie photos, posts, video messages, texts — and yes, sexts — are our current tools for instantaneously updating the world about our lives. But often we don't consider that the Internet is an indelible medium and that there is a potential danger in posting personal information that can get hacked or negatively affect our reputation, including the ability to get hired or keep a job. The question is: Do we gain more than we lose when we voluntarily give up our privacy and dignity to cyberspace on a global and permanent basis? It's an analog question each of us at any age should ask and answer for ourselves.

**Making relationships mean something.** Social isolation is one of the greatest health threats to both older and younger people, not just because it can deny access to physical support but also because the loneliness and lack of opportunity to contribute to society can lead to physical illness and depression. Fortunately, networking is one of the activities that the Internet has exponentially improved, and it can be an effective and empowering way to increase one's presence and knowledge and to share one's talents and services with others. That being said, it's worth our while to understand that there are levels to intimacy and commitment, that friending or being followed by thousands of people may make us popular but not more cherished, and that by spending time casting our relationship nets too widely we might begin to neglect tending to our closest relationships, those with people we value the most. Using social media to keep in touch with family and *real* friends is a smart way to age in a digital world.

These three analog habits are simple and reflect values that worked well in the past and can still apply today. Anyone, regardless of age, can embrace them.

Aging well means aging smartly, choosing the right high- or low-tech product or behavior to serve one's purpose at any given time. It also means perceiving — and honoring — older adults as humans who, having lived decades in an analog past, are seeking to make their way in a digital future.

# THE (OLD) WORLD ACCORDING TO BETTY WHITE

As the entertainment world was preparing to celebrate Betty White's 100th birthday on January 17, 2022, she passed away on New Year's Eve, to the shock of millions of fans. The sadness was palpable, and not only among older adults or even middle-aged people. The reaction among young people — many of whom weren't yet born when she starred in the television series *The Mary Tyler Moore Show* and *The Golden Girls* but likely knew her from reruns and/or her most recent TV show, *Hot in Cleveland* — was quite emotional. And surprising to me.

Her social media reach was impressive. On the day she died, she had 1.6 million followers on Twitter, 1.8 million followers on Instagram, and 4.5 million followers on Facebook. On New Year's Day, NBC re-aired a *Saturday Night Live* episode from 2010 that White hosted as the result of a Facebook campaign in which nearly 500,000 fans petitioned the show to recruit her.

As a 70-something person who sometimes questions how appreciated (or not) people like me are for having lived two or more decades beyond middle-age, I've been fascinated by the scope of White's fan base, a sizable number of whom were one-third her age.

What was her secret? Surely no one could claim that she was denying her age or devaluing herself for being of advanced years. In fact, she embraced those years every step of the way. And it clearly showed. The world according to Betty White was a place where being old should be accepted unabashedly as par for the course — in a game lasting way longer than 18 holes.

And so for me, Betty White was a fine role model of elderhood. Here's why:

**She was always herself.** A queen of quips, she had a great sense of humor, especially about her own life (to see what I mean, Google "Betty White quotes"). People may have been shocked or even entertained by an old woman's ability to swear like a sailor, revel in innuendo, or tell sexual jokes, but White didn't adopt those traits to appear young and hip. She behaved that way throughout her life. In such cases, others' stunned reactions simply revealed their own biased belief in age-appropriateness and a need to embrace "old person" stereotypes.

**She was generous and compassionate.** A strong ally of the LGBTQ+ community, White was best known for her advocacy for the rights of animals and humanitarian work on their behalf. While most of us older adults are not lucky enough to have White's financial wealth, we can still be inspired by her efforts to improve the lives of others and find our own ways to do the same.

**She continued to work at what she loved.** In the entertainment business, it's more than a challenge for women to remain employable in middle age, let alone in their 60s and beyond. And in the rest of the business world, women's "sell-by date" usually occurs a lot earlier. White always acknowledged her luck in continuing to be sought after for her talents. Nevertheless, many of us older adults, men as well as women, who need or want to continue to work can keep her in mind as an example of how skill and experience, rather than age, should determine ongoing employability.

**She insisted on staying relevant.** Whether it was on the radio, on TV, or in movies, whether she was doing a Snickers commercial for Super Bowl XLIV,[1] appearing at a WWE wrestling match,[2] or rapping with Luciana in the video "I'm Still Hot,"[3] she engaged with people of all ages. She was open to using her talents in all kinds of opportunities. That's an attitude to cultivate, no matter one's age.

Betty White's passing was more than the loss of an exceptional comedy star and humanitarian. As I see it, her greatest contribution as a cultural icon is the way in which she defined being old in the world: never apologetically, but rather, always brazenly joyous.

Today, if I could, I'd ask her advice about what we older adults should tell ourselves and others as we hopefully add decades to our lives.

"I'm me. I'm here. Deal with it!" she'd probably say, with a wide smile and twinkle in her eyes.

# THE TONY BENNETT EFFECT

I'll gladly confess it: I was always a huge fan of Tony Bennett. Not just because he was a phenomenal vocalist (even Frank Sinatra called him "the best singer in the business") or because he and I came from the same New York City neighborhood of Astoria, Queens. The truth is, I have loved his style in so many ways beyond the musical. To state it plainly: How he chose to live exemplifies three basic realities of the older adult experience: adaptability, resourcefulness, and generativity.

Bennett rocketed to pop superstar fame in the 1950s, but it didn't last long. The rise of rock music in the '60s left him struggling for gigs and record deals, despite the fact that younger artists and groups such as Elvis Presley, The Four Seasons, and The Beatles were including in their albums standards from The Great American Songbook.

A change came in the late '80s, when the renditions of the 20-something Harry Connick Jr. served as background music to the popular movie *When Harry Met Sally*. Suddenly there seemed to be a newfound appreciation for tunes by Cole Porter, Irving Berlin, and George and Ira Gershwin. Coincidentally, that's also when Bennett realized that he could adapt to the changing times and, more importantly, that he wanted to. And that's when his resourcefulness kicked in. He knew very well what his talents were and how they could be more widely shared, given a new audience. So beginning in the 1990s, he started appearing on MTV and newly "hip" late-night talk shows. And the hit albums and public appearances returned.

Yet for Bennett, then in his 60s, it wasn't enough to make a comeback. He saw the value in finding an enduring way to share his passion for great American music by creating a legacy that could serve future musicians — a later-years impulse that developmental psychologist Erik Erikson called "generativity." He began to record a series of *Duets* albums, collaborating with iconic Gen X and Millennial singers such as Lady Gaga, John Mayer, Amy Winehouse, Michael Bublé, and Queen Latifah, as well as with Latinx performers such as Maria Gadú and Vicentico.

In 2001, he founded the Frank Sinatra School of the Arts public high school, in his beloved old neighborhood. These acts of consummate humanity and generosity boosted his public appreciation even higher, and in 2017 at age 91 he was awarded the Library of Congress Gershwin Prize for Popular Song, the first non-songwriter to win the honor.

And perhaps his most poignant and generous contribution came at the end of his life, when he and his family openly shared with his fans the reality of his challenges as a person with Alzheimer's disease. Always the gentleman, he endured his final years with grace, dignity, and a quiet joy that retained his passions — for music, as well as for drawing and painting, at which he also excelled.

Adaptability, resourcefulness, and generativity are personality traits available to us at any age, but most especially in our later years, depending on how much wisdom we glean from our cumulative experiences and how much psychological effort we invest in being more self-aware and other-directed.

How can each of us better hone and apply these traits in our lives as we age? And what benefits might we reap when we do? In Tony Bennett's case, he acquired a new relevance in the music world, stretched himself as a performer as he collaborated with younger vocal stylists, and broadened the appeal of The Great American Songbook for generations to come.

Not a bad deal for a guy from Astoria, Queens. And not a bad role model for us older folks, either.

# ON THE CARE AND FEEDING OF POWER

I bought my first house when I was 51 years old. Up until that time, I was always an apartment dweller. Long after the transaction, I remained in awe of what I'd done. For along with the responsibilities of home ownership came a strange and unsettling sense of power.

I owned everything on that 0.27-acre property, including a beautiful Japanese cherry tree that blossomed in early spring. For three weeks it produced a gorgeous riot of pink flowers that later gradually floated to the ground to be replaced by new leaves. And even in that stage, their dots of color created a beautiful pointillistic scape on the lawn. I was in Impressionist heaven.

I don't know how old that tree was, but it certainly had experienced years of life before I ever arrived on its scene. Someone else had nurtured it as a sapling and pruned, watered, and protected it. And it now dawned on me that at a moment's notice and with one mindless or arrogantly selfish stroke of a chainsaw, I could cut down that wondrous growth. That sense of power humbled me. It scared me, too, not because I would ever consider ending the life of that amazing bit of nature, but rather because I was aware that any other homeowner in a similar situation might choose to do so.

Like many other Americans, I've been thinking a lot about the nature of power, about what it can do for us — and to us. I've been pondering the longstanding cultural values we Americans have cherished and the innovative social programs we have established — values and programs that are now quite vulnerable to a sinister collective will and that could be cut down or uprooted at any time, should we decide to take such actions.

And I'm humbled and scared, too, by the dangerous talk that is getting louder about privatizing Medicare, defunding Medicaid, repealing the Affordable Care Act, and cutting benefits to Social Security. Before we take a chainsaw to any policies and programs that have a track record of securing the greater good for our fellow citizens, we must stop and decide which efforts we want to maintain and which we conclude are necessary to abolish. After all, it's impossible to resurrect a sawed-off tree. At best, it can take years for new shoots to sprout from the remaining stump and reach full growth. And uprooted trees can require lots of stabilizing support and still be too shocked to thrive after any efforts to replant them.

Just because we have the power to do something drastic doesn't mean that we should use that power. Instead of handing over a program to be administered solely by for-profit companies or disenfranchising entire groups of people who desperately rely on supportive services, let's explore making moderate adjustments and improvements that won't throw our social ecosystem into chaos. In other words, let's consider any changes to these programs as efforts to prune unruly branches and fertilize slowly depleting soil rather than adopt policies that promote full-scale deforestation.

And much more importantly, let's use greater discretion and self-control as we care for and feed our own impulses to power. Let's trim back our partisan tendencies and nourish our sense of compassion. For once we destroy our will and ability to act responsibly toward our fellow Americans, it will take many years indeed to reestablish our roots as mature, competent citizens.

We must remain conscientious stewards as we tend the landscape of our society. We have no other choice, if we are to survive — let alone flourish — as a nation.

# HOW SHOULD WE CELEBRATE OLDER AMERICANS MONTH?

May is Older Americans Month.

Most people don't know that. In fact, the ones who do are more likely to work for a company or organization that provides aging goods or services or promotes public policy affecting older adults.

"Truthfully, I don't pay attention to Older Americans Month," says New York Times columnist Paula Span. "When you write a column called *The New Old Age* [as I do], every month is elders month. Besides, this one seems to exist mostly for public relations people pushing various products and requests for coverage. I doubt one person in 100 could even tell you which month is Older Americans Month or would know that it exists."[4] The way American society designates a National Day, Week, or Month is an arbitrary process — sometimes it's done by the government,[5] but as Span points out, it's usually established by a PR or advertising campaign as a tool for fundraising, putting on a conference, or selling products and/or services.

The commemorations cover a spectrum from the lighthearted to the lofty. In May alone, there's National Lumpy Rug Day, National Etiquette Week, and National Asparagus Month. On the other hand, there's also National Foster Care Day, Teacher Appreciation Week, and Asian American and Pacific Islander Heritage Month.

No matter the level of significance, all of these celebrations have one thing in common: They are time limited. As a result, our collective attention to any of these events (if we think about them at all) is tentative and temporary as we move on to another one. It's like taking out the good china from the hutch cabinet to set the table for an annual celebratory meal. The dinnerware, never used the rest of the year, adds to the aura of the special occasion. Afterward, not being considered proper or practical for everyday use, the set is immediately stored away and easily forgotten once the event is over.

And that's a problem when the commemoration concerns a population that experiences discrimination. Whether it's Black History Month (February), Women's History Month (March), LGBTQ Pride Month (June), National Hispanic Heritage Month (mid-September to mid-October), National Disability Employment Awareness Month (October), or National Native American Heritage Month (November), each gesture of symbolic honor is instead a social indictment of the ways in which we categorize and marginalize that specific group.

Unfortunately, that is often how such national celebrations work. And because of this, they don't fulfill a potentially greater social goal — one that, if celebrated in the right way, should eventually eliminate their very existence.

In the case of Older Americans Month, the designation is a trivial distinction that inadvertently sends the message "If old people are really valuable — and valued — we wouldn't have to set aside 31 consecutive days each year to remind ourselves that this is true."

In addition, as a group, older adults are unique. "It's puzzling that we feel the need to celebrate older Americans, as if they are somehow peculiar and different from the rest of us," says Paul Irving, senior advisor at the Milken Institute Center for the Future of Aging. "In fact, all of us are older or will be older. Unlike gender, race, sexuality, religion, or political belief, growing old is common ground, something uniting, not differentiating."[6]

Should we then stop celebrating Older Americans Month and similar commemorations?

Wendl Kornfeld, founder of Community as Family educational groups and an activist for solo agers, strongly believes that they serve a social purpose. "There could well be reasoned opposition to stopping specially designated months," she explains. "For example, parents and teachers may feel that Black History Month is essential to educating children about Black history, providing strong role models, inspiring emulation, and actively working toward equality in every aspect of American life."[7]

In the case of older adults, Kornfeld suggests that "older adults (who often feel invisible) may think their designated month brings attention to their continuing positive contributions to society, as well as identifying what still must be done to adequately serve this demographic's particular needs.… We all have to be in the fabric of American life."[8]

If older adults are threads in the fabric of American life, they are merely loosely woven into it, mainly due to the myopic perception that people in later life are a needy population in ongoing, inevitable decline and no longer productive in the same ways younger and middle-aged people are. If and when elders are recognized at all, it is usually regarding how much of an economic burden they place on younger generations and how to forestall it.

Case in point: The American Jobs Plan[9] of the 2021 Biden Administration "to put $400 billion toward expanding access to quality, affordable home- or community-based care for aging relatives and people with disabilities" was meant to improve, in a passive way, the quality of life of people as they age without much consideration for how they also could and should engage with their communities by actively participating in them.

Fortunately, President Biden's "A Proclamation on Older Americans Month, 2021"[10] recognized that during the pandemic "older Americans have stepped up to support their families, friends, and neighbors. They are among our essential workers, volunteers, and donors, bolstering their communities and inspiring others to do the same." The President was "committed to ensuring older adults are central in our country's recovery efforts."

While the goals of the proclamation are honorable, the document doesn't acknowledge the widespread fear of aging and resulting prejudice and discrimination against old people that necessitate calling Americans' attention to ageism in the first place. Such omissions can cause what Kornfeld calls a "Don't take my month away from me"[11] reaction among members of a group who struggle against social marginalization.

We need to rethink what these commemorations are really about. Social justice advocates should use these days, weeks, and months to hold "reverse" public relations campaigns that call for a future in which these celebrations will no longer be necessary. That will happen only when these groups' needs, values, and skills become integral to everyone else's lives.

"It's hard to 'celebrate' Older Americans Month in any traditional way when the pandemic exposed how rampant ageism is," says Janine Vanderburg, senior strategist and master trainer for the Changing the Narrative campaign. "We're using the opportunity to coalesce a group of advocates to amplify our collective voices on social media. Our goal? To increase awareness of ageism and the potential contributions of older adults to communities and workplaces…and to advocate for effective solutions, including stronger age-discrimination laws, and the inclusion of older adults in stimulus-funding workforce development programs."[12]

If a national commemorative celebration of a particular subpopulation is to mean anything at all, it must call attention to the ways in which we regularly overlook the members of that group and inspire us to work harder at fully engaging with them. It's time to put away the good china once and for all and instead give all people, including older adults, a seat at the daily table.

"Instead of age," asserts Irving, "let's celebrate our diversity, roles and responsibilities, challenges and accomplishments. Well-intentioned pats on the back for nothing more than living long send the wrong message. It's not about the number of years we live, but what we do with them."[13]

In other words, May is Older Americans *Month*…but it needn't be.

# SEVEN WAYS ELDERS CAN SAVE THE WORLD

For his book *What Are Old People For?* geriatrician Bill Thomas chose the subtitle "How Elders Will Save the World." To some, this phrase might appear overly romantic and dramatic, for aren't we all, no matter our age, responsible for improving the quality of life on our planet in general and in our societies in particular?

But I'm with Thomas on this claim, because I believe that older adults are our largest untapped human resource, possessing a huge trove of varied experiences and honed skills cultivated over a lifetime as only elders have done. *Any* elder, regardless of income, physical and/or cognitive ability, level of education, or geographic home can make a productive difference in the way all of us function as a culture. The only thing holding us back is the acceptance of this premise, by ourselves as individuals and by society as a whole. We elders *can* save our societies and the world…but only if we accept the challenge and everyone else cooperates in creating opportunities to do so.

But how, exactly, can this come to pass?

One of the most inspirational paradigms that answers this question came from Maggie Kuhn, founder of the Gray Panthers, a multigenerational organization established in the 1970s whose mission has been to "work for social and economic justice and peace for all people."[14] She believed that there are five major roles older adults can play in society: mentors, mediators, monitors, mobilizers, and motivators. [15]

Let's consider each of these five roles.

**Mentors**. Of the five roles, this may be the one most often associated with elder wisdom. After all, it's easy for us to imagine that the older a person gets, the more s/he has experienced and has learned from such experience. We may have mental images of elders coaching youngsters in reading, tutoring them in math, helping them build birdhouses, or teaching them to cook. But do we, perhaps, define mentorship too narrowly by limiting such interactions to those between leisured retirees and children? What about working elders taking new, younger employees under their wings? Or established entrepreneurs advising young startup businesses? Or Korean and Vietnam War veterans counseling and supporting veterans of our latest wars? Think how much accumulated knowledge and wisdom in all fields might be shared if we encouraged all older adults, especially those who are lonely and/or isolated, to share what they know with at least one other person.

**Mediators.** Any of us who have experienced a calm grandparent stepping in to ease flaring tempers during a parent-child argument can appreciate the compassionate understanding and affirmation that an elder can bring to the issues of both parties. With specific training, elders can take advantage of their unique, multiperspective problem-solving skills in order to mediate conflicts within more formal settings, such as neighborhoods, schools, workplaces, houses of worship, and organizations.

**Monitors.** This is an ideal role for many older adults, one that engages them socially and/or politically, especially if they have strong concerns about how their neighborhoods are being served and their tax money is being spent. But monitoring can include more than attending public meetings of a city council or county commission or reviewing pending state and congressional legislation. Elders can monitor polling places to make sure that voter registrations and elections are administered fairly. They can also serve on nonprofit and corporate boards of directors to ensure that organizations are adhering to their missions and operating within their budgets. This ongoing scrutiny by older adults can preserve the integrity of all social operations on all levels.

**Mobilizers**. The next time you see a video of a public demonstration or campaign rally, check out the ages of the people who are there. The chances are likely that you will see a healthy share of older adults participating in the action. Many elders and empty nesters find that they have more free time to enlist in meaningful causes in ways they might not have been able to do before. But free time isn't all they have at their disposal. Their past experiences managing obligations of family, jobs, and finances can serve them as efficient organizers and recruiters — just the kind of folks you would want to have on your team. Smart organizations and fundraisers know the value of looking to older volunteers for their engagement and support.

**Motivators**. Because older adults have lived longer and have had more experiences, they have had the opportunity to evolve into people who can see the bigger picture of what it means to be human, a spiritual perspective that appreciates the interconnectedness and interdependence of all generations. They tend to seek a greater purpose in life, one involving the creation of a personal legacy based on giving back to society. They can help younger generations by encouraging them to act compassionately, help others in need, and create policies and programs that serve all members of their communities. They can be the gadflies that urge leaders to make course corrections when they lose track of their basic obligation to serve the greater good.

These are Kuhn's five roles through which elders can save society, as workers or as volunteers. They are brilliant options. Think about it: Just about every older adult can assume at least one of them.

But what about elders who have extreme dementia or are otherwise greatly physically challenged? Are they to be written off as unable to contribute to changing our culture? Is there no role that they can play?

Actually, I believe that there are two more roles, which have the potential to be the most effective of all: Older adults can be **Models** and

**Mirrors** of aging for the rest of us to consider when we think about how to improve ways of perceiving and serving older adults. They can remind us of their enduring personhood and to treat it with respect and reverence. They can show us that a life, during any stage in which it is lived, has intrinsic value. And they can hold up a mirror to our own fears about aging, calling us to revise our prejudices and to act with diligence and speed to improve the quality of life of those who are in their later years.

Every single elder can save the world. This ideal is more than romantic and dramatic. It's up to all of us to turn it into a fact.

# THE CASE FOR GERIATRICIANS

Imagine that you have recently bought a vintage house, built in the early 1940s. A distinguished residence filled with original architectural elements, the home was never renovated but kept in its original condition. And while the structure continues to retain its charm, it requires updating of its plumbing, electrical wiring, and roof. Of course, you want to make these renovations with care in order to maintain the character and integrity of the dwelling. So which contractor will you hire to do the work: someone who creates and assembles prefabricated units, a builder of commercial structures, or a specialist in historic homes?

Our bodies are our most essential "homes." However, most of us know so little about the aging body that we assume an older one is just like a middle-aged one…only existing much longer. And for many elders who are in absolute tiptop condition, such a comparison may appear to be quite valid. But in general, an 80-year-old is unlikely to be as muscular, flexible, and free of chronic disease as a 40-year-old.

And just as we don't assume that children are merely physically and cognitively small adults (hence the need for pediatricians), we should likewise have a different understanding of the specific requirements of older bodies. More importantly, we must value older people enough to make sure that there are plenty of well-trained physicians, known as geriatricians, who can give them the best personalized care possible.

But the unfortunate reality is that the U.S. has a serious shortage of geriatricians. One assessment from March 2023 estimated that a total of 7,300 physicians — fewer than 1% of all doctors — were board certified in geriatrics.[16] Compare this with a May 2022 U.S. Bureau of Labor Statistics report citing the employment of 33,430 pediatricians.[17] Given the fact that in 2022 there were about 25% more children under the age of 18[18] than adults 65 and older,[19] our current health care system should have more than 25,000 geriatricians to meet an equivalent need. In addition to this total, to keep pace with the growing older population, we'll need at least 5,000 more by 2030.[20]

In a keynote address in mid-March 2023, Age Wave CEO Ken Dychtwald bemoaned the dire state of U.S. geriatric education. "As of last week," he said, "…we have 183 medical schools in America, only 11 full departments of geriatrics. Like, *excuse me*?"[21]

Why the huge discrepancy between the supply and the demand? Geriatrician Michael Wasserman, chair of the Public Policy Committee of the California Association of Long Term Care Medicine, puts it succinctly: "There are a few primary reasons. First, lack of geriatric medicine training. Hence, few role models. Second, poor reimbursement. Geriatrics is the lowest paid specialty. Third, most experiences with older adults occur in hospitals, where patients are generally at their worst. There is a need for positive primary care experiences."[22]

Let's consider these reasons one by one.

**Lack of geriatric training.** To what kind of specialized training is Wasserman referring? "Classic internal medicine is about diagnosis, treatment and cure," he says. "Geriatric medicine is about function and quality of life."[23]

To be sure, simultaneously addressing function and quality of life can be a challenging endeavor, nevertheless it's crucial to the treatment of older people. In a 2023 article published by the American Society on Aging, geriatric physician assistant Steven D. Johnson explained his work in the context of the relationship he has with his patients: "The care of the older adult tasks us with the responsibility to consider all the physical, medical, emotional and social relationships and offers us the opportunity to transcend the clinician/patient roles and find in that relationship our shared humanity."[24]

The American Geriatrics Society adds another dimension:

In getting to know older adults and caregivers in a more personal way, geriatrics healthcare professionals learn about the connections between overall well-being and what individuals ultimately want and need from their own care. Geriatrics bridges an important connection between clinical best practices and the recognition that an older person may have unique care preferences and expectations that warrant adjusting individual plans.[25]

The dearth of geriatric training didn't suddenly appear on the national scene. It's always existed. However, with the continuous growth of the older population, it's become more obvious and urgent. In 2019, a bill known as The Geriatrics Workforce Improvement Act, authorizing funds to train more geriatricians, was introduced in the U.S. Senate but was never voted on and died in 2020.[26] Tragically, the government's response to this state of urgency has been to do nothing.

**Poor reimbursement.** Because of its holistic approach to the diagnosis and treatment of older patients who often present with multiple complex chronic conditions, the very nature of geriatric care requires longer and more involved office visits[27] than the average 15 to 20 minutes most internists spend with younger adult patients. One 2021 analysis puts the dilemma succinctly:

A major driver of persistently low physician recruitment into geriatrics is compensation. In addition to incremental debt associated with geriatric fellowship training, a board-certified geriatrician can expect to make US$20,000 yr less than an internist largely because all geriatric patients are on Medicare, which pays less than the commercial insurance common in a general internist's practice.[28]

Being one of the lowest-paid medical specialties isn't exactly the kind of incentive that would attract health care practitioners to the field of geriatrics.

**Lack of broader interaction with older patients.** If medical school students encounter patients of advanced age primarily in hospital settings under highly stressful, acute circumstances, it's unlikely that they will be inspired to specialize in geriatrics. While their hospitalized patients of all ages experience stress, those med students may assume that there is little upside in treating a subpopulation that doesn't have much longer to live and therefore it's futile to try.

Ironically, such negative assumptions keep potential practitioners from discovering the psychological and professional rewards of working with older adults that make geriatrics one of the most personally satisfying medical specialties. Or, as the American Geriatrics Society explains:

In several studies, geriatrics ranks among the most satisfying health professions. In fact, one study reported that geriatricians had the highest job satisfaction of physicians practicing in any subspecialty. Geriatrics health care professionals cite their encounters with inspirational older adults, the deep and meaningful relationships they develop, and the typically steady work hours as significant factors adding to their job satisfaction.[29]

Wasserman would agree. "I've always loved being around older adults and was very close to my grandparents," he says. "My greatest satisfaction has always been getting to know my patients. Older adults appreciate a clinician who hears their concerns and is honest in focusing on their function and quality of life."[30]

There may be an even deeper reason why geriatricians are in short supply. Maybe, just maybe, it's because our society doesn't value old people enough. As we discovered during the COVID pandemic, widespread cultural ageism based on the fear and dread of getting old and dying leads many of us to believe that elders are less "productive" in midlife economic terms and thus pose a great financial burden on the health care system.

What we fail to recognize is the immense social contribution of older adults to maintaining economic and emotional stability in their families, purchasing consumer products and services, volunteering at nonprofits, and safeguarding businesses' institutional knowledge and practices.

Older adults, like people of all other ages, deserve the best health care, one that is tailored to their needs and desires for a quality life. And just like vintage buildings, their bodies and minds house treasures worthy of being cherished and protected.

Who's better than a most highly trained specialist to handle the job?

# ACCESSIBILITY FOR ALL

In the 1970s as a college English major, I took several education courses under the assumption that I would someday teach at the high school or university level. When it was time for my student-teaching experience, I was assigned to a local elementary school to assist a first-grade teacher who thought I could be best used to tutor one of her underperforming students with "a behavior problem" who needed extra help with his studies.

His name was Omar, the child of Egyptian immigrants. A small boy of slight build and unbounded energy, he sat in the last row of the class, put there because he was constantly restless, getting up out of his seat, talking with the kids around him and looking at their papers. The teacher thought he'd be less distracting to most of his classmates if he weren't in their line of sight.

For my first day, I sat behind Omar and observed his squirrely behavior. Soon the teacher allowed me to take him each day to the empty school cafeteria to work with him in a one-on-one session before lunchtime. She left it up to me to determine how I'd address his needs.

I found Omar to be an exceptionally bright boy. He asked me a lot of good questions as we worked on his ability to add numbers and to decipher letters and form them into words. And here's where I got my clue about how to help him. Because his hands were always fidgeting as he spoke, I thought it might help him to focus if I gave him something to hold while he was reading the picture book we chose together.

The next day I brought in a bundle of pipe cleaners and put one in his hands. The strategy worked. Bending and unbending the pipe cleaner, he immediately calmed down and moved his face closer to the page.

During reading, when he got stuck on a particular letter, I identified it and modeled its phonetic sound. Then I asked him to use the pipe cleaner to form its shape, to then say its name, and reproduce its sound. Soon we went through the entire alphabet together, forming all the letters' shapes and voicing their sounds. We did the same thing with numerals from 1 to 9. He was delighted at his accomplishment.

Before long we were laying out those pipe cleaner letters and numerals on the cafeteria table to make entire words and create simple math problems. Day after day, Omar continued to make progress. He was no longer squirming. But I did notice that he continued to put his face unusually close to whatever page he was looking at.

I relayed my observation to his teacher and asked if Omar was ever tested for eye problems. She didn't know and asked his parents. They told her that Omar had never been seen by an eye doctor and promptly had him examined. It turned out that the boy wasn't a hyperactive child with behavior problems after all but instead had severe astigmatism, which kept him from seeing both the blackboard and what was right in front of him. That was why he was constantly moving around, asking his classmates what they were copying from the board and writing down. Omar was fitted with glasses and moved to the front of the class to give him greater accessibility to the board — and to his teacher. And he thrived.

Omar's story is one we all share because it reflects our need for accessibility, no matter our age or physical condition. At every stage of life from birth onward, we continually approach doorways to new experiences and opportunities and must be able to open those portals to have access to what is on the other side.

Some issues of access are simple and easily solvable, such as placing several thick telephone books (remember those?) on a dining room chair so a small 1950s me could reach my plate of food. Even today, a still short, much older me benefits from setting my otherwise dangling feet on the occasional, welcomed footrest attached to a bus or train seat in front of me.

But most accessibility issues — especially for older adults — are far more complex, serious, and challenging to resolve because, unlike those involving children, they address the needs of people who would otherwise be fully autonomous and responsible for their actions were it not for the barriers that society places in their way. These issues fall under three categories: products/services, opportunities, and relationships. Let's consider each one:

Access to **products and services** is usually determined by the physical limitations we may develop as we age. Our sight, hearing, balance, endurance, or flexibility may become more impaired. These pose difficulties when some of us try to do such things as read small print, faint-typeface online screen texts, and subtitles that flash by quickly on TVs and videos; listen to unclear public address systems or try to have conversations in noisy restaurants; wend our way on unevenly paved sidewalks and cross wide streets within 10 seconds before the WALK signs change; and trek for long distances in places that have no public benches on which to rest. Furthermore, some of us older adults are challenged within our own homes when bottle tops, milk carton flaps, and round doorknobs become harder to manipulate by arthritic hands, and stairs and bathtubs get harder to climb or climb over.

As for **opportunities**, access to them is blocked for us when our résumés are passed over, we can't get job interviews, and we're pressured to retire from the workplace, even though we still have ideas and skills to share; we're ignored as potential subjects in medical clinical trials as biological outliers and denied costly treatments for our conditions because of low Medicare reimbursement rates; we're considered too old and therefore unappealing to play leading roles in movies and TV series and we are ignored in marketing campaigns promoting high-tech products, the assumption being that we are reluctant or unable to use them. The list goes on.

But perhaps the most insidious form of inaccessibility arises when we are blocked from having **relationships** that affirm our dignity as people living into our later years. I'm talking about the isolation that results from the denial of access to those products/services (the things we want and need) and opportunities (the things we want/need to do).

For example, it happens when well-meaning but compassionately ageist (and simultaneously ableist) staff of long-term-care communities prevent memory-care and/or assisted living residents from mingling with independent living residents in the dining room and during events. Access to relationships is also denied when others assume that older adults have little interest or competence in participating in activities that can benefit others.

A case in point: I once had an appointment with the activities director of an independent living community to discuss presenting educational programs for the residents. Although I arrived on time, the woman was harried and stressed, being on a deadline to put together the monthly community newsletter, which involved writing brief articles, including profiles of the newest residents, as well as taking photos of some of the events for that month.

I wondered why she was doing all of this alone, and moreover, why the residents themselves weren't involved in creating the newsletter. Surely, I said to her, there must be folks who enjoy writing who could produce those articles and resident profiles, as well as someone who might enjoy being the community's photographer. What she said next absolutely stunned me:

"I never thought of that. Come to think of it, two of our residents are former English teachers, and a retired Life magazine photographer lives here, too!"

Granted, those people may have had no desire to work on the news-letter, but not even offering them the chance for such involvement and interaction is a perfect example of the denial of access.

Thinking too narrowly and in stereotypical ways about older adults, seeing us as homogenous members of an amorphous group instead of perceiving us as individuals and addressing our situations on a case-by-case basis, are acts akin to assuming that young Omar had a behavior problem (why else would he have been so hyperactive and disruptive?) instead of looking deeper.

It's only by imagining and designing for the needs and desires of individuals *as individuals* and incorporating as many of those options as possible that true universal accessibility is accomplished. WALK signs that allow enough time for elders to cross streets also allow enough time for a parent pushing a baby stroller while holding the hand of a young child; a young, injured athlete using crutches; and two teachers leading a class of young elementary students to get to the other side. Building doors that have latch handles instead of round knobs, making it easier for arthritic hands to grasp, also allow people carrying two full bags of groceries to use their elbow to gain entry.

Accessibility involves more than universal design for all. It involves universal *acceptance of all*.

The paradox it presents is something we should all contemplate. To truly empower us as we age, we need to be able to open whatever doors to new experiences we encounter. By providing us older adults with greater access to society, *society gets greater access to us* — our talents, skills, ideas, perceptions, experience, and acquired wisdom.

What culture would want to close its portals to all of that?

# HOW SHOULD WE CHANGE AGING?

The time around each New Year's Day is one during which we are pressured culturally to make a fresh start in our lives. It's an annual rite that supports the adage "Mighty oaks from little acorns grow."

Right off, I'll admit that I'm terrible at keeping New Year's resolutions, probably because they are made on January 1. Any acorns I've planted on that day have never turned into saplings, let alone trees. I'm far more likely to commit to goals when I make them at any time of the year and for reasons inspired by immediate needs and introspection rather than prodded by social convention.

However, years ago I established for myself a set of four resolutions that I have managed to keep on a regular (if not exactly daily) basis. I promised myself to try, as often as possible, to 1) create something, 2) maintain something, 3) repair something, and 4) let go of something.

"Creating" can mean just about anything: writing a letter to a friend, reading a certain book for the first time, following a new recipe — you get the gist.

"Maintaining" is preserving the value or integrity of something, such as when attending regular meetings of a group, changing the oil and filter on a car, or following an exercise routine.

"Repairing" is easiest to identify; something is broken, and we fix it, such as gluing together the vase that accidentally fell from the table or apologizing to a friend for having said something thoughtless or judgmental.

"Letting go" can be the toughest resolution to keep, because we get attached to things, relationships, beliefs, and even beliefs and emotions. Fortunately, many of us have experienced the physical value and mental relief of occasionally cleaning out the closets of our homes, or minds.

By now you may have realized that these categories overlap. For example, by maintaining an exercise routine, you also might be repairing your body in some way (*e.g.,* losing weight or rehabilitating a joint). By creating a letter to a friend, you help to maintain that relationship. And discovering (creating) or revising (repairing) options for your life can help you in letting go of older ones that no longer work for you.

All of these are personal, individual commitments. But what if we applied these four types of resolutions to the way our society views aging and interacts with older adults? As we're all well aware, aging is usually viewed as something to dread and avoid as long as possible. However, there are many ways we can resolve to change aging on both personal and societal levels by applying my four resolutions:

**Repair something.** There's so much that needs repairing regarding how we treat elders in our culture, but for starters, I'd suggest that we fix the notion that older adults can't do things as well as younger people. We need to develop a more nuanced view of aging that recognizes some of the gradual physical and cognitive losses that can occur with age and then balance them with a newer and stronger appreciation of the *gains* that aging brings — you know, those greater multiperspective problem-solving skills and that wisdom gleaned from accumulated knowledge and experience. Personally, I resolve to help in this repair process by kindly calling out anyone who makes an ageist joke or comment in my presence and explaining some of those gains.

**Maintain something.** We need to keep supporting organizations and individuals dedicated to the pro-aging movement. If we look around diligently, we'll find many people and groups to support. As an individual, I resolve to more actively share with others any supportive links or valuable articles that I find.

**Let go of something.** No contest here: As a culture, we need to let go of our obsession with youth. Yes, young people are wonderful and do wonderful things. But the same can and should be said about older adults. And yes, "new and improved" products and services can benefit our lives, but so can a wiser use of traditional products and services that have a track record of success. And, please, can we get rid of our disdain for wrinkles and gray hair? That emotion reflects the greater fear of being classified as a member of a group whose "club" society as a whole has deemed uncool. Appreciation of youth and old age needn't be an either-or proposition. Both can be honored for their proper places in the lifespan. Personally, I resolve to connect more directly and more often with younger people so that I might help dispel some of their dread of old age, and might learn something new about them and myself in the process.

I'm hopeful that sticking to such resolutions will result in **creating something**: a more humane society that reaps the benefits provided by elders' unique abilities and perspectives.

Mighty revolutions from little resolutions grow. So I ask you: How should we change aging right now, before the next New Year? What should we create, maintain, repair, and let go of?

And what might *you* do to help achieve these goals?

# Aging Right-Side Up

The real voyage of discovery…consists not in seeking new landscapes but in having new eyes.

—Marcel Proust

**WHEN INTRODUCING *AGING SIDEWAYS*,** I explained that this book was about perception and direction and used Betty Edwards' innovative Upside-Down Drawing exercise as an analogy for the process of developing "new eyes" to view the landscape of aging in more positive, realistic ways. Throughout these chapters, I provided messages and metaphors that hopefully challenged some myths and stereotypical ideas you had about getting older, pleasantly nudging your thoughts "sideways" enough to shift your vision in meaningful ways.

It's now time to put that new pro-aging perception into action to move in a new direction for the rest of your life — in other words, to age "right-side up."

Moving in a right-side-up direction means exercising a set of cognitive muscles you may not even know you possess. It can feel awkward at first and may result in some sore moments, but if you stick with it, I'm confident that you'll never want to go back to former assumptions and behaviors that may have been limiting your ability to grow into a more proactive, dignified, fulfilling elderhood.

The question is: How to do it?

Remember those four effective "sideways" strategic skills I listed in the Introduction? They are actions you can take when coming to terms with your own aging process as well as with others' reactions to you. I've purposely demonstrated each one through the approaches I used in more than a few essays throughout this book.

Here are just a few examples (and the essays that illustrate them):

*Sideways Skill #1: Sidestepping a deeply embedded obstacle you're approaching rather than retreating from it or futilely trying to remove it.*

One of the biggest obstacles to empowered aging is to fear or deny the likelihood of some form of decline in physical or cognitive health. By now, however, you've been exposed to more accurate depictions of aging that also include the growth of some important mental abilities and the long-term development of social and professional skills.

Therefore, you should feel free to reject the zero-sum myth of one-sided loss and embrace ways in which you can put those abilities and skills to greater use ("What's Your 'And'?"). You can minimize the focus on your chronological age ("On Asking 'the Question'") and instead choose to be a catalyst for personal and social change ("Seven Ways Elders Can Save the World").

*Sideways Skill #2: Redefining a term or concept in a way that makes its meaning more accurate or more relevant to you.*

When you believe that an established image or stereotype relating to age or aging is false or no longer advantageous to use, it can be liberating to reject it and substitute one that makes more sense to you because it reflects your experience or understanding.

In my case, I have chosen to depict the massive population of older adults as a pent-up "reservoir" of knowledge and talent waiting to be released into society rather than as a huge, destructive wave ("Turning the Tide on the 'Silver Tsunami'"). I also believe that aging requires the development of spirits of steel rather than of a malleable, delicate, precious metal ("Where Are the Golden Years?"). I also propose considering us elders as Master Climbers continually striving to achieve goals that we define for ourselves ("Let's Get Over Being 'Over the Hill'") as well as appreciating that we live in a varied social ecosystem inhabited by people of all ages ("A Forest of Generations").

*Sideways Skill #3: Looking peripherally as you move forward rather than only straight ahead or in the rearview mirror.*

This skill involves the willingness and imagination to think "outside the box" and find other ways to perceive and act. For example, I consider old people as wild, unwanted plants often overlooked or outright rejected by society but having a special inherent value ("On the Value of Weeds"). I also assert that aging requires us to wear the best metaphorical "shoes" that will enable us to move forward in fulfilling ways ("The Aging Equivalent of High Heels").

*Sideways Skill #4: Being open to the unexpected rather than controlling what you encounter in the moment.*

There is a freedom in being flexible and resilient when encountering the challenges of older age. For example, you can see aging as an enemy, stranger, neighbor, or friend; the choice is up to you ("What's Your Relationship with Aging?"). You can decide that admitting to — and maybe even declaring that — reaching elderhood is a good thing ("Old

Person — No Longer in Training"). And you can be open to learning from others as they talk about their experiences ("Old Stories, New Lives").

I realize that having quirky takes like mine on all kinds of aging issues may not be your style. That's fine. What's important for changing your perspective about aging is to ask right-side-up questions whenever you encounter any age-related belief, statement, or behavior that makes you uncomfortable, offends you, limits your potential, diminishes your autonomy, or denies your identity. And this also applies to when it happens to others around you, no matter their age. I'm talking about questions like these:

- Where/When have I seen this happen before?
- Who benefits from this negative situation/condition?
- Does what I'm witnessing/experiencing have to do with age, or is it about something else?
- Why is this belief/behavior considered acceptable?
- What if this situation/condition didn't exist?
- What can I/others do to manage/change this situation/condition?

The challenge to aging right-side up is for you to encourage any of these questions and their answers to come into your mind automatically, thus becoming a natural reflex. As you are more able to do this and to act on the answers that you get, you'll be better able to help others see the landscape of aging with "new eyes" and develop a perspective that's less ageist and more pro-aging.

That's the road I envision all of us traveling together from now on. There's a lot of work we need to do to change the minds of many others about what it means to grow older. As you share with others some of the same ideas I've shared with you, I hope you'll join me in inspiring those around you to briefly step off the habitual path of belief they've been on and instead look for signposts showing other, more self-affirming directions in which to go.

It begins with nudging their thinking so that it comes from a different perspective.

Sideways.

# Notes

## Introduction: Aging Sideways

1   Allen, Julie Ober; Solway, Erica; Kirch, Matthias; *et al.* "Experiences of
Everyday Ageism and the Health of Older US Adults," *JAMA Network Open*
(2022), 5(6): e2217240.

2   Organisation for Economic Co-operation and Development. "Life
Expectancy at 65," (2021). https://data.oecd.org/healthstat/life-
expectancy-at-65.htm

3   Vespa, Jonathan; Medina, Lauren; and Armstrong, David M. "Demographic
Turning Points for the United States: Population Projections for 2020
to 2060," U.S. Census Bureau P25-1144 (Issued March 2018, Revised
February 2020). https://www.census.gov/content/dam/Census/library/
publications/2020/demo/p25-1144.pdf

4   *Ibid.* https://www.cnbc.com/2018/03/14/retirees-will-outnumber-kids-for-
the-first-time-in-us-history-report.html

5   *Ibid.*

6   Stamford, Bryant. "The Fastest Growing Group Is People over 85. It's
Possible to Live Long and Well, but How?" *Currier Journal,* May 26, 2022.
https://www.courier-journal.com/story/life/wellness/health/2022/05/26/
fastest-growing-age-group-people-over-85-live-long-well/7389772001/

7    Creamer, John; Shrider, Emily A.; Burns, Kalee; and Chen, Frances. "Poverty in the United States: 2021," Report P60-277. (United States Census Bureau, September 13, 2022): Table A-1: "People in Poverty by Selected Characteristics: 2020 and 2021." https://www.census.gov/library/publications/2022/demo/p60-277.html

8    Administration for Community Living. "2020 Profile of African Americans Age 65 and Older," (no date) p. 4. https://acl.gov/sites/default/files/Profile%20of%20OA/AAProfileReport2021.pdf

9    Administration for Community Living. "2020 Profile of Older Americans," (May 2021) p. 13. https://acl.gov/sites/default/files/aging%20and%20Disability%20In%20America/2020Profileolderamericans.final_.pdf

10    *Ibid.*, p. 7; HealthinAging.org. "Nursing Homes." https://www.healthinaging.org/age-friendly-healthcare-you/care-settings/nursing-homes

11    Dimock, Michael. "Defining Generations: Where Millennials End and Generation Z Begins," Pew Research Center, January 17, 2019. https://www.pewresearch.org/fact-tank/2019/01/17/where-millennials-end-and-generation-z-begins/

12    Edwards, Betty. *Drawing on the Right Side of the Brain: A Course in Enhancing Creativity and Artistic Confidence* (New York: Tarcher/Perigree, 2012), p. 52.

## Chapter 2: What's Age Got to Do with It?

1    Chopik, W.J.; Bremner, R.H.; Johnson, D.J.; and Giasson, H.L. (2018). "Age Differences in Age Perceptions and Developmental Transitions," *Frontiers in Psychology, Vol. 9 Article 67, p. 8.*

2    Schmauck-Medina, T.; Molière, A.; Lautrup, S.; Zhang, J.; et al. "New Hallmarks of Ageing: A 2022 Copenhagen Ageing Meeting Summary." *Aging* (Albany NY). 2022 Aug 29;14(16):6829–6839.

3    Population Reference Bureau. *Fact Sheet: U.S. Dementia Trends* (Washington D.C., 2021). https://www.prb.org/resources/fact-sheet-u-s-dementia-trends/

4    The Lancet Commission. *Dementia Prevention, Intervention, and Care: 2020 Report of the Lancet Commission.* https://www.thelancet.com/article/S0140-6736(20)30367-6/fulltext

5    Applewhite, Ashton. *This Chair Rocks: A Manifesto Against Ageism*. (New York: Celadon Books, 2016), p. 8.

6    AARP (2022). "Age Is Just a Number When It Comes to Technology," *AARP 2022 Tech Trends Fact Sheet*. https://www.aarp.org/content/dam/aarp/research/surveys_statistics/technology/2022/2022-technology-trends-older-americans-tech-usage-age-factsheet.doi.10.26419-2Fres.00493.014.pdf

7    Schachter-Shalomi, Zalman and Miller, Ronald S. *From Age-ing to Sage-ing: A Revolutionary Approach to Growing Older* (New York: Grand Central Publishing: 2014), p. 25.

8    *Ibid*, pp. 5–6.

9    *Ibid*, p. 73.

10   *Ibid*.

11   *Ibid*., Chapter 4, pp. 81–106.

12   *Ibid*., pp. 93–105.

13   Gendron, Tracey. *Ageism Unmasked: Exploring Age Bias and How to End It* (Lebanon, New Hampshire: Steerforth Press, 2022), p. 5.

14   WFAE-90.7. Charlotte and the Aging Boom: Are We Ready?" *Charlotte Talks with Mike Collins*, July 8, 2015. https://www.wfae.org/show/charlotte-talks-with-mike-collins/2015-07-08/charlotte-and-the-aging-boom-are-we-ready

15   Jeste, Dilip V.; Depp, Colin A.; and Vahia, Ipsit V. "Successful Cognitive and Emotional Aging," *World Psychiatry*. 2010 Jun; 9(2): p. 78.

16   Mcleod, Saul. "Erik Erikson's 8 Stages of Psychosocial Development," *Simply Psychology*. Updated on January 25, 2024. https://www.simplypsychology.org/Erik-Erikson.html

## Chapter 3: Seeing with Fresh Eyes

1    Crossan, John Dominic. *A Long Way from Tipperary: What a Former Irish Monk Discovered in His Search for the Truth* (New York: HarperOne, 2000), p. 101.

2    Larson, Doug. "Doug's Dugout" (daily column), *Green Bay Press Gazette*. https://www.azquotes.com/author/19669-Doug_Larson

3    Adler, Warren. "Lying About My Age," *ChangingAging.org*, August 13, 2015. https://changingaging.org/blog/lying-about-my-age/

4   *Ibid.*

5   America Counts staff. "2020 Census Will Help Policymakers Prepare for the Incoming Wave of Aging Boomers," *Census.gov.*, December 10, 2019. https://www.census.gov/library/stories/2019/12/by-2030-all-baby-boomers-will-be-age-65-or-older.html

6   Knapp, Kenneth A. "The Fallacy of the Lump of Labor: Adding to the Costs of Ageism," *Issue Brief,* December 2007. International Longevity Center–USA https://www.issuelab.org/resources/11891/11891.pdf

7   National Oceanic and Atmospheric Administration. "Tsunami Warning System," *Ocean Explorer* (page revised February 12, 2013). https://oceanexplorer.noaa.gov/edu/learning/9_ocean_waves/activities/tsunami.html

8   Google Images. https://www.fontainesauction.com/auction-lot/roddy-mcdowall-photograph-of-bette-davis-old-ag_49741A9A7C


## Chapter 4: Aging on Our Minds

1   Hall, Alena. "53% Of U.S. Adults Don't Fear Growing Old—Study Finds People Actually Fear Less As They Age," *Forbes Health* (Oct 19, 2022). https://www.forbes.com/health/medicare/fear-of-aging-survey/

2   Applewhite, *This Chair Rocks: A Manifesto Against Ageism.* (New York: Celadon Books, 2016), p. 206.

3   *Ibid.*, p. 207.

4   Hall, *op cit.*

5   *Ibid.*

6   Population Reference Bureau. *Fact Sheet: U.S. Dementia Trends* (2020). https://www.prb.org/resources/fact-sheet-u-s-dementia-trends/

7   Hudomiet, Péter; Hurd, Michael D.; and Rohwedder, Susann. "Trends in Inequalities in the Prevalence of Dementia in the United States." *PNAS* 119 (46) e2212205119 (November 7, 2022). https://www.pnas.org/doi/10.1073/pnas.2212205119

8   Population Reference Bureau. *op cit.*

9   Livingston, G.; Sommerlad, A.; Orgeta, V.; *et al.* "Dementia Prevention, Intervention, and Care," *The Lancet*, 2017; 390 (10113) pp. 2673–2734.

10   Interview with Andrea Creech, March 28, 2019.

11   Interview with Thomas Kamber, April 9, 2019.

12   Interview with Tim Carpenter, April 15, 2019.

13   Interview with Carrie Andreoletti, April 12, 2019.

14   Creech, *op. cit.* interview.

15   Kamber, *op. cit.* interview.

16   Creech, *op. cit.* interview.

17   Kamber, *op. cit.* interview.

18   Gerontological Society of America. "Age-Friendly University (AFU) Global Network." https://www.geron.org/programs-services/education-center/age-friendly-university-afu-global-network

19   Dublin City University. "Age-Friendly Principles and How to Join." https://www.dcu.ie/agefriendly/principles-age-friendly-university

20   Andreolotti, *op. cit.* interview.

21   *Ibid*.

22   Carpenter, *op. cit.* interview.

23   Park, Denise C. "Cognitive Ability in Old Age Is Predetermined by Age 20 y," *PNAS* 116 (6), pp. 1832–18 (January 30, 2019).

24   Salthouse, Timothy A. "When Does Age-Related Cognitive Decline Begin?" *Neurobiology of Aging*, April 30, 2009, (4) pp. 507–14.

25   Applewhite, *This Chair Rocks*, p. 63.

26   Museum of Modern Art. "Conversation with Gene Cohen of the Center on Aging, Health & Humanities and Gay Hanna of the National Center for Creative Aging," *Perspectives*, p. 68. https://www.moma.org/momaorg/shared/pdfs/docs/meetme/Perspectives_GCohen-GHanna.pdf

27   CBS. "I Was Sure I Could Do It," *60 Minutes* interview with Katie Couric. February 8, 2009. https://www.youtube.com/watch?v=rZ5HnyEQg7M

28   Couric, Katie. "Capt. Sully Worried About Airline Industry," CBS News. February 10, 2009. https://www.cbsnews.com/news/capt-sully-worried-about-airline-industry/

29   Salthouse, *op cit.*

30   Interview with Dr. Louise Aronson, April 23, 2017.

31   Interview with Tim Carpenter, April 20, 2017.

32    Robbins, Gary. "We All Have Some Wisdom. But What Is It?" *The San Diego Union-Tribune,* April 2, 2015. https://www.sandiegouniontribune.com/news/science/sdut-brain-wisdom-explained-2015apr02-story.html

33    Jeste, Dilip. "Seeking Wisdom in Graying Matter." TEDMED2015. https://tedmed.com/talks/show?id=526815

34    Aronson, *op cit.* interview.

35    Jeste, *op cit.* TEDMED2015.

36    Carpenter, *op cit.* interview.

37    Leonard, Dorothy; Swap, Walter; and Barton, Gavin. "What's Lost When Experts Retire," *Harvard Business Review,* December 2, 2014. https://hbr.org/2014/12/whats-lost-when-experts-retire

38    Panopto. "Inefficient Knowledge Sharing Costs Large Businesses $47 Million Per Year," *The Workplace Knowledge and Productivity Report.* (July 16, 2018). https://www.panopto.com/company/news/inefficient-knowledge-sharing-costs-large-businesses-47-million-per-year/

39    *Ibid.*

40    Michelangelo's Pieta in St. Peter's Basilica in the Vatican. Original file by Stanislav Traykov. https://commons.wikimedia.org/wiki/File:Pieta_de_Michelangelo_-_Vaticano.jpg

41    Andreasen, Nancy C. "Secrets of the Creative Brain," *The Atlantic,* July/August 2014. https://www.theatlantic.com/magazine/archive/2014/07/secrets-of-the-creative-brain/372299/

42    Runco, Mark A. "'Big C, Little c' Creativity as a False Dichotomy: Reality Is Not Categorical," *Creativity Research Journal,* 26 (1), pp. 131–32 (2014).

43    Andreasen, *op. cit.*

44    Galenson, David W. "The Nature of Creativity in Old Age," Working Paper No. 2019-67. Becker Friedman Institute for Economics at the University of Chicago, May 2019, p. 3. https://bfi.uchicago.edu/wp-content/uploads/BFI_WP_201967.pdf

45    Kerka, Sandra. "Creativity in Adulthood," *ERIC Digest* No. 204, p. 4. https://files.eric.ed.gov/fulltext/ED429186.pdf

46    Cohen, Gene D. *The Creative Age: Awakening Human Potential in the Second Half of Life* (New York: Avon Books, 2000), p. 30.

47    Michelangelo, Pietà Firenze. Original file by Hans-Juergen Luntzer. https://commons.wikimedia.org/wiki/File:Michelangelo_Pieta_Firenze.jpg

## Chapter 5: A Life of One's Own


1   Woolf, Virginia. *A Room of One's Own*. (Orlando, Florida: Harcourt, 1989), p.4.

2   Van Vleck, Morgan. "'Kids These Days': Why Youth-Directed Ageism Is an Issue for Everyone." Washington University in St. Louis Institute for Public Health. October 26, 2021. https://publichealth.wustl.edu/kids-these-days-why-youth-directed-ageism-is-an-issue-for-everyone/

3   Quinn, Holly. "What Does Ageism in Tech Look Like?" *Technical.ly.* February 7, 2022. https://technical.ly/diversity-equity-inclusion/ageism-in-tech/; Walsh, Emily. "A Tech Firm's Call to Hire 'Old People' Highlights a Troubling Trend in Silicon Valley." *Business Insider,* August 26, 2021. https://www.businessinsider.com/we-hire-old-people-ageism-tech-inudstry-2021-8

4   Berman, Phillip L. and Goldman, Connie, eds. *The Ageless Spirit* (New York: Ballantine Books, 1992), pp. 126–27.

5   Allen, Julie Ober; Solway, Erica; Kirch, Matthias; *et al.* "Experiences of Everyday Ageism and the Health of Older U.S. Adults," *JAMA Network Open*, 2022 Jun 1; 5(6):e2217240.

6   Officer, Alana; Amuthavalli Thiyagarajan, Jotheeswaran; Schneiders, Mira Leonie; Nash, Paul; and de la Fuente-Núñez, Vânia. "Ageism, Healthy Life Expectancy and Population Ageing: How Are They Related?" *International Journal of Environmental Research and Public Health* 17, no. 9: 3159. May 1, 2020.

7   D'Arrigo, Terri. "Ageism Takes Toll on Physical, Mental Health," *Psychiatric News*, August 22, 2022. https://psychnews.psychiatryonline.org/doi/10.1176/appi.pn.2022.09.9.5

8   Levy, Becca R.; Slade, Martin D.; Kunkel, Suzanne R.; and Kasl, Stanislav V. "Longevity Increased by Positive Self-Perceptions of Aging," *Journal of Personality and Social Psychology*, 2002, Vol. 83, No. 2, 261–70.

9   *Ibid*, p. 268.

10  Levy, Becca R.; Slade, Martin D.; Pietrzak, Robert H.; and Ferrucci, Luigi. "Positive Age Beliefs Protect Against Dementia Even Among Elders with High-Risk Gene," *PLOS One,* February 7, 2018.

11  Woolf, *op cit.*, p. 24.

12  Nolan, Emma. "Why Hollywood Is Finally Over Method Acting," *Newsweek*, April 22, 2022. https://www.newsweek.com/why-hollywood-finally-over-method-acting-1700143

13   Dowd, Maureen. "Spare Me the Purity Racket," *New York Times*, July 27, 2019. https://www.nytimes.com/2019/07/27/opinion/sunday/maureen-dowd-trump-impeachment.html

14   Vaupel, James W. "Biodemography of Human Ageing," *Nature*. March 25, 2010, 464 (7288), pp 536–42.

## Chapter 6: Here, There, and Everywhere

1   *Bronfenbrenner, Urie. "Toward an Experimental Ecology of Human Development," 1977, American Psychologist. 32 (7): 513–531.*

2   Gendron, Tracey. *Ageism Unmasked: Exploring Age Bias and How to End It,* (Lebanon, N.H.: Steerforth Press, 2022), p. 4.

3   Levy, Becca. *Breaking the Age Code: How Your Beliefs About Aging Determine How Long & Well You Live.* (New York: HarperCollins, 2022), p. 152.

4   Kim, Janet and McCollough, Rachel. "When It Comes to Aging, Intersectionality Matters," Caring Across Generations, July 8, 2019. [link defunct]

5   International Lesbian, Gay, Bisexual, Trans and Intersex Association. "Intersections of Ageism and Age Discrimination with Cisheteronormativity, Homophobia and Transphobia, and Discrimination Based on Sexual Orientation, Gender Identity and Gender Expression," *ILGA World*, April 2021, p. 2.

6   Fulmer, Terry and Morton, Grace. "How Ableism and Ageism Affect Older Adults," Next Avenue, October 17, 2022. https://www.nextavenue.org/how-ableism-and-ageism-affect-older-adults/

7   Crenshaw, Kimberlé. "Demarginalizing the Intersection of Race and Sex: A Black Feminist Critique of Antidiscrimination Doctrine, Feminist Theory and Antiracist Politics," *University of Chicago Legal Forum*, Vol. 1989: Issue 1, Article 8. https://chicagounbound.uchicago.edu/cgi/viewcontent.cgi?article=1052&context=uclf

8   Levy, *Breaking the Age Code*, p. 153.

9   Applewhite, *This Chair Rocks*, p. 12.

10   Eisen, Ben. "Older Americans Stockpiled a Record $35 Trillion. The Time Has Come to Give It Away," *The Wall Street Journal*, July 2, 2021. https://www.wsj.com/articles/older-americans-35-trillion-wealth-giving-away-heirs-philanthropy-11625234216

11   Fengler, Wolfgang. "The Silver Economy Is Coming of Age: A Look at the Growing Spending Power of Seniors," The Brookings Institution, January 14, 2021. https://www.brookings.edu/blog/future-development/2021/01/14/the-silver-economy-is-coming-of-age-a-look-at-the-growing-spending-power-of-seniors/

12   Engel, Mary. "American Girl in Italy 1951," Ruth Orkin Photo Archive. https://www.orkinphoto.com/photographs/american-girl/

13   Gendron, *op. cit.,* pp. 96–97.

14   Yuhas, Alan. "'Not My Choice.' A TV Anchor Is Ousted, and Viewers Ask: Was Sexism to Blame?" *The New York Times*, August 30, 2022. https://www.nytimes.com/2022/08/30/world/canada/lisa-laflamme-ctv-departure.html

15   Talbot, Michael. "'Women with Grey Hair Are Being Edged Out of the Workplace': Dove," *City News,* August 23, 2022. https://ottawa.citynews.ca/2022/08/23/women-with-grey-hair-are-being-edged-out-of-the-workplace-dove-5729840/

16   Devereux-Evans, Olivia. "Wendy's Canada Changes Its Mascot's Iconic Red Hair to Gray in Support of News Anchor Who Claims She Was Fired 'Because She Stopped Dying Her Hair'," *Daily Mail*, August 31, 2022. https://www.dailymail.co.uk/news/article-11164107/Wendys-Canada-changes-mascots-iconic-red-hair-gray-support-news-anchor.html

17   Smith, Mitch and Glueck, Katie. "Kansas Votes to Preserve Abortion Rights Protections in Its Constitution," *The New York Times,* August 2, 2022. https://www.nytimes.com/2022/08/02/us/kansas-abortion-rights-vote.html

18   Knowles, Hannah and Kitchener, Caroline. "In Sprint to November, Democrats Seize on Shifting Landscape over Abortion," *The Washington Post*, September 6, 2022. https://www.washingtonpost.com/politics/2022/09/05/abortion-roe-midterms/

19   Levin, Yuval. "Why Are We Still Governed by Baby Boomers and the Remarkably Old?" *The New York Times*, June 3, 2022. https://www.nytimes.com/2022/06/03/opinion/baby-boomers-gen-x-us-politics.html

20   Philbrick, Ian Prasad. "Why Does America Have Old Leaders?" *The New York Times,* July 16, 2020. https://www.nytimes.com/2020/07/16/opinion/america-presidents-old-age.html

21  Woolf, Steven H.; Masters, Ryan K.; and Aron, Laudan Y. "Changes in Life Expectancy Between 2019 and 2020 in the U.S and 21 Peer Countries," *JAMA Network Open* 2022;5(4):e227067, April 13, 2022, p. 4.

22  Library of Congress. "117th United States Congress: A Survey of Books Written by Members," *Research Guides.* https://guides.loc. gov/117th-congress-book-list

23  The White House. "The Cabinet." https://www.whitehouse.gov/ administration/cabinet/

24  Britannica.com. "Mortality Demography." https://www.britannica.com/ science/mortality-demography

25  Tridimas, George. "Constitutional Choice in Ancient Athens: The Evolution of the Frequency of Decision Making," *Constitutional Political Economy* 28, 209–230 (2017), p. 210.

26  History.com Editors. "Ancient Greek Democracy," *History.com,* August 19, 2019. https://www.history.com/topics/ancient-greece/ ancient-greece-democracy

27  Britannica.com. "Gerousia Council." https://www.britannica.com/topic/ gerousia

28  Capasso, Luigi; D'Anastasio, Ruggero; Pierfelice, Lia; Di Fabrizio, Antonietta; and Gallenga, Pier Enrico. "Roman Conquests, Lifespan, and Diseases in Ancient Italy," *The Lancet,* Volume 362, Issue 9384, August 23, 2003, p. 668.

29  Davis, Jennifer. "The Roman Senate as Precursor of the U.S. Senate," *Library of Congress Blogs,* September 30, 2020. https://blogs.loc.gov/law/2020/09/ the-roman-senate-as-precursor-of-the-u-s-senate/

30  PBS.org. "Senators," *The Roman Empire in the First Century.* https://www. pbs.org/empires/romans/empire/senators.html

31  Andrlik, Todd. "How Old Were the Leaders of the American Revolution on July 4, 1776?" Slate, August 20, 2013. https://slate.com/news-and- politics/2013/08/how-old-were-the-founding-fathers-the-leaders-of-the- american-revolution-were-younger-than-we-imagine.html

32  Lau, Tim. "Citizens United Explained," *Brennan Center for Justice,* December 12, 2019. https://www.brennancenter.org/our-work/ research-reports/citizens-united-explained

33    Young, Robin and Mitchell, Jack. "40 Years In 5 Minutes: Age Simulation Suit Aims to Increase Empathy in Building Design," *WBUR Here & Now*, June 3, 2019. https://www.wbur.org/hereandnow/2019/06/03/age-simulation-suit

34    Google Images. "Aging Simulation Suit." https://www.google.com/search?q=aging+simulation+suit&tbm=isch&hl=en&sa=X&ved=2ahUKEwi2n6_b-sH4AhXZAjQIHVboC7wQBXoECAEQOg&biw=947&bih=641

35    MIT AgeLab. "AGNES (Age Gain Now Empathy System." https://agelab.mit.edu/methods/agnes-age-gain-now-empathy-system

36    Produkt + Projekt Wolfgang Moll. "Instant Aging Suit GERT: GERT Creates the Experience [sic] Old Age." https://www.age-simulation-suit.com/download/Instant_aging_suit.pdf

37    Gerhardy, Thomas H.; Schlomann, Anna; Wahl, Hans-Werner; and Schmidt, Laura I. "Effects of Age Simulation Suits on Psychological and Physical Outcomes: A Systematic Review," *European Journal of Ageing* 19, 953–976 (2022).

38    Statistica. "Percent of Adults Aged 45 Years and Older with Vision Impairment in the U.S. from 2017 to 2017, by Age." https://www.statista.com/statistics/1018377/vision-impairment-older-adults-us-by-age/

39    National Institute on Deafness and Other Communication Disorders. "Quick Statistics About Hearing, Balance, and Dizziness." https://www.nidcd.nih.gov/health/statistics/quick-statistics-hearing

40    Freiberger, Ellen; Sieber, Cornel Christian; and Kob, Robert. "Mobility in Older Community-Dwelling Persons: A Narrative Review," *Frontiers in Physiology*, Volume 11, 15 September 2020.

41    Tavares, Jane L.; Cohen, Marc A.; Silberman, Susan; and Popham, Lauren. "Chronic Inequities: Measuring Disease Cost Burden Among Older Adults in the U.S.: A Health and Retirement Study Analysis," Leading Age LTSS Center @UMass Boston, and the National Council on Aging, April 2022, p. 5.

## Chapter 7: Lessons from a Pandemic

1    World Health Organization. "Coronavirus Disease (COVID-19) Pandemic." https://www.who.int/europe/emergencies/situations/covid-19

2    Centers for Disease Control and Prevention. "End of the Federal COVID-19 Public Health Emergency (PHE) Declaration," May 11, 2023. https://archive.cdc.gov/#/details?url=https://www.cdc.gov/coronavirus/2019-ncov/your-health/end-of-phe.html

3    Smith-Schoenwalder, Cecelia. "WHO, CDC Study: Vast Majority of COVID-19 Deaths Among Older Adults," *U.S. News and World Report,* February 2, 2023. https://www.usnews.com/news/health-news/articles/2023-02-02/who-cdc-study-vast-majority-of-covid-19-deaths-among-adults-aged-60-and-older

4    Cha, Ariana Eunjung and Keating, Dan. "Covid Becomes Plague of Elderly, Reviving Debate Over 'Acceptable Loss'," *The Washington Post,* November 28, 2022. https://www.washingtonpost.com/health/2022/11/28/covid-who-is-dying/

5    Rueda, J. "Ageism in the COVID-19 Pandemic: Age-based Discrimination in Triage Decisions and Beyond," *History and Philosophy of the Life Sciences,* July 13, 2021; 43(3): 91–97.

6    *Ibid.,* p. 93.

7    *Ibid.,* p. 95.

8    Alsina, Deborah. "Joint Statement on Treatment Rights of Older People During Pandemic," *Independent Age,* March 30, 2020. https://www.ageuk.org.uk/latest-press/articles/2020/03/rights-of-older-people-during-pandemic/

9    Aronson, Louise. "'Covid-19 Kills Only Old People.' Only?" *The New York Times,* March 22, 2020. https://www.nytimes.com/2020/03/22/opinion/coronavirus-elderly.html

10    Vitale-Aussem, Jill; Pearson, Caroline; and Thomas, Bill. "If You Hated 2020, You're Going to Despise Old Age," Nexus Insights. https://www.linkedin.com/pulse/you-hated-2020-youre-going-despise-old-age-nexus-insights/

11    Thomas, Dylan. "Do Not Go Gentle into That Good Night," *The Poems of Dylan Thomas,* Centenary Edition. (New York: New Directions, 2017), p. 193.

12    Stieb, Matt. "Texas Lt. Gov. Dan Patrick: 'Lots of Grandparents' Willing to Die to Save Economy for Grandchildren," *New York Magazine,* March 23, 2020. https://nymag.com/intelligencer/2020/03/dan-patrick-seniors-are-willing-to-die-to-save-economy.html

13 Yourish, Karen; Lai, K.K. Rebecca; Ivory, Danielle; and Smith, Mitch. "One-Third of All U.S. Coronavirus Deaths Are Nursing Home Residents or Workers." *The New York Times,* May 11, 2020. https://www.nytimes.com/interactive/2020/05/09/us/coronavirus-cases-nursing-homes-us.html

14 Leland, John. "They Survived the Holocaust. Now They're Confronting the Virus," *The New York Times,* May 4, 2020. https://www.nytimes.com/2020/05/04/nyregion/holocaust-survivors-coronavirus.html

15 Barry, Ellen. "They Survived the Worst Battles of World War II. And Died of the Virus," *The New York Times,* May 24, 2020. https://www.nytimes.com/2020/05/24/us/they-survived-the-worst-battles-of-world-war-ii-and-died-of-the-virus.html

16 Chappell, Bill. "U.S. Could Have Saved 36,000 Lives If Social Distancing Started 1 Week Earlier: Study," National Public Radio, May 21, 2020. https://www.npr.org/sections/coronavirus-live-updates/2020/05/21/860077940/u-s-could-have-saved-36-000-lives-if-social-distancing-started-1-week-earlier-st

17 Yoran, Varda. "Just Because I'm 90 Doesn't Mean I'm Ready To Die ⊠ Or Disposable," *HuffPost,* April 29, 2020. https://www.huffpost.com/entry/i-am-old-not-disposable-coronavirus-pandemic_n_5ea7295dc5b6a30004e67306

18 Span, Paula. "Should Youth Come First in Coronavirus Care?" *The New York Times,* July 30, 2020. https://www.nytimes.com/2020/07/31/health/coronavirus-ethics-rationing-elderly.html

19 Farrell, Timothy W.; Ferrante, Lauren E.; Brown, Teneille; Francis, Leslie; *et al. "*AGS Position Statement: Resource Allocation Strategies and Age-Related Considerations in the COVID-19 Era and Beyond," *Journal of the American Geriatrics Society,* Volume 68, Issue 6, June 2020, pp. 1136–42.

20 *Ibid.,* p. 1137.

21 *Ibid.,* p. 1138.

22 Span, *op cit.*

23 Flynn, Maggie. "Nursing Homes in Every State Report PPE Shortages, With Up to 60% Lacking a Week's Supply," *Skilled Nursing News,* Oct. 14, 2020. https://skillednursingnews.com/2020/10/nursing-homes-in-every-state-reports-ppe-shortage-with-up-to-60-lacking-a-weeks-supply/

24  Helfand, Benjamin K.I.; Webb, Margaret; Gartaganis, Sarah L.; *et al.*
"The Exclusion of Older Persons From Vaccine and Treatment Trials for
Coronavirus Disease 2019 — Missing the Target," *JAMA Internal Medicine,*
2020;180(11), pp. 1546–49.

25  Weech-Maldonado, Robert; Lord, Justin; Davlyatov, Ganisher;
Ghiasi, Akbar; and Orewa, Gregory. "High-Minority Nursing Homes
Disproportionately Affected by COVID-19 Deaths," *Frontiers in Public
Health,* March 22, 2021; 9:606364.

26  Institute for Healthcare Policy and Innovation. "Everyday Ageism and
Health: Older Adults' Experiences with Everyday Ageism," University of
Michigan, July 2020. https://www.healthyagingpoll.org/reports-more/
report/everyday-ageism-and-health.

27  Coughlin, Joseph. "COVID-19 Now We All Know What It's Like To Be
Old & Alone," *Forbes,* March 18, 2020. https://www.forbes.com/sites/
josephcoughlin/2020/03/18/in-covid-19-age-were-all-getting-a-taste-of-
social-isolation-many-older-adults-experience-daily/?sh=42643c231e7b

28  AARP Research. "2023 Tech Trends and adults 50+," January 2023.
https://www.aarp.org/content/dam/aarp/research/surveys_statistics/
technology/2023/2023-tech-trends.doi.10.26419-2Fres.00584.001.pdf

29  Burr, D.A.; Castrellon, J.J.; Zald, D.H.; and Samanez-Larkin, G.R. "Emotion
Dynamics Across Adulthood in Everyday Life: Older Adults Are More
Emotionally Stable and Better at Regulating Desires," *Emotion,* (2021) *21*(3),
pp. 453–64.

30  Mcleod, Saul. "Erik Erikson's 8 Stages of Psychosocial Development," Simply
Psychology. https://www.simplypsychology.org/erik-erikson.html

## Chapter 8: Sending the Right Messages

1  Lindland, Eric; Haydon, Abigail; Kendall-Taylor; and Fond, Marissa.
"Gauging Aging: Mapping the Gaps Between Expert and Public
Understandings of Aging in America," FrameWorks Institute, June 18, 2015,
pp. 6–7.

2  Leardi, Jeanette. "How Photos Showing Older Adult Hands Reveal Cultural
Bias," Next Avenue, January 12, 2022. https://www.nextavenue.org/
what-the-hands-are-doing/

3    Leardi, Jeanette. "Selling the Idea of Pro-Aging Advertisements," Next Avenue, July 15, 2022. https://www.nextavenue.org/selling-the-idea-of-pro-aging-ads/

4    AARP Research. "Media Image Landscape: Age Representation in Online Images," September 2019. https://www.aarp.org/content/dam/aarp/research/surveys_statistics/life-leisure/2019/age-representation-in-online-media-images.doi.10.26419-2Fres.00339.001.pdf

5    Amica Senior Lifestyles. "Study: Senior Actors and Characters in Hollywood," December 2021. https://www.amica.ca/conversations/senior-actors-in-hollywood [defunct link]

6    *Ibid.*

7    Markov, Čedomir and Yoon, Youngmin. "Diversity and Age Stereotypes in Portrayals of Older Adults in Popular American Primetime Television Series," *Ageing & Society*, Volume 41, Issue 12, December 2021, pp. 2747–67.

8    O'Neil, Moira and Haydon, Abigail. "Aging, Agency, and Attribution of Responsibility: Shifting Public Discourse About Older Adults," *FrameWorks Institute*, 2015, pp. 23–25.

9    Spohr, Mike. "These Kids Dressed Up As 100-Year-Olds Are Too Cute To Handle," *BuzzFeed*, Feb 8, 2017. https://www.buzzfeed.com/mikespohr/19-kids-who-look-hilariously-like-your-grandparents

10   Flamion, Allison; Missotten, Pierre; Jennotte, Lucie; Hody, Noémie; and Adam, Stéphane. "Old Age-Related Stereotypes of Preschool Children," *Frontiers in Psychology*, Volume 11, Article 807, April 28, 2020.

11   Providence Mount St. Vincent. "Intergenerational Learning Center." https://www.providence.org/locations/wa/mount-st-vincent/facility-profile/intergenerational-learning-center

12   AARP Experience Corps. https://www.aarp.org/experience-corps/

13   For All Ages. "Age-Positive 100th Day of School Program Ideas." https://forallages.org/100th-day-of-school

14   Rodgers & Hammerstein Foundation. https://rodgersandhammerstein.com/song/south-pacific/youve-got-to-be-carefully-taught/

15   Kogan, N.; Stevens, J.; and Shelton, F.C. (1961). Age Differences: A Developmental Study of Discriminability and Affective Response. *The Journal of Abnormal and Social Psychology, 62*(2), 221–30.

16   Flamion, *et al., op cit.*

17   Interview with Lindsey McDivitt, July 8, 2022.

18   McDivitt, Lindsey. "A Is for Aging, B Is for Books…." https://www.lindseymcdivitt.com/

19   McDivitt, *op. cit.* interview.

20   Interview with Tracey Gendron, January 29, 2020.

21   Lundebjerg, Nancy E.; Trucil, Daniel E.; Hammond, Emily C.; and Applegate, William B. "When It Comes to Older Adults, Language Matters: Journal of the American Geriatrics Society Adopts Modified American Medical Association Style," *Journal of the American Geriatrics Society,* Volume 65, Issue 7, July 2017, pp. 1386–88.

22   Interview with Julie Sweetland on February 6, 2020.

23   Gendron, *op cit.* interview.

24   *Ibid.*

25   Dictionary.com. "The Language of Ageism: Understanding How We Talk About Older People." https://www.dictionary.com/e/ageism-terms/

26   California Assisted Living Association. "Elevate Aging Through Language: A Usage and Style Guide." https://www.topsixtyoversixty.com/wp-content/uploads/sites/24/2020/05/elevate_aging_style_guide.pdf

27   *Ibid.*

28   Schoeneman, Karen. "Mayday," *The Language of Culture Change,* Pioneer Network, October 2016. https://www.pioneernetwork.net/wp-content/uploads/2016/10/The-Language-of-Culture-Change.pdf

29   Thomas, Bill. "About That OTHER Word," *ChangingAging,* January 30, 2013. https://changingaging.org/blog/about-that-other-word/

30   Gendron, *op. cit.* interview.

31   Sweetland, *op. cit.* interview.

32   Gendron, *op. cit.* interview.

33   Sweetland, *op. cit.* interview.

## Chapter 9: Talkin' 'Bout Our Generations

1   *On Rhetoric: A Theory of Civic Discourse.* 2nd edition. Translated by George A. Kennedy (New York: Oxford University Press, 2007), p. 149.

2   Shakespeare, William. *As You Like It,* Act II Scene VII, lines 163–66.

3    The Who. "My Generation." 2014 Stereo Mix. https://www.youtube.com/watch?v=f-p_oyMYPP4

4    Cohen, Philip N. "Generation Labels Mean Nothing. It's Time to Retire Them," *The Washington Post*, July 7, 2021. https://www.washingtonpost.com/opinions/2021/07/07/generation-labels-mean-nothing-retire-them/

5    Dimock, Michael. "5 Things to Keep in Mind When You Hear About Gen Z, Millennials, Boomers and Other Generations," *Pew Research Center*, May 22, 2023. https://www.pewresearch.org/short-reads/2023/05/22/5-things-to-keep-in-mind-when-you-hear-about-gen-z-millennials-boomers-and-other-generations/

6    Duffy, Bobby. *The Generation Myth: Why When You're Born Matters Less Than You Think*. (New York: Basic Books, 2021), p. 1.

7    *Ibid.*, p. 4.

8    *Ibid.*

9    *Ibid.*, p. 7.

10    *Ibid.*, p. 17.

11    *Ibid.*

12    Palmer, Kim. "How Pew Research Will Report on Generations Moving Forward," Pew Research Center, May 22, 2023. https://www.pewresearch.org/short-reads/2023/05/22/how-pew-research-center-will-report-on-generations-moving-forward/

13    Thomas, Bill. "About That OTHER Word," ChangingAging, January 30, 2013. https://changingaging.org/blog/about-that-other-word/

14    Interview with Eunice Lin Nichols, January 20, 2020.

15    Interview with Stephen Katz, January 3, 2020.

16    Weber-Raley, Lisa. "Burning the Candle at Both Ends: Sandwich Generation Caregiving in the U.S.," *National Alliance for Caregiving*, November 2019, p. 9.

17    AARP Research. "The Value of Experience: AARP Multicultural Work & Jobs Study Chartbook for Total Respondents," p. 61.

18    Sevilla, Cate. "Everyday Ageism in the Tech Industry." https://www.cwjobs.co.uk/advice/ageism-in-tech

19    Interview with Candace Steele Flippin, January 8, 2020.

20    Katz, *op. cit.*, interview.

21    Nichols, *op. cit.*, interview.

22   Flippin, *op. cit.,* interview.

23   *Ibid.*

24   *Ibid.*

25   Katz, *op. cit.,* interview.

26   DiNubile, Nicholas A. "Boomeritis." https://drnick.com/resources/boomeritis/

27   CoGenerate. https://cogenerate.org/

28   Generations United. https://www.gu.org/

29   AmeriCorps Seniors. https://americorps.gov/serve/americorps-seniors

30   AARP. https://www.aarp.org/experience-corps/

31   Sages & Seekers. https://sagesandseekers.org/

32   Stanford Social Innovation Review. "Meeting the Multigenerational Moment." https://ssir.org/meeting_the_multigenerational_moment#

## Chapter 10: Growing Older Your Way

1   Bakan, David. *The Duality of Human Existence: Isolation and Communion in Western Man,* (Boston: Beacon Press, 1966).

2   McAdams, *Dan P. The Stories We Live By: Personal Myths and the Making of the Self,* (New York: William Morrow & Co., 1993), p. 71.

3   Leardi, Jeanette. "How Photos Showing Older Adult Hands Reveal Cultural Bias," Next Avenue, January 12, 2022. https://www.nextavenue.org/what-the-hands-are-doing/

4   National Institutes of Health Clinical Center. "Patient Bill of Rights." Updated May 24, 2021. https://clinicalcenter.nih.gov/participate/patientinfo/legal/bill_of_rights.html

5   AARP. "Advance Directive Forms." https://www.aarp.org/caregiving/financial-legal/free-printable-advance-directives/

6   Shaw, Gina. "Advance Directives," *WebMD,* February 5, 2022. https://www.webmd.com/palliative-care/advance-directives-medical-power-attorney#1

7   National POLST. "Honoring the Wishes of Those with Serious Illness and Frailty." https://polst.org/

8   MedlinePlus. "Do-Not-Resuscitate Order." https://medlineplus.gov/ency/patientinstructions/000473.htm

9    Alda, Alan. *If I Understood You, Would I Have This Look on My Face?: My Adventures in the Art and Science of Relating and Communicating.* (New York: Random House, 2017), p. 61.

10   Applewhite, Ashton. *This Chair Rocks: A Manifesto Against Ageism.* (New York: Celadon Books, 2016), pp. 58–59.

11   Lee, Michelle. "*Allure* Magazine Will No Longer Use the Term 'Anti-Aging'," August 14, 2017. https://www.allure.com/story/allure-magazine-phasing-out-the-word-anti-aging

12   Lee, Michelle. "Editor's Letter: The End of "Anti-Aging," One Year Later," *Allure*, October 9, 2018. https://www.allure.com/story/editors-letter-anti-anti-aging-one-year-later


## Chapter 11: Empowering Aging


1    "Snickers Super bowl XLIV 2010 Commercial with Betty White and Abe Vigoda." https://www.youtube.com/watch?v=VLy4qzV1gL0

2    "Betty White guest stars on Raw: Raw, Feb. 10, 2014." https://www.youtube.com/watch?v=cI6V1b1sNCc

3    "Betty White Sings OFFICIAL 'I'm Still Hot' Music Video w/Luciana HD for The Lifeline Program." https://www.youtube.com/watch?v=dEh_asEffoQ

4    Interview with Paula Span, May 1, 2021.

5    Congressional Research Service. "Commemorative Days, Weeks, and Months: Background and Current Practice." Updated June 27, 2019. https://sgp.fas.org/crs/misc/R44431.pdf

6    Interview with Paul Irving, May 2, 2021.

7    Interview with Wendl Kornfeld, May 1, 2021.

8    *Ibid.*

9    The White House. "Fact Sheet: The American Jobs Plan," March 31, 2021. https://www.whitehouse.gov/briefing-room/statements-releases/2021/03/31/fact-sheet-the-american-jobs-plan/

10   The White House. "A Proclamation on Older Americans Month, 2021," May 3, 2021. https://www.whitehouse.gov/briefing-room/presidential-actions/2021/05/03/a-proclamation-on-older-americans-month-2021/

11   Kornfeld, *op. cit.,* interview.

12   Interview with Janine Vanderburg, April 25, 2021.

13   Irving, *op. cit.,* interview.

14   Temple University Libraries. "Gray Panthers," Temple
University Special Collections. https://archive-it.org/home/
TempleSpecialCollections?q=Gray+Panthers&page=1&show=Sites

15   Schachter-Shalomi, Zalman and Miller, Ronald S. *From Age-ing to Sage-ing:
A Revolutionary Approach to Growing Older* (New York: Grand Central
Publishing: 2014), p. 73.

16   Shahidullah, Jeffrey D. "Why the U.S. Health Care System Must Address the
Shortage of Geriatricians Now," Next Avenue, March 30, 2023. https://www.
nextavenue.org/healthcare-must-address-geriatrician-shortage/

17   U.S. Bureau of Labor Statistics. "Occupational Employment and Wages, May
2022, 29-1221 Pediatricians, General," April 25, 2023. https://www.bls.gov/
oes/current/oes291221.htm

18   Federal Interagency Forum on Child and Family Statistics. "POP1 Child
Population: Number of Children (in Millions) Ages 0–17 in the United
States by Age, 1950–2021 and Projected 2022–2050." https://www.childstats.
gov/americaschildren/tables/pop1.asp

19   United States Census Bureau. "The Older Population in the United States:
2022." https://www.census.gov/data/tables/2022/demo/age-and-sex/2022-
older-population.html

20   Shahidullah, *op cit.*

21   Dychtwald, Ken. "Searching for the Fountain of Health." Keynote address,
NextMed 2023 conference, March 14, 2023. https://www.youtube.com/
watch?v=fOGU5wGVW-s&t=1492s

22   Interview with Dr. Michael Wasserman, September 4, 2023.

23   *Ibid.*

24   Johnson, Steven D. "Geriatric Medicine Is, in Essence, About
Relationship(s)," American Society on Aging, *Generations
Today,* May 17, 2023. https://generations.asaging.org/
geriatric-medicine-about-relationships

25   American Geriatrics Society. "Is Geriatrics Right for You" 2023. https://
www.americangeriatrics.org/geriatrics-profession/why-geriatrics/
geriatrics-for-you

26   GovTrack. "S. 299 (116th): Geriatrics Workforce Improvement Act." https://
www.govtrack.us/congress/bills/116/s299

27   Tatum, Paul E. III; Talebreza, Shaida; and Ross, Jeanette S. "Geriatric Assessment: An Office-Based Approach," *American Family Physician*, 2018;97(12), pp. 776–784.

28   Rowe, John W. "The U.S. Eldercare Workforce Is Falling Further Behind," *Nature Aging,* 1, 327–329 (2021).

29   American Geriatrics Society, *op cit.*

30   Wasserman, *op cit.* interview.

# Acknowledgments

**I'VE READ LOTS OF BOOKS IN MY LIFE,** which means I've also read lots of Acknowledgments pages — the formal, the witty, the terse, the overblown, the humble, but always, the invariably grateful.

When I consider all the people who helped me birth this book, I'm overwhelmed by the myriad ways they have contributed to my work. And, more especially, by their willingness to do so. Their contributions fall into two categories: the tangible forms, the ways in which this manuscript became a book; and the intangible ones, the ways in which I was supported throughout the process.

First, the Tangibles.

Some of the essays that compose *Aging Sideways* first appeared as blog posts on the website ChangingAging.org. A few others appeared in the defunct online magazine Stria. For these initial opportunities, I'm grateful.

This book would most likely still be a stack of pages without the generous support of Geoffrey A. Rose, MD, and Katherine A. Rose, MD.

Richard Eisenberg's was the first pair of eagle eyes to review my entire manuscript. A highly experienced journalist and editor, he offered numerous insightful suggestions, always framed in kind and patient feedback, all of which inspired me to believe that I was moving along on the right track.

Two powerhouse gerontologists, Tracey Gendron, PhD, who graciously wrote the Foreword, and Kate de Madeiros, PhD, combed through the text for accuracy, rigor, and context. Each pointed out different issues requiring my attention and highlighted additional relevant sources to consider. Together they provided verification and validation…in stereo.

Polly Letofsky of My Word Publishing efficiently, effectively, enthusiastically, and empathetically led me through the potential minefield of publishing, which I greatly appreciate.

Anyone who believes that you can't judge a book by its cover (or visual interior) hasn't yet worked with graphic designer extraordinaire Victoria Wolf of Wolf Design and Marketing.

As for the Intangibles, these are the people who kept up my spirits, listened to my various frustrations, offered advice and reality checks, provided professional connections, accompanied me on mind-clearing walks, and did many other good deeds.

For these contributions, I thank Ashton Applewhite; Mary Bachran; Sky Bergman; Yung-Ping (Bing) Chen, PhD; Nicole Christina; Tonine Davis; Stella Fosse; Kathe Fradkin; Jan Golden; Carl Honoré; Wendl Kornfeld; Anthony Leardi; Carol Marak; Bonnie Marcus; David Molinaro; Barbara Raynor; Teddy Seegers; Janine Vanderburg; and Cricket Weston.

While at times *Aging Sideways* seemed to me to be writing itself, I know it's mainly the good vibes of the aforementioned people that kept me focused and persistent in working toward my goal.

Finally, to reiterate this book's dedication, I'm grateful to my long-departed parents and maternal grandmother, each of whom helped set me on the path to a greater understanding of the challenges and gifts of growing older.

# About the Author

**JEANETTE LEARDI** is a social gerontologist, community educator, writer, editor,
public speaker, and aging wellness leader
who has a passion for later life empowerment
and finds special personal fulfillment helping
older adults identify and share their wisdom
with others. 

Her decade of experiences as the primary caregiver to both of her
parents inspired her encore career goals of changing perceptions about
the aging process and helping people appreciate elders' inherent dignity,
wisdom, and unique value as mentors and catalysts for social change.

She accomplishes this through her publications, including her *Ageful
Living* blog, appearances on numerous podcasts, and engaging presen-
tations and classes on such topics as journaling, memoir writing, ethical
will creation, brain fitness, health literacy, ageism, intergenerational
communication, creativity, and caregiver support to people of all ages.

Leardi has a master's degree with honors in English from Rutgers
University and a graduate certificate in gerontology from the University

of North Carolina at Charlotte. Her journalism experiences include positions at Newsweek, Life, People, Condé Nast Traveler, Sesame Workshop, and The Charlotte Observer. Her articles on aging have appeared in national print and online publications.

You can learn more about her work by visiting her website at www.jeanetteleardi.com.

Printed in Great Britain
by Amazon

57595484R00195

Printed in Dunstable, United Kingdom

## Bulk order & collaboration

FOR INQUIRIES ON BULK DISCOUNTS AND COLLABORATION, PLEASE CONTACT US AT ARKANDANCIENT@OUTLOOK.COM



AUTHOR: JOYCE CAROL
COVER ILLUSTRATOR: MIJA LUKS
LAYOUT DESIGNER: FAYE T.

# Your Words Matter

I ALWAYS WANT TO HEAR WHAT YOU
ARE GOING TO SAY ABOUT...

# I am proud of you

BECAUSE...

# 34

# CELEBRATING YOU

## The Best of you
### PART 2

MY FAVORITE THING YOU HAVE EVER TAUGHT ME IS ...

MY FAVORITE WAY WE SPEND TIME TOGETHER IS ...

MY FAVORITE THING YOU DO WITHOUT REALIZING IS...

33

EVERY TIME I
SEE YOU, I AM
REMINDED OF...

78

# ICONIC & SAVAGE

## YOUR ONE-LINERS DESERVE THEIR OWN MERCH!

HERE ARE YOUR FUNNIEST CATCHPHRASES, SAVAGE COMEBACKS, OR PHRASES THAT LIVE RENT-FREE IN MY HEAD:

# 31

# UNIQUELY YOU

## ALL THE THINGS THAT MAKE YOU UNIQUE!

I SEE YOU, AND ALL THE THINGS
THAT MAKE YOU, YOU.
I LOVE THAT YOU ...

30

# SUPERHERO

your greatest superpower is

IF YOU WERE A SUPERHERO,
YOU WOULD LOOK LIKE ...

67

I LOVE HEARING
STORIES ABOUT
YOUR ...

# Stronger Together

A CHALLENGE WE FACED TOGETHER AND OVERCAME WAS ...

I LOVE HOW YOU NEVER ...

SOMETHING I LEARNED ABOUT YOU THROUGH THIS WAS ...

# 27

# CELEBRATING YOU

## The Best of you
### PART 1

MY FAVORITE THING ABOUT YOU IS ...

MY FAVORITE WAY YOU MAKE ME FEEL LOVED IS ...

MY FAVORITE TRADITION WE HAVE IS ...

97

I KNOW YOU LOVE ME
SO MUCH BECAUSE ...

# 25

you always made me feel safe ...

# Our Funniest Moment

THIS IS THE FUNNIEST THING WE HAVE DONE, AND I WANT TO DO IT AGAIN WITH YOU SOON. I STILL LAUGH WHEN I THINK ABOUT IT.

87

# PERSONALITY HEIST

## 4 THINGS I'D STEAL FROM YOUR PERSONALITY IF I COULD:

77

# GRATITUDE

## Grateful Hearts

I AM GRATEFUL FOR HOW
YOU ALWAYS...

1

2

3

# 21

In one word

IN ONE WORD,
YOU ARE:

07

BECAUSE OF YOU, I
BELIEVE I CAN ...

# 19

# I am enough

YOU HAVE ALWAYS MADE ME FEEL
LIKE I WAS ENOUGH...

# 18

# ALL ABOUT YOU

I love how you believe in ...

I am humbled by your ...

17

# BUCKET LIST

## Our Bucket List

ALL THE THINGS I DREAM OF DOING WITH YOU.

PLACES I WANT TO VISIT WITH YOU:

FOOD I WANT TO TRY WITH YOU:

THINGS I WANT TO DO WITH YOU:

# 16

# WEIRD & ADORABLE

YOUR WEIRDEST HABIT THAT I SECRETLY FIND ADORABLE:

YOUR WEIRDEST OBSESSION THAT I SECRETLY FIND ADORABLE:

# 15

This is you being awesome !

# HERE IS A PICTURE
# OF YOU BEING
# AWESOME!

# 14

YOU INSPIRE ME TO ...

# 13

IF YOU WERE A SEASON, YOU WOULD BE ...

# 12

# CHEF'S KISS

## No one cooks like you do

- THE TASTE OF HOME -

I AM CRAVING YOUR COOKING,
ESPECIALLY YOUR...

I LIKE IT SO MUCH BECAUSE...

IT MAKES ME FEEL...

II

# TWIN FLAMES

You and I are
similar in ...

# 10

# DRAMA KING/QUEEN

## YOU ARE 50% DRAMA, 50% ANGEL, 100% HUMAN.

YOUR MOST DRAMATIC MOMENT AWARD GOES TO...

YOU ARE NOT OVERREACTING. YOU ARE JUST ADDING FLAVOR TO LIFE.

6

# SCENT OF YOU

If you were a scent.
YOU WOULD BE:

8

# AWARD-WINNING

*you deserve an award for …*

YOU DESERVE AN AWARD FOR
BEING THE GLUE, THE GLITTER,
AND THE CALM IN THE STORM.

WE ARE PROOF THAT BEING
WEIRD TOGETHER IS THE
BEST KIND OF FUN!

## OUR GOOFY Portrait!

DRAW HIM/HER, BUT MAKE IT SUPER
SILLY AND WEIRD! ADD FUNNY HAIR,
BIG GLASSES, OR WACKY EXPRESSIONS.

NO MATTER WHERE LIFE TAKES YOU,
I HOPE YOU ALWAYS REMEMBER ...

No matter what

5

# SOUNDTRACK

IF I HAD TO DESCRIBE YOUR PERSONALITY
USING ONLY ANIMAL NOISES, IT WOULD BE:

# Words to Live By

THE BEST ADVICE YOU HAVE EVER GIVEN ME IS ...

IT HELPED ME WHEN ...

ONE WAY I WILL CARRY THIS WITH ME AS I GROW IS ...

# ALL STAR

## A tribute to you

YOUR WORLD-CLASS SARCASM:

YOUR RANDOM OBSESSIONS:

AWARD-WINNING LOOKS:

7

# POEM

THE MOST BEAUTIFUL THING ABOUT YOU,
IS THE KINDNESS YOU SHARE,
THE LOVE SO CLEAR.
IT'S IN YOUR LAUGHTER, WARM AND BRIGHT,
A LITTLE SPARK THAT FILLS THE NIGHT.

IT'S IN YOUR WORDS, GENTLE AND TRUE,
THE WAY YOUR HEART SEES THE BEST IN YOU.
NOT JUST IN SMILES OR THE WAY YOU STAND,
BUT IN THE WARMTH OF YOUR HELPING HAND.

SO WHEN YOU WONDER,
JUST KNOW IT'S TRUE,
THE MOST BEAUTIFUL
THING ABOUT YOU ...
IS YOU.

The most beautiful

THING ABOUT YOU IS ...

TO

_______________________

FROM

_______________________

## Want a freebie?

SEND US YOUR SECRET CODE "LV231" ON
INSTAGRAM @ARKANCIENTCO
AND WE WILL SEND YOU A SURPRISE!